THE RADIANT HOUR

REPRESENTING AMERICAN CULTURE
A series from University of Exeter Press
Series Editor: Mick Gidley

Representing American Culture exists to publish lively, accessible and up-to-date studies of the culture of the United States. Whether devoted to topics in popular, middlebrow or high culture, books in the series explore the ways in which ideological assumptions may be seen to be represented. The series is edited by Mick Gidley, Professor of American Literature at the University of Leeds.

REPRESENTING AMERICAN CULTURE

Narratives and Spaces: Technology and the Construction
of American Culture
David E. Nye (1997)

Green Screen: Environmentalism and Hollywood Cinema
David Ingram (2000)

THE RADIANT HOUR

Versions of Youth in American Culture

Edited by Neil Campbell

UNIVERSITY
of
EXETER
PRESS

First published 2000 by
University of Exeter Press
Reed Hall, Streatham Drive
Exeter, Devon EX4 4QR
UK
www.ex.ac.uk/uep/

British Library Cataloguing in Publication Data
A catalogue record of this book is available from the British Library

ISBN 0 85989 647 1

Typeset in 10/13pt Jansen Text by
Kestrel Data, Exeter, Devon

Printed and bound in Great Britain by
Short Run Press Ltd, Exeter, Devon

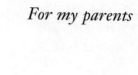

For my parents

Contents

Contributors

Charles Acland is Assistant Professor in the Department of Communication Studies, Concordia University, Montreal, where he teaches media and cultural studies. He is co-editor of *Harold Innis in the New Century: Reflections and Refractions* (1999), and author of *Youth, Murder, Spectacle: The Cultural Politics of 'Youth in Crisis'* (1995). His articles on film, television, taste and cultural history have appeared in *Cultural Studies, Communication, Wide Angle*, and *Canadian Journal of Film Studies*.

Neil Campbell is subject leader for American Studies at the University of Derby. He is co-author of *American Cultural Studies* (1997), author of *The Cultures of the American New West* (2000), and has written recent book chapters on Paul Bowles and transatlantic studies, and Cormac McCarthy.

Henry Giroux teaches at Penn State. His most recent books include: *Fugitive Cultures: Race, Violence, and Youth* (1996); *Channel Surfing: Racism, the Media, and the Destruction of Youth* (1997); *Stealing Innocence: Youth, Corporate Power, and the Politics of Culture* (2000); *Impure Acts: the Practical Politics of Cultural Studies* (2000).

David Holloway teaches American Studies at the University of Derby, and has published articles on Cormac McCarthy in *Southern Quarterly* and *Borderlines*. He is curently completing a book on McCarthy for publication in 2001.

Jon Lewis is Professor of English at Oregon State University. His books include: *The Road to Romance and Ruin: Teen Films and Youth Culture*

(1992), *Whom God Wishes to Destroy . . . Francis Coppola and the New Hollywood* (1995) and the edited anthology *The New American Cinema* (1998).

Simon Philo teaches American Studies at the University of Derby, and has published a chapter on MTV in *The Global Village: Dead or Alive?* (ed. Browne and Fishwick) (1999) and other articles on popular culture and the media. He has a chapter forthcoming on The Simpsons in *Must See TV* (ed. Jancovich and Lyons).

Jenny Robinson is a teacher of English and American Studies at the University of Derby and Burton College and is currently writing a PhD on American writing for girls.

Elizabeth Young is a freelance writer who has published widely, writing essays and reviews on contemporary culture and fiction for, amongst others, the *Guardian*, and is co-author of *Shopping in Space* (1992).

Acknowledgements

Firstly, I would like to thank all the contributors to this collection for their generosity, patience and good nature. Secondly, many thanks to all the students who have read, discussed and enjoyed youth texts as part of the American Studies course *The Radiant Hour* at the University of Derby, England. It is from this course that the book takes its title. In the words of Adrienne Rich, 'As teachers, we have to become students again, continually'.

I would like to thank Serpent's Tail and Elizabeth Young for their permission to re-publish 'Children of the Revolution', which first appeared in *Shopping in Space: Essays on American 'Blank Generation' Fiction*, by Elizabeth Young and Graham Caveney (1992).

Note to readers

Readers will find notes and a bibliography at the end of each individual chapter. These will enable further reading and the development of the ideas suggested in the section.

INTRODUCTION
The Radiant Hour: On Youth Cultural Studies

Neil Campbell

To read the pronouncement of Peter Sealey, Director of Global Market-ing for Coca Cola, that 'The time is right; the world has changed. There are global media now, like MTV. And there is a global teenager. The same kid you see at the Ginza in Tokyo is in Piccadilly Square [sic] in London, in Pushkin Square, at Notre Dame',[1] is to realize how far youth has been embedded into corporate America. It is also an occasion to recognize that such a bold assumption may misunderstand the complex relations of youth interacting with the multiple social forces and institu-tions that surround them. Even accepting there might be such a concept as a 'global teenager', this supposed marketing target audience for Coca Cola has its own ideas, forms of expression and may or may not fulfil the category assigned it by the corporation. These fundamental relationships of representation and power, and the assumptions about control, defini-tion and status are central to the consideration of the place of youth in American culture to be discussed in this collection of essays.

The concept of youth itself is complex because it is bound up with cultural practices, definitions and values that have constructed its multiple meanings over time. As Stuart Hall reminds us: 'It is by our use of things, and what we say, think and feel about them—how we represent them —that we give them a meaning . . . the words we use about them, the stories we tell about them, the images of them we produce, the emotions we associate with them, the values we place on them' (Hall 1997: 3). Youth is, therefore, defined within different discursive formations circulating within culture, where culture is seen as a process and a set of practices that produce and exchange meanings through the members of a social system, and where discourses are 'ways of referring to or constructing knowledge about a particular topic of practice: a cluster (or formation) of ideas, images and practices, which provide ways of talking about, forms of knowledge and conduct associated with a particular topic, social activity or institutional site in society' (ibid: 6). Hence, discourses, such as popular music, fashion, television, advertising, fiction, journalism, education and medicine produce 'knowledge' about what constitutes 'youth', about how we should interpret it and define it within our particular historical moment. In addition, and alongside these powerful discourses, America has a particularly resilient cultural attachment to the idea of youth, viewing itself as a mythic nation of youthfulness formed out of the rejection of the Old World 'parent' culture and creating itself anew. Ponce de Leon's search for the Fountain of Youth brought him from Europe to Florida to attain immortality, just as George Washington's youthful energy would 'cut down' his father's English cherry tree in a symbolic myth of honest, destructive severance of the fresh, New World from the stale, Old (parental) World (see Chapters 5 and 6). Amid such embedded cultural creation myths, America has remained fascinated by constantly reinventing representative narratives of youth and recasting them as the dominant discourse or cultural mood of the age demands. In turn, however, other 'excluded' groups intervene, such as women, Chicano/as or African-Americans, to produce and circulate their own stories of youth which might run counter to the mainstream, but which utilize certain patterns in youth representation to promote particular notions of community or serve other political purposes. Thus youth signifies desire, hope, and promise as well as fear and suspicion as it is constructed in the discourses of the adult world.

Discourse constructs concepts of youth in any given situation by approving or disapproving of the languages used to talk, write or represent it within society. At any time certain discourses will become dominant, carry more power and influence within society, and as a result, their versions and uses of youth will assume greater cultural weight and significance. Hence, as various authors in this collection testify, youth is often defined as a 'problem', a 'crisis' or as 'trouble' to be managed by parent-culture's institutions of power (education, family, media, judiciary), and yet elsewhere it is framed by notions of pleasure, fun and exoticism (see Chapters 1, 3 and 8). These definitions or uses of youth are not mutually exclusive and often interrelate in different ways. For example, images of a fun-loving, self-gratificatory youth can be interpreted as irresponsible, anti-social and 'slack' within a dominant adult discourse that values the work ethic and strict social codes of behaviour. However, as discourses continually shift, change and alter, it is likely that any dominant view can be, at times, challenged by emergent discourses that represent youth in different ways. Hence, fun can be reinterpreted as a healthy and positive release from stress and overwork, like the popular television series *Ally McBeal*'s recuperation of 'song and dance' and animation as signifiers of 'youthful', carefree, zany exuberance and as release from the heady, 'adult' world of the attorney's office; or the cycles of Hollywood films, like the work of John Hughes in the 1980s (*Ferris Bueller's Day Off, The Breakfast Club*), that presented youth as potentially disruptive, but ultimately reconciled, in its own interest, to American core values like family, home, school and friendship. Tension and instability are, however, part of the understanding of how discourses work within society, for they are rarely fixed and unassailable, but exist as part of a system of power relations in which contest and negotiation take place. The notion of hegemony, derived from Antonio Gramsci, helps explain this process, for it refers to a situation in which 'a provisional alliance of certain social groups can exert "total social authority" over the other subordinate groups' by winning and shaping consent and agreement about values (Hebdige 1979: 15–16). However, it is provisional precisely because it requires consent, and therefore, exists as a 'moving equilibrium' liable to be challenged, modified, negotiated, resisted or even overthrown by other cultural configurations (see Hall and Jefferson 1991: 11–12). Thus texts which define and explore notions of youth with an 'apparent universality' (Brake 1987: 5), have to be examined, as in this collection, from a range of perspectives as revealing documents or sites, not just about youth itself, but about the multiple discourses that contribute to its construction and how these are, in turn, used hegemonically within society. In studying youth as a cultural construct, therefore, one examines significant relations, negotiations and struggles over meanings, power, hegemony, ideology, representation and authority circulating within American society.

Studying Youth: Some Key Elements

The concept of adolescence developed with urbanization and industrialization in the nineteenth century, as children attended school more regularly and age differences became specifically organized as a social tool. As high schools developed in the USA, children remained longer in formal education and the term 'adolescent' came into the common vocabulary to mark them off from the step into work and the temptations of city life. With parents living longer and having less reliance on their children to work to support the family, attention focused upon the years between childhood and adulthood and how these could be best managed to produce a 'good citizen'. This 'in-between-time' was quickly defined as one of potential trouble where the problems of being on the edge of two worlds gave rise to immense 'storm and stress' from which the adolescent emerged as an adult, either reconciled or antagonistic towards the existing, 'parent' culture.

In America, G. Stanley Hall, professor of psychology at Clark University, wrote *Adolescence and Its Relation to Psychology, Anthropology, Sociology, Sex, Crime, Religion, and Education* (1904) in an effort to explain and account for the turmoil of youth. He believed that adolescence was 'a new birth, a wiping clean of the slate of childhood', but still a time full of struggle and pain which had to be allowed free play in order that the subject made a 'safe passage to maturity' (Kett 1977: 217). Following Freud, Hall felt any repression of instincts, of which youthful conflict was an example, was unhealthy and would ultimately hamper a 'normal' transitional development. Hall felt that the individual developed like the nation, resting his work on a version of the theory of recapitulation which claimed that the child's passage through life followed the course already taken by his 'race' and nation. Thus, adolescence corresponded to a prehistory of the race characterized by migrations and upheavals in which myths and sagas reflected these traumatic movements that led to a kind of quasi-religious awakening. Hall's work demonstrates how youth was always bound up and defined through various discourses, as his book's title suggests, making links between adolescence and 'race', 'nation', sexuality and gender, and also demonstrating in its contradictoriness the problems with any all-encompassing attempt to explain youth. Hall advocated a dual freedom and control; the former allowing the adolescent to discover his/her potential whilst the latter enabled him or her to be channelled towards the social good. Yet Hall asserts the need to watch and guide youth through these troubled times because there is the potential within such an energized and problematic group for deviance and anti-social behaviour. The influence of Hall on youth studies was significant, encouraging adult-sponsored organizations like the Scouts, parents' manuals to advise on bringing up troubled adolescents, and high school management systems to 'train' them for adulthood, and therefore, to overcome such deviant possibilities.

These interests and concerns over youth development led to a trend for parental guidebooks, such as the 'Childhood and Youth Series', with titles like *Honesty* (1914), *The High School Age* (1915), and *Self-Reliance* (1916), offering advice on how best to overcome the 'problems' constantly associated with youth. Thus, in *The High School Age*, boys are being 'round[ed] . . . out into efficient manhood' and find in adults 'sympathy and help rather than condemnation' (in Kett 1977: 230). This is a part of a tradition in which youth is surveilled and guided to adulthood and a useful and productive future determined by the 'parent' culture and its class-related attitudes. Acland calls this the 'ideology of protection' where 'strategic interventions by state and others' guarantees the 'smooth reproduction of social relations' and, therefore, of hegemony (1995: 25). In fact, the assumed danger of youth, as Acland argues, justified and encouraged the hegemonic social order to assert its authority even more and set the boundaries of the acceptable, both discursively and legally. This interrelationship of youth with adult cultures was made more visible as the former manifested itself as *sub*cultural groups, that is, as informal and organic groups which existed beneath, but within—as *sub*terranean, *sub*ordinate, *sub*altern and potentially *sub*versive—the mainstream, dominant culture (see Gelder and Thornton 1997).

The Chicago School of Sociology, formed in 1892, developed a reputation for a specific form of urban studies interested in the 'interaction of people's perceptions of themselves with others' views of them' (Gelder and Thornton 1997: 11). By the 1920s the Chicago School, using participant observation, gathered and published materials on youth gangs and deviant groups (criminals, bootleggers), and through a number of subsequent works developed approaches to those 'subcultures' which exist alongside the broader American culture. Although not purely concerned with youth studies, this work clearly recognized the significance of subcultural youth formations and their relations with the 'parent' culture, and began to structure research questions to explore these areas in more depth. This can be seen in the influential studies by Thrasher (1927), Whyte (1947), Albert Cohen (1955) and Howard Becker (1963), in which youth opposed and reversed many of the values and customs of the mainstream culture through the distinctive styles, rituals, values and languages they created. The Chicago School, and its later developments, began to explore working-class youth subculture and its links to territory, class, ethnicity and culture in ways that valued and examined the lived experience of youth in cities. Looking back on some of their findings, John Irwin wrote that 'subcultural pluralism and relativism' affects everyday interaction because, '[o]ne's values, beliefs, and cultural meanings are no longer taken for granted . . . one is involved in consciously comparing, negotiating and sharing these with others . . . [and] the subculture is becoming an explicit and important action system' (in Gelder and Thornton 1997: 69).

Following a conference at the University of Chicago in 1941 and discussions with The Committee on Human Development, A. B. Hollingshead started his study *Elmtown's Youth* (1949).[2] Although not *of* the Chicago School, aspects of its approaches filter into the study, and in particular its exploration of class and status systems within the youth community. The 'hypothesis' for the study claims that 'The social behavior of adolescents appears to be related to the positions their families occupy in the social structure of the community' (Hollingshead 1961: 9). Living in the community of Elmtown and using participant observation and interviews, the research 'often led us into the back alleys Elmtowners [i.e. adults] preferred to ignore', building a picture of a divided, hypocritical community (ibid.: 10). The study found that class was at the root of subcultural behaviour, with adolescents reflecting the status and power of their parents. The conclusions were that 'the ideals embodied in the democratic creed of official American society are being compromised by the operation of the class system in the schools . . . the churches, the lodges, the economic system, recreation, and leisure time organizations' (ibid.: 447). The embedded ideologies of Elmtown; 'reverence for the past, the status quo, and private property' determine 'high social prestige —wealth, family, and power' whilst those who challenged such notions are defined as 'enemies' and 'traitors' to both community and nation. Hollingshead reported that the 'system sifts and sorts [people] according to their "social worth" . . .' in a hegemonic process that appears an 'eternal truth', as if produced 'by the laws of nature' ensuring that the community's upper classes maintain unquestioned authority and 'control' (ibid.: 450–1). Hollingshead's analysis of a class-driven hegemony is a radical indictment of the methods used to control youth and spare them 'the shock of learning the contradictions in the culture' through a process of segregation from 'the real world that adults know' under the belief that they are being saved from 'conflict and contradiction' and so kept 'pure' (ibid.: 149). His research begins to suggest that, as others later would argue, youth cultures might be a form of 'collective compensation for those who could not succeed' in the routes laid down for them by their parents, educators and state (Hall and Jefferson 1991: 29).

Kenneth Keniston's *The Uncommitted: Alienated Youth in American*

Society (1965) wrote similarly of the 'failure of acculturation' to 'the American way of life' as a characteristic of youths who rejected the values of their parents and often longed for a more authentic, sincere world. Using a psycho-social approach, Keniston saw alienated youth as 'ambivalent, apolitical, and uncommitted' (Lewis 1992: 10), but acknowledged that this might be a response to a social order that offered them little, and against which they might be offering some resistance (see Chapter 8). Indeed, ignoring the class-related conclusions of Hollingshead, much American work concerned itself with youth's deviancy from social norms, or its oppositional qualities—what it was against, rather than what it was in its own right. This is echoed in the lines from the youth movie *The Wild One* (1954) when Marlon Brando is asked 'What are you rebelling against?', to which he answers, 'What have you got?' Matza (1961) argued that there were three subterranean traditions that defined the rebelliousness youth desired: delinquency, bohemianism and radicalism. In the 1950s and 1960s these often combined in versions of American youth culture that rejected the 'lonely crowd' of suburban America (Riesman *et al.* 1951; see Chapter 1) in favour of the 'Beat' generation and the counter-culture. In both examples, the idea of 'youthfulness' rather than the 'young' was an important factor symbolizing alternatives to the mainstream and registering an anti-establishment perspective that signalled a gradual movement away from the assumed consensus that Hollingshead had discovered in Elmtown, and towards a sense of youth 'disaffiliation', becoming 'active agents of social breakdown' (Hall and Jefferson 1991: 72). Friedenberg's *Coming of Age in America* (1965) demonstrates the reasons for youth disaffiliation by commenting on the 'massive intervention' by adults in the 'growth' of the adolescent which served to 'establish and maintain hegemony' and to 'colonise' and 'contain' the young (1965: 4). Clearly influenced by the civil rights and decolonization movements, Friedenberg aligns himself with aspects of Paul Goodman (1960) and Erik Erikson's (1951, 1968; see Chapter 8) work by calling for a liberationist education system that encouraged development rather than 'training' along officially sanctioned lines of economic necessity. His views are radical at times—anti mass education, compulsion and vocational curricula—and yet patronizing about the status of youth who, he assumes, need a kind of protection against 'trashy goods and shallow, meretricious relationships' because, he argues, youth cannot grow as part of 'mass society' (Friedenberg 1965: 249, 266) Charles Reich, however, in his influential *The Greening of America* (1972), saw youth as an international social bloc with 'an entire culture, including music, clothes and drugs', capable of radical potential because 'the message of consciousness went with it . . . capable of changing and destroying the Corporate State without violence' (in Shuker 1994: 228). These varied relations of education, mass society and subcultures emerging in the 1960s would, however, become an increasingly important area of youth studies as new voices sought to understand the multiple interactions of the discursive formations surrounding and defining 'youth' as a politically charged category in the post-war world.

Outside America, in, for example, Stanley Cohen's *Folk Devils and Moral Panics* (1972), the work of the Chicago School was expanded upon in order to explore how deviancy was constructed by 'labelling' through social institutions such as the legal system or the media. He looked at the reactions in the press to British seaside subcultural violence in 1964 and 1966, and how 'moral panics' were created and subsequent calls for controls instigated. His examination of media exaggeration, stereotyping and moral outrage led him to analyse 'Societal Control Culture' as a key response to perceived youth dangers. His work focused much attention on issues of representation and response, suggesting that there were multiple reactions and 'uses' of the events he described, ranging from 'moral panic' to spectacle and nostalgia. This range of interpretation and cultural analysis had an important influence on the development of youth studies in its next phase.

Elements of subcultural studies from the Chicago School, in particular Howard Becker's *Outsiders: Studies in the Sociology of Deviance* (1963), the examination of class and community relations seen in *Elmtown's Youth*, and Cohen's analyses of mediation, were developed in Britain via the various works of the Birmingham Centre for Contemporary Cultural Studies founded in 1964 (see Chapters 1 and 8). Initially, utilizing a Marxian, Gramscian approach, the Centre's increased social, political dimension to youth studies can be seen operating across a range of works, but found one of its earliest statements in Hall and Jefferson's collection *Resistance through Rituals* (1975) where attention is drawn to the idea that 'deviance was a social creation, a result of the power of some to label others', and the product of complex, social interactions around class, status and community (Hall and Jefferson 1991: 5). Importantly, youth is located within a wider definition of culture—not as was so often the case in the past, a segregated, protected sub-group of the adult world. Culture is defined as:

that level at which social groups develop distinct patterns of life, and give *expressive form* to their social and material life-experience . . . The 'culture' of a group or class is the peculiar and distinctive 'way of life' of the group or class, the meanings, values and ideas embodied in institutions, in social relations, in systems of beliefs, in *mores* and customs, in the uses of objects and material life.

(ibid.: 10)

A culture provides the 'maps of meaning' making the world intelligible to its members, but society consists of diverse cultures unequally accorded power and influence 'in relations of domination and subordination', with certain 'maps of meaning' having a more dominant, because authoritative, position. They manage and determine the hegemonic position through which their views are promoted and centralized as the 'core' values of the social order—forming an ideological consensus. Youth cultures, according to the Birmingham School, are always related to the dominant culture in complex, dynamic dialogues, perhaps reproducing established patterns (see Willis 1977) or 'winning space' within the social order by intervening within the hegemonic process through acts of resistance, negotiation and gestures of style (see Hebdige 1979). Youth responded to broad social shifts, to disintegrating and changing family roles, employment patterns and leisure, through their varied subcultural groups, but they could not solve these issues: 'They "solve", but in an imaginary way, problems which at the concrete, material level, remain unresolved' (Hall and Jefferson 1991: 47–8) This suggests that the subcultural activities of youth produced 'imaginary' or 'symbolic' victories through those avenues of life they had some control over (matters of style, music, language) whereas the 'real' political causes of their disaffection remained unresolved and located in another cultural realm.

Importantly however, the Birmingham School refused to see youth as alienated from society, preferring a Marxian idea of cultural production in which identity is formed by the 'use one makes of, and the meanings one ascribes to, the "raw materials" of existence' (Gelder and Thornton 1997: 84). As a result, youth became 'expressive, meaningful, significant' and could be 'read' through their actions, style and values, as complex cultural texts moving into and out of the mainstream (ibid.). The Birmingham approach took youth seriously as an interactive component in the complex workings of contemporary society, acknowledging in the process the importance of mass culture and leisure as key sites of youth, often emphasizing fashion, music, 'going out' and drug use in its studies. The overall influence of the Birmingham School has been immense, in Europe, the USA and globally, and has led to developments in cultural studies that have extended out from youth studies into issues of gender, ethnicity, race, place and cultural identity. The focused attention on class relations, structural questions and the spectacular aspects of youth expression are often cited as criticisms of the Birmingham School, as are its interests in style and its lack of awareness about youth's contradictions and the movements in and out of subcultures. These issues, however, have provided others with areas of research in terms of youth pleasures, identities and postmodernism. Sarah Thornton, for example, derives her ideas from a variety of sources, including the Birmingham and Chicago Schools, writing of 'subcultural capital' within rave culture. Borrowing the concept of 'cultural capital' from Pierre Bourdieu, she argues that youth 'measures' its credibility in terms of media coverage and notoriety, engaged as it is in an elaborate relationship between image and identity, resistance and incorporation. Thornton works out a fluid, dynamic, complex relationship of power at work within youth culture as it interacts diversely with society. Far from simply oppressed, youth exists in 'a media-made culture and a culture that makes media' (Lewis 1992: 4) seeking to utilize this reality in the construction of symbiotic relationships with diverse aspects of the 'parent' culture. There is a movement in Thornton's work away from reductionist oppositional, binary interpretations of youth identity or power relations, towards a more changeable, unstable and pragmatic inter-connectedness that develops notions of youth studies in some new, interesting directions that I shall discuss more later.

Studying Youth: Some Developments

The climate of interest in youth, subcultures and the various expressive practices that have emerged from and about these groups is reflected in the variety of approaches now being utilized in their examination. One productive way of understanding how representations of youth function is to view them as *dialogic*, as existing in an 'agitated and tension-filled environment . . . weav[ing] in and out of complex interrelationships, merg[ing] with some, recoil[ing] from others', but always 'leav[ing] a trace', sometimes 'harmonizing' and sometimes 'striking a dissonance' (Bakhtin 1990: 276–7). Texts, inscribed with discursive formations, must be interrogated so the powerful defining 'languages' might be understood, their 'interrelationships' unravelled, and their inclusions and exclusions revealed, challenged and resisted. For Bakhtin, dialogue means that Otherness, so often a definition of youth, does not exist in order to be submerged and incorporated eventually into a unified consciousness or social order, but it has a vital, consistent role in the production of meaning. In dialogue everything is defined through relations between differences, rather than determined by a single, authoritarian version at the centre. In dialogue, things coexist simultaneously, in tension and contestation, and no one meaning can ever dominate for it will always exist in relation to other meanings and so be liable to alteration and change. Thus, applying some of these ideas, youth can be viewed as always in dialogue with the marketplace, both feeding off and appropriating elements, whilst having its products incorporated and sold back by the same market.

Looking back to the late 1950s again, one can see the one-sided, or 'monologic' nature of youth discourse in a widely circulated socio-scientific study published in 1957, Remmers and Radler's *The American Teenager*. Carrying the weight of Margaret Mead's endorsement, the book was perceived as 'of supreme importance' because it surveyed high school age Americans and believed that its scientific method, or 'continued careful probing of his [sic] attitudes and behavior' (1957: 259), would result in greater understanding of the young mind. The liberal intentions of the study are, in many ways, laudable, but ultimately flawed, as so many youth studies are, by its insistence upon explanation and control. This liberal discourse concludes with three statements that reveal much about how youth was defined and contained in the late 1950s. It argues that youth is 'exasperating . . . unpredictable . . . inspiring', but that scientific knowledge 'will ultimately cut down his unpredictability . . . [and] he'll no longer be so exasperating', so the inspiration 'will become apparent' (ibid.: 259). The future of this one-dimensional, socialized youth is related to 'democracy's real promise'—'As we progress, this potential progresses too'—until 'the debt will be more than repaid' (ibid.). The language exposes the underlying connections between youth and national ideology, seeing it as the potential carrier of the dream of progress, democracy and good investment as long as the unpredictability and exasperation has been brought under control. More recently, as we have seen, cultural studies has related the 'inspiration' of youth to its very 'unpredictability' and its adeptness at intervening in the very discourses that seek to manage and define it. As Lipsitz writes, youth 'can only fight in the arenas open to them; [and so] they often find themselves forced to create images of themselves that interrupt, invert or at least answer the ways in which they are defined by those in power' (Lipsitz in Ross and Rose 1994: 20). Rather than erase unpredictability, youth representations, voices, and texts are not simply raised to be controlled, but might carry influence and weight as knowledges in their own right and produce innovative and dynamic forms of expression. Recent American youth studies (Giroux 1996; Grossberg 1992; Gaines 1992) in particular have been active in their willingness to explore these 'histories' and to assert them against their silencing in the official mainstream. Very much in the tradition of other marginalized groups, such as women, African-Americans and Native Americans, diverse youth groups contribute to productive counter-histories (see Chapter 6) that might find some valid space in an extended, evolving cultural dialogue. As Foucault wrote, there are

> a whole set of knowledges that have been disqualified as inadequate to their task or insufficiently elaborated: naive knowledges, located low down in the hierarchy, beneath the required level of cognition or scientificity . . . differential knowledge incapable of unanimity and which owes its force only to the harshness with which it is opposed by everything surrounding it.
>
> (Foucault 1980: 82–4)

These are the very unpredictable 'knowledges' of youth that need to be included in a wider cultural dialogue, a Foucauldian genealogy, aimed at recording 'struggles' and 'conflicts' but without 'the tyranny of globalising discourses with their hierarchy' and the 'centralising powers' that seek to explain, order and control (ibid.). Youth studies can represent this new history as a genealogy that 'must record the singularity of events outside of any monotonous finality . . . in the most unpromising places, in what we tend to feel is without history . . . ' (Foucault 1993: 139). This can be seen, for example in Donna Gaines' *Teenage Wasteland*, which examines the suburban 'psychic space' of disaffected youth by articulating their 'secret histories . . . lived histories shared in places coded with secret meanings' (Gaines 1992: 47). In a time of despair when the world appears to be 'shrinking' and 'your capacity to dream has reached a dead end', all that is left is to 'disappear', to 'shut down, tune[d] out; you're gone' as a way of resisting and establishing 'community' (ibid.: 101). Gaines' histories, like Foucault's and Giroux's, are about 'border crossing', projecting and representing specific youth voices into the mainstream—'to travel back and forth, tripping discourses, translating and presenting the social self where it usually fears to tread . . . in settings and situations we thought we had escaped when we decided to defect to the world of higher knowledge' (in Ross and Rose 1994: 229). In this way, Gaines' work is a first step in a cultural project concerned with defining and altering 'the power dynamic and try[ing] to humanize people', by 'working on the front lines' with youth and the institutions that traditionally seek to manage and shape their lives (ibid.: 229, 228).

Another way of constructing a 'genealogy' whilst examining the power of discursive formations and their dialogic relations, is through 'youth' texts which represent and narrativize, in diverse ways, the relations of youth within society. Hence, novels and films often articulate those discourses that define youth as a problem to be organized, controlled and surveilled; as a potentially wayward group in need of rules and adult-endorsed codes of practice to bring them into line and within the social fold (Foucault's 'centralising powers'), whilst also dialogically suggesting the contrary impulse toward self-definition and empowerment (Foucault's 'subjugated knowledges'). To borrow a commonly used image from fictional youth texts (see Campbell and Kean 1997), discourses 'script' young lives, providing a preordained, approved guide that defines and controls what can and can't be done. Bakhtin might call these 'scripts' monologic structures, since they define youth in a one-dimensional language—of class, race, gender, for example. As these 'scripts' become widely circulated, reinforced and assume the role of 'commonsense' (are made to appear natural) they achieve immense authority and centripetal, hegemonic power to define and to manage youth differences. Much of youth cultural studies, as we have seen, has been concerned with the dynamics of these relations, of the production and circulation of scripts/discourses, and their social power as boundary-setters and definers of youth norms and deviance. What tends to be squeezed out in this process of definition are the differences and 'unpredictabilities' that exist across the broad category 'youth', including important distinctions of race, gender, sexuality, and class. Cultural studies' interest in youth cultures has been, in part, a determined effort to resituate these differences and to examine the nuances and resistances inherent in the subcultures of plural youth. Youth cultural studies is a field for the analysis of opposition to the mainstream, to questionings of the preferred 'scripts' of adult culture, for analysing alternative modes of address and representation, subjugated knowledges, or what Henry Giroux (1996) called 'fugitive cultures'. Thus, youth studies, as we have seen, is often concerned with agency or the possibility of resistance and intervention in the systems of meaning sanctioned by the adult mainstream. Various forms of popular music have become sites for the analysis of youth's resistance and opposition to the mainstream, emerging most visibly with rock and roll in the 1950s (see Hebdige 1979; Shuker 1994; Grossberg 1992; Ross and Rose 1994).[3] As Grossberg writes, 'Rock emerged as a way of mapping the specific structures of youth's affective alienation on the geographies of everyday life', offering 'new possibilities of identification and belonging' and to 'increase its own sense of control' (1992: 179). Tricia Rose goes further, claiming some rap can serve as communal counter-memory constructing 'oppositional transcripts' as cultural responses to oppression and the stories told from within the closed circle of a preferred, official discourse. Rap resists 'dominant public transcripts', offering the oppressed a public arena through which to air their 'hidden transcripts' and so to give voice to a history not often told: 'a contemporary stage for the theatre of the powerless' (Rose 1994: 100, 101). This echoes both Hebdige (1988) and Gaines, the latter noting that 'we act every chance we get, everywhere we are, every day' (in Ross and Rose 1994: 234), suggesting the performance of identity as an oppositional action, just like the overt gestural styles of hip hop.

> Rap's capacity as a form of testimony, as an articulation of a young black urban critical voice of social protest has a profound basis for a language of liberation . . . Rap's poetic voice is deeply political . . . but rap's hidden struggle, the struggle over public space, community resources, and the interpretation of black expression constitutes rap's hidden politics.
>
> (Rose 1994: 144–5)

Critical to all this is that the dialogical process by which youth interacts with the established mainstream or centre is not overlooked or hidden away. This is not simply about noting the oppositional 'us/them' nature of youth's role in society, but seeing that dialogue is always more that a binary relation containing within it a more complex understanding based on how language works socially. There is an utterance, a reply, and the relations between these two elements. When applied to youth culture this is a productive reminder that it is more than opposition and resistance to adult authority (the 'reply'), it is about a third process between the utterance and the reply, or between the dominant discourse and the countering perspective. Increasingly, youth studies might become more interested in this third, dialogic element, the space between simplistic antagonistic definitions of adult/youth dichotomies and concerned much more with the hybrid space where youth and adults interrelate, learn from each other, listen, and exchange. Perhaps the conflict model of youth culture needs to be rethought again to recognize the varied, complex interactions and 'crossings' between the generations and across class, gender and ethnic lines.

One of the issues that this collection addresses, from different perspectives, is the need to acknowledge the 'fugitive', unofficial, subjugated histories of youth as part of a broader framework—a new genealogy— for democratic communities which must also hear the voices of other previously marginalized or oppressed groups. This is not simply political correctness or academic fashion, but a means of revitalizing the democratic process by inclusion and expansion and by unsettling old regimes of representation through a process of hybridization. Rap, new writing, graffiti, or dance styles represent voices heard within a more open, dialogic, understanding of culture in which meaning is not singular and fixed, but created in the interaction and interplay of diverse expressions. Youth's multiple mixed voices, varied representations—its 'heteroglossia' —to borrow a term from Bakhtin, should be seen as part of the complex dialogue of culture and not isolated as merely a 'phase' or a period of transition to be managed by the official, adult culture. This potentiality of youth and its ability to radicalize and critique, is, as we have seen above, often interpreted as a threat to the existing, established cultural centre where youth is defined as a danger and mediated as images of crisis and moral panic. In these terms, the differences within youth cultures that might signal what Acland terms 'fresh contacts' (see Chapter 1), are viewed instead as overt rejections of an already authorized present system and as dangers to be policed, controlled and diminished. Youth, in these terms, is dealt with as merely oppositional, a counter-force to be contained in some way. If we relate this back to the notion of scripting discussed earlier, the word 'authority' connects clearly with the sense of 'to author', and so binds power to authoring as a means of defining the norms and boundaries of existence and approving its terms of reference. The struggle is against the scripting of identity by others and the desire, however futile, to be the author of one's own self or to expand the acceptable frames of reference through which youth is 'written' into the social script. However, as Holloway reminds us (see Chapter 5), the 'bourgeois self-authoring myth' is itself ideological and masks a system of values and assumptions that need to be examined by other versions of identity, such as collectivity and community, which youth may, indeed, give access to. Grossberg puts it well: 'Youth was subordinated to its already defined place within a social narrative that was told before it arrived' (Grossberg 1992: 179). Thus central to the signification of youth has always been the search for empowerment from this position of subordination and alienation and from an adult-defined set of social norms which imposed a monologic authority.

Yet, of course, it is not quite as simple as this might appear since youth circulates as an aspiration within contemporary America not just as an identifiable transition between childhood and age. The generations that grew up in the 1950s and 1960s, the Baby Boomers, refuse to let go of 'youth' as a lifestyle choice and hold on to it through their choices of music, fashion, their struggles over body-image, their attitudes and, to an extent, their politics (especially environmentalism, multiculturalism, etc.). As Grossberg writes, youth can be viewed as 'an identity defined solely by and for the adults who, in a variety of ways, invest in it and use it to locate themselves' (ibid.: 176). Youthfulness of body and mind has separated itself off from youth alienation and subordination, whilst retaining some of the feelings associated with it, in order to represent a social position and a bundle of attitudes that signify vitality and fun, a desire for alternatives and a willingness to step outside the social average. Grossberg sees youth in these terms 'as an affective identity stitched onto a generational history' (ibid.: 183), a space which is increasingly occupied by those who 'feel' young and wish to identify themselves with its more positive social connotations. Youth is a commodified aspiration too that can be sold to any market, unrestricted to a particular age group; as lifestyle, as body-image, as outlook. What this might indicate, further to the discussion above, is that the old oppositional strategies of 'us/them', 'old/young', dominant and subculture are in the process of perpetual revision since the relations of youth and adult have themselves become less distinct, dialogized or even 'symbiotic' (Thornton in Ross and Rose 1992: 188). Some of the old want to be young and some of the young want to be old; subcultural style is *haute couture* and many of the perceived certainties of youth culture (its own metanarratives) have become far less clear within a popular cultural context where retro-reinvention and rediscovery means that disco resurfaces as cool and flares can be once again fashionable as youth imitates and mutates its earlier subcultural modes.

The ambiguous, hybrid crossing over between youth and age is part of the current cultural ground whereby youth cultures are perceived as forming 'coalitions across racial and ethnic lines' (Lipsitz in Ross and Rose 1994: 24), and beginning to break down or blur older, social barriers or stereotypes. As McRobbie argues, 'youth remains a site of cultural innovation' and through its ever-changing, mobile interactions with traditional borders and boundaries, has the capacity for 'different, youthful, subjectivities' (McRobbie 1994: 178–9). Rather than being contained within the single category of 'youth', McRobbie finds evidence of overlapping interest groups and alliances which contribute to the 'new ethnicities in relation to youth' (ibid.: 188) that she parallels with newer concepts of identity formation discussed in cultural studies (see Hall in Morley and Chen 1998; Gilroy 1993). Youth is always engaged in 'fragile, "shaggy", hybridic identities . . . at the forefront of exploring and inventing . . . categories' (ibid.: 192) and thereby, reflects notions of subjectivity that value unresolved and unfixed selves, 'always open to change, to transformation and to realignment' (ibid.: 192). In this vision, McRobbie is akin to Guillermo Gomez-Pena's New Border youth who mix and match the forms of different cultures so as to be of both and something else as well, '*en route* to other selves and other geographies' (Gomez-Pena 1996: 2). I would relate this sense of possibility back to the idea discussed earlier, that youth studies might, like Gomez-Pena, be interested in exploring notions of a mobile, 'third space' between conventional binary positions, ethnicities, subjectivities and classes, where, in the interstitial folds of society, something new and fresh might emerge.

In these speculations, youth is seen as always related to society in complex struggles over power and space, but within this process engaged in dynamic, innovative and productive redefinitions of identity, culture and authority. Cultural studies must develop its analyses to both record and understand the complex relations across these blurring lines and borders so as to recognize the expansion and development of 'youth' cultures and representations into many avenues of society (via race, class, gender, sexuality), across nations and across new media and technological forms (see Chapter 1).

Studying Youth: Case Studies

Many of these debates about youth can be seen by looking at how, in 1999, on the edge of the millennium, representations of American youth were both prevalent and contradictory, approving and disapproving, but always visible across a range of media texts. I wish to examine three diverse 'high school' media 'texts' which can be contrasted with my earlier examples, *Elmtown's Youth* and *The American Teenager*: (1) 'The Gap' advertisement pleading for a new consumer democracy of 'Everybody in vests', with multicultural youths promising to 'wrap us up in their love'; (2) news stories endlessly creating and feeding off the moral panics surrounding the safety of high schools in the wake of killings in Jonesboro, Arkansas, or Littleton, Colorado; (3) Hollywood's renewed enthusiasm for suburban high school movies like *10 Things I Hate About You*, *Cruel Intentions*, *Never Been Kissed*, *American Pie* and *Rushmore*.

Reading across these contemporary 'high school' texts, I am struck by the diverse messages they circulate about youth in America. The Columbine killings, for example, focused the world's media on issues of 'today's youth', violent anomie and prejudice amongst affluent teenagers. The shock surrounding the events at Columbine was emphasized because they took place in a well-to-do, primarily white, Colorado suburban school, with a strong academic and sports record; a school whose motto reads, 'The finest kids in America pass through these halls'. Beverly Fanganello of Denver City Council claimed, 'This is where everybody moves to be safe. This is middle America', horrified that the crisis, expected of inner city schools, should have apparently spread to leafy Littleton. Suddenly, the assumed order and success of white suburban kids—the signifiers of progress, democracy and sound futures, (according to the rhetoric of Boomer critics Remmers and Radler 1957)—was disrupted by the realization that the high school itself was possibly a tribal system of subcultures, with rivalries and hostilities mixing Nazism, Goth rock and the fascination with guns that adult culture either knew nothing about, or chose to overlook. Suddenly, the 'other' world of youth problems, its 'unpredictabilities', always imagined as inner city and non-white, intervened in the managed environment of Littleton. Cindy Brown, executive director of a group founded to combat school violence, said that the reason for the killings was 'real simplistic . . . troubled youths with access to weapons and access to schools' (*Guardian*, 22 April 1999: 1) Ironically, what she omits is any discussion of the complex nature of what that 'trouble' might be and of its causes within the wider society. The social causes are screened behind the predictable emphasis on individual eccentricities and the 'Trenchcoat Mafia', whilst the reporting revealed a pervasive regret for the loss of some idealized, suburban notion of youth as decent, athletic and hard-working. As writers like Giroux (1996) and Acland (1995) have consistently argued, issues of social control, imposed hierarchy, homogeneity, consumption, divisions of class, race and gender may all contribute to the 'troubles' that youth experience as they attempt to find a place in capitalist cultural formations which signal their approval on certain paths and not for others. Yet little serious discussion has taken place of these issues since the media seems fixated upon stories of lost innocence, corrupted youth and the dangers of unchecked internet access, preferring to ignore the rather more diverse nature of high school relations. Youth was the problem to be solved, for the sake of the nation, rather than an examination of the multiple forces that surrounded and constructed them in their daily lives at home and school.

In the film *10 Things I Hate About You* (dir: Gil Junger, 1999), set in Padua High School, Oregon, a similar picture is given of a school divided into multiple groups, from jocks and prom queens to white Rastafarians, cowboys and snobbish Ivy Leaguers. The discovery of these cliques is a source of humour in one sequence of the film, but in the media's shocked recognition at Columbine, it became a major factor in explaining the tragic events. Ironically, a cleverly written film script by Karen Lutz and Kirsten Smith, offers more insight to the 'troubled youth' than most of the 'moral panic' journalism that spilled out following the killings in Colorado. If the high school is a microcosm of the future, then the film sees America as far from united, democratic or progressive. In Padua (the film is a reworking of Shakespeare's *The Taming of the Shrew*), the school mirrors an equally divided and bizarre social system, where teachers and parents are the eccentric ones, seeking to control and monitor youth and shape them to their particular vision, whilst supporting education which appears to neither satisfy nor challenge its pupils. Even the 'hip' black English teacher sends Kat (Julia Stiles) out of class at every conceivable opportunity for presenting alternative views and thinking for herself. Home and school are comfortable but imprisoning spaces with a father, obsessed with his own body-image, desperate to keep his daughters from sexuality, and a school counsellor who neglects her 'troubled' students in order to write her own erotic novel. The film reminds us that any notion of youth is always contested, with parents and teachers holding on to their version of it—as health, as eroticism, as liberal teaching methods—whilst adolescents struggle to define themselves within the economic and social order through acceptance and popularity (Bianca), success and glamour (Joey) or through alternative behaviour and style (Kat and Verona), and within systems of home and school that present them with rules and regulations that appear perverse and restrictive. As so often in youth texts, the spaces of home and school represent disciplinary power and what is sought is an alternative space where youth might define itself as 'other' than the scripts played out in adult culture. Significantly, Kat sits on the porch of her house, is most free at school on the soccer field, and only relates to Verona (her 'suitor') when they are away from both spaces of home and school. It is no surprise that Kat reads Sylvia Plath's *The Bell Jar* to articulate her own inner troubles since the novel is a brilliant dissection of youth's struggle to overcome the controlling, reductive discourses of education, parents and patriarchy and to assert the possibility of self-expression and agency. In a wonderful image, Plath's serious novel echoes the comic intent of Kat's struggle for independence, referring to its heroine Esther Greenwood as feeling like a 'scrawled over letter' who 'hated the idea of serving men in any way [for she] wanted to dictate [her] own thrilling letters' and not simply repeat the words of others (Plath 1972: 21, 79).

In these two examples, high school and youth are both central and yet dealt with very differently. The youth of Columbine are mediated as victims in need of further protection, to be surveilled, counselled, and policed, whose transition from childhood has been rudely interrupted by violence. Perhaps symbolically, *Time* reported that as the school reopened, the library, where much of the killing took place, 'no longer officially exists' as it had been 'gutted . . . then sealed' behind 'two rows of blue lockers' (16 August 1999). Rather like the causes of the killings themselves and any productive discussion of youth troubles, the space in which they occurred has been hidden away, leaving other cultural texts, such as films, novels, cartoons, music, web sites etc. to address the underlying concerns of youth and its relations with the mainstream, adult culture.[4] As Mike Davis has said, youth has become such a regulated, curfewed and controlled social group in the late twentieth century, that 'the only legal activity . . . is to consume' (Davis 1995: n.p.). The adult gaze, after events like Columbine, falls on their imagined worst fears, that youth is out of control, and as a result, the response is to assert greater controls rather than to engage in deeper understanding. In one comment recorded in *Time*, a tourist remarked that Littleton is 'so clean-cut and sterile . . . There are so many things you have to be out of touch with before something like this can happen' (26 August 1999). Rather than listen to the voices that, however misguided, were present in the Trenchcoat Mafia and other groupings within the school, the forces of normalization closed ranks and 'took back the school', still remaining 'out of touch' with the roots of the very problem they claim to be concerned about.

This brings us back finally to The Gap's advertising campaign with its alternative to the Trenchcoat Mafia and Marilyn Manson images of troubled youth, preferring instead to represent youth as calm, orderly consumers singing of love, as if to reiterate an earlier desire expressed by

Coca Cola 'to teach the world to sing in perfect harmony'. The Gap's hip, multicultural campaigns have the same message wrapped up in different clothing, edging us towards what Charles Acland terms 'one-worldness' or globalism (see Chapter 1). Going 'Back to School' in this advertisement is nothing to do with new security measures and CCTV, but all about street chic, and the classic assertion of capitalist contradictions: individual sameness, 'Everybody in vests' (pun intended?). The advertisement's backdrop is white, sterile and its protagonists cool and almost static as they sing the lyrics of the song. However, The Gap corporate policy sees youth as part of a 'global community', like Peter Sealey's comment that opened this introduction, in which selling is only part of a wider commitment to youth issues. The Gap claims 'It's not easy growing up in today's world' and the corporation engages in 'youth learning programs that help kids develop self-esteem, stay in school . . . so they can grow up to lead rewarding and fulfilling lives' (http://www.gapinc.com). The corporation's social policy and its advertising articulates the Baby Boomers' dream of carefree, affluent, liberated youth and sells street fashion—with 'total access' (ibid.)—in a sanitized, pre-washed form to the next generation, the so-called Baby Boom Echo, Millennium Generation, Generation Y or Nexus Generation (see Chapter 1, 7, 8), whose diverse membership might participate in its consumption fully, choose to modify it in some creative manner, or reject it altogether. Whoever these texts 'target', however they are 'hailed' by their sophisticated languages, it is reassuring to remember that the sheer multiplicity within youth cultures means that the message is already being dialogized in some way, 'cut and mixed', sampled, reinvented or simply ignored.

Consistently, youth consumes and is consumed by these visions of what it should be, but equally youth has the capacity to resist, to alter, to reject, to ironize and to critique the very same structures that appear to define and control the boundaries of their lives. This is the instability I spoke of earlier and the reason that youth cultural studies has proven such a popular area within contemporary research. In one sense, youth is always a site of struggle, of resistance, of indifference, of creative thinking and disagreement, and therefore a place where cultural critics find scope to examine both the structuring forces of society and their counter-forces and oppositions. Although youth cultural studies may not offer any final, radical alternatives, perhaps its enduring interest is its capacity to present new, fresh, transgressive territories through which to enter and analyse the mainstream. As a form of dialogical Otherness, youth still has the capacity, as Tricia Rose says of rap, 'to unnerve and simultaneously revitalize American culture' (Rose 1994: 185). And yet, youth's status within the culture it dialogues with, is always ambiguous, always fluctuating between positions. As Dick Hebdige wrote in 1988 about youth subcultures, they are

> neither simply affirmation nor refusal, neither 'commercial exploitation' nor 'genuine revolt'. It is neither simply resistance against some external order nor straightforward conformity with the parent culture. It is both a declaration of independence, of otherness, of alien intent, a refusal of anonymity, of subordinate status. It is *in*subordination. And *at the same time* it is also a confirmation of the fact of powerlessness, a celebration of impotence.
>
> (Hebdige 1988: 35; my emphasis)

This tense dialogue between insubordination and impotence characterizes the way youth exists both in and out of the social system, necessarily 'other' within a cultural order that appears to endow them with visibility, for it never stops talking about youth, and yet is reluctant to convert that visibility into status and political power. Youth may be talked about and represented, but too often this cultural presence is controlled or put in parenthesis, as a necessary spectacle which can be easily discounted as a transitory phase soon to be incorporated into the normalized mainstream.

Youth in this collection is never simply one thing, but viewed instead as an important focal point for writers, film-makers, television producers and others to analyse ideologies, identities and themes in American life. Youth is a discursive site, crossed and recrossed with multiple meanings and representations that reveal a great deal about social order, power relations, social myths, institutions, and also about the capacity for pleasure, resistance, and the endless possibility for reinvention. Above all, as Hebdige recognized, youth is multiple, unstable and exists simultaneously in a variety of guises. It is no longer only about a particular age group, but has taken on immense cultural energy as a complex aspirational signifier maintaining its capacity for wonder and surprise, for a deep connection to feelings of 'faith, hope and refuge', as well as still provoking edgy fear and moral panic (Ross and Rose 1994: 3).

This Collection of Essays

This collection aims to examine how 'versions' or representations of youth have circulated within American culture through expressive texts, in particular through literature, film and television. The essays combine 'framing' chapters, which open up discussions on a range of important debates around the subject of American youth's relationship to the culture of which it is a significant element, and chapters which examine more specific groups of narratives for clues to how representations work within that culture. This collection extends debates about youth narratives and representations in different directions and through different critical voices, by reflecting a mixture of established critics in the field alongside newer, emerging writers. The collection aims, firstly, to reflect upon the critical meanings of youth and generation within the context of American cultural representation and, secondly, to trace these meanings through a range of texts—film, television and literature—in such a way that their ideological implications are emphasized. Thirdly, as I believe most of these essays demonstrate, there is a necessary political engagement that emerges when one considers the representations of youth. As these essays show, youth is always ideological because it is bound up with a whole series of social discourses, power relations, hierarchies and institutions, and, therefore, as one examines these forces in individual texts or groups of texts, one is drawn into an exploration of what Fredric Jameson (1981) would term 'the political unconscious' of America. Over the years, as I have shown earlier, 'youth' as an idea has been studied, commodified, demonized, saluted, appropriated and rejected, but, as a consequence, has rarely been far from the American psyche. For this reason, youth is a significant aspect of contemporary cultural politics with its attention to debates over identity and subjectivity, gender, sexuality, ethnicity, class, pedagogy and representation. Indeed, a key element in cultural studies has been the argument over who authorizes the narratives that are privileged in any culture, whose history is most prominent, whose versions are official and legitimized, and whose are subordinated and erased (see Jordan and Weedon 1995), and this is of particular prescience when we think of youth, since it is precisely within these struggles that so many of its representations are located.

Charles Acland's essay examines the development of the concept of 'generation' within the classification and analysis of youth cultures and sees its relevance to the debates over how youth is changing as we move into a new millennium. The impact of 'the waning of the specificity of youth', of globalization and transnationalism is traced through recent representations within the media, and the young are seen as 'a key site' within which capital and culture struggle for meaning and power. Identifying the 'dynamic' between individual consumer and 'transnational sameness', Acland ponders the contradictions inherent in these new trends as a source of critical analysis and for 'fresh contacts'. Henry A. Giroux's chapter is a passionate plea for political and pedagogical change anchored in an analysis of urban race representation in Hollywood films like *187*. He argues for a critical cultural politics that interrogates texts such as this and uses the process as a form of political education to break down the dominant discourses that frame youth, and in particular, urban youth of colour, in a narrow, limiting manner. It is a call for 'social investment' and the rejection of 'stereotypes and myths' of containment so that youth might be revised and included within a true democratic process rather than excluded from it and demonized as a danger to its survival.

Elizabeth Young's powerful essay, first published in 1992, surveys the changing literature of youth through the important decade of the 1980s by focusing upon the radical writings of now-familiar authors like Bret Easton Ellis, as well as the less well known work of the 'Downtown' New York group. Young contextualizes the fiction within the economic and social changes of the 1980s and reads it as a series of postmodern responses to an increasingly mediatized, simulated and excessive environment. Style magazines, comic books and music provided new sources for youth voices and these became rapidly integrated within the formal qualities of the 1980s novel whose authors saw these elements 'inextricably intertwined' in their dissections of postmodern culture. Jenny Robinson's chapter charts some of the earliest literary representations of youth in girls' fiction, and in particular Susan Coolidge's *What Katy Did*, with a view to exposing how these ambiguous cultural texts both map a 'trail' for patriarchy's notion of femininity and offer sites of resistance and pleasure for its female (and male) readers. Like Giroux's piece, this is a political and a personal journey whose conclusions are very relevant to contemporary debates on gender, power and representation. David Holloway's chapter uses the work of S.E. Hinton as a focus for an analysis of 'embedded class tensions' that are displaced by the unifying ideology of youth that has been persistent within American culture. Using the ideas of the often forgotten, but highly significant Randolph Bourne, Holloway unlocks the ideological elements of the discourse of youth both as 'negative' and, ultimately as a potentially explosive, 'utopian' force through which to expose and critique bourgeois myths of self and social order.

In contrast to the urban focus of many youth texts, Neil Campbell writes about the rural West in *Montana 1948* and the dramatic education of a boy growing up after the war. The fiction becomes, however, another channel through which significant youth themes are examined, and in particular the construction of history and masculinity. Through its youthful narrator, the novel interrogates how history and subjectivity are constructed, offering imaginative parallels between revisionist, ethnic history and life-writing, to show, as in Holloway's essay, that the *bildungsroman*, the most familiar of youth genres, can be a source of alternative thinking and subtle political analysis. The book closes with chapters examining recent visual media, Generation-X films and 'teen-something' TV. Simon Philo argues for a fuller reading of *Dawson's Creek* and other youth TV, demonstrating their continuity with earlier youth texts and their support for traditional values, such as the family and responsible sexuality. Contrary to Michael Medved's fear of promiscuity and the end of core values, Philo sees these TV texts as unthreatening and conservative, presenting far more complex renditions of youth experience than is usually attributed to them. Jon Lewis's essay on Gen-X film takes us back, in part, to the first essay in the collection, with its attention to earlier notions of youth from the 1960s related to those prevalent images that saturate the media today. Analysing trends within a range of films, Lewis sees connections to Keniston's and Erikson's adolescence theory as well as glaring differences that demonstrate Gen-X's abiding interests in timeless youth themes: school, work, family, sexuality, the environment, sincerity and apocalypse. Faced with the 'part-time, dead-end' future, voices in these films fluctuate between despair and ambition, anxiety and irony, and despite their supposed indifference to the state of things, seem to care a good deal.

The ideological tensions uncovered and analysed in these chapters refer back to the collection's title whose roots lie in a collage of images from F. Scott Fitzgerald's *The Beautiful and the Damned* (1922). Fitzgerald emerged in the 1920s defining the era of 'flaming youth', and articulated elements that would become central to all future representations of youth: frankness, style, music, rebellion, conformity, sexuality, dream and disappointment. Maury Noble, in *The Beautiful and the Damned*, ruminates on happiness as the 'first hour after the alleviation of some especially intense misery', then comments on Anthony Patch's look as 'one of those immortal moments which come so radiantly that their remembered light is enough to see by for years'; and finally, Gloria and Anthony's desire is described as the ability to 'slip off the blinders of custom . . . [so] each would find in the other almost the quintessential romance of the vanished June' (Fitzgerald 1974: 108–8, 150). Across these words, Fitzgerald's romanticism captures, I feel, the ambivalence of American youth as 'intense misery', 'immortal moments' and a rejection of 'custom'—a kind of radiant hour of promise, anxiety and desire in the life of the individual embedded within a social order. Although 'youth', as I have argued, may no longer be simply the preserve of the young, its attributes and moods are aspired to by all those who seek to identify themselves with youthfulness. These aspirations may be added to with dreams of health, sexuality and social acceptance or rebellion, but at the heart of the appropriation of youth is the desire to feel, if only occasionally, connected to the matrix of radiance: intensity/misery/immortality/rebellion/desire. To feel life in all its complex, ambiguous wonder. As Patricia Meyer Spacks wrote in 1981,

> The young embody our most profound vulnerabilities and our most intimate strengths. They speak to us of our past and our future. We can imagine them as licensed transgressors, surrogates for ourselves, or as prophets of salvation; as violators or precursors of system. (1981: 296)

These essays contribute to the necessary and important debates over the meanings of youth representation within American culture, as both 'violators' and 'precursors of system', the past and the future, profit and loss, salvation and transgression, indifference and care, self and community. In so doing, the collection deliberately asserts the contradictions in youth representations and, therefore, denies any easy definitions that only serve to compound stereotypes or sustain vested interests. Without any single vision or approach, these essays show how the cultural politics of youth are no longer only about being young but rather associated with both personal and public values, aspirations and ideologies that extend way beyond any simple consideration of the self. As a consequence, the radiant hour is both brief and endless.

Notes

1 Quoted at http://carmen.artsci.washington.edu/cmu418/lecture8/coke.html
2 In the Preface, for example, Hollingshead credits Louis Wirth, a leading figure in the Chicago School.
3 Music is not discussed at length in this collection, as its focus is upon narratives and representations of youth. The amount of research and publication on

music and youth culture has been, however, one of the most productive areas in recent years. See the Bibliography for some key texts.

4 Columbine has generated a mass of Internet discussion, and now has vast web-sites and 'memorials' which reflect the journalism, individual and communal reactions, public and political outcries, and various other issues related to the events. See, for example, *Columbine: Tragedy and Recovery* http.//www.denverpost.com/news/shotarch.html for many links.

Bibliography

Acland, Charles (1995) *Youth, Murder, Spectacle: The Cultural Politics of "Youth in Crisis"*, Boulder and Oxford: Westview Press.

Bakhtin, M. (1990) *The Dialogic Imagination*, Austin: University of Texas Press.

Becker, H. (1963) *Outsiders: Studies in the Sociology of Deviance*, New York: Free Press.

Brake, M. (1987) *Comparative Youth Culture*, London: Routledge.

Campbell, N. and Kean, A. (1997) *American Cultural Studies*, London: Routledge.

Cohen, A.K. (1955) *Delinquent Boys*, London: Collier Macmillan.

Cohen, S. (1972) *Moral Panics and Folk Devils*, London: MacGibbon and Kee.

Davis, Mike (1995) On-line interview with *Escape Velocity*, no page.

Erikson, E. (1951) *Childhood and Society*, London: Imago.

——(1968) *Identity: Youth and Crisis*, New York: Norton.

Fitzgerald, Scott. F. (1974 [1922]) *The Beautiful and the Damned*, Harmondsworth: Penguin.

Foucault, M. (1980) *Power/Knowledge: Selected Interviews and Other Writings 1972–1977*, London: Harvester Wheatsheaf.

——([1997], 1993) *Language, Counter-Memory, Practice: Selected Essays and Interviews*. Ithaca, NY: Cornell University Press.

Friedenberg, E.Z. (1965) *Coming of Age in America*, New York: Vintage.

Frith, S. (1983) *Sound Effects: Youth, Leisure and the Politics of Rock 'n' Roll*, London: Constable.

Frith, S. and Goodwin, A. (eds) (1990) *On Record: Rock, Pop and the Written Word*, London: Routledge.

Gaines, Donna (1992) *Teenage Wasteland: Suburbia's Dead End Kids*, New York: Harper Perennial.

—— (1994) 'Border crossing in the USA', in A. Ross and T. Rose, *Microphone Fiends: Youth Music and Youth Culture*, London: Routledge.

Gelder, K. and Thornton, S. (eds) (1997) *The Subcultures Reader*, London: Routledge.

Gilroy, Paul (1993) *The Black Atlantic*, London: Verso.

Giroux, H.A. (1996) *Fugitive Cultures: Race, Violence and Youth*, London & New York: Routledge.

Gomez-Pena, G. (1996) *The New World Border*, San Francisco: City Lights.

Goodman, Paul (1960) *Growing Up Absurd*, New York: Random House.

Grossberg, L. (1992) *We Gotta Get Out of this Place: Popular Conservatism and Postmodern Culture*, London: Routledge.

Hall, G. Stanley, (1904) *Adolescence: Its Psychology and Its relation to Physiology, Anthropology, Sociology, Sex, Crime, Religion and Education*, New York: D. Appleton and Co.

Hall, S. and Jefferson, T. (eds) (1991 [1975]) *Resistance through Rituals: Youth Cultures in Post-War Britain*, London: HarperCollins.

Hall, S. (1996) 'New ethnicities', in D. Morley and K.H. Chen (eds) *Critical Dialogues in Cultural Studies*, London: Routledge.

——(1997) *Representation*, London: Sage.

Hebdige, D. (1979) *Subculture: The Meaning of Style*, London: Methuen.

——(1988) *Hiding in the Light*, London: Routledge.

Hollingshead, A.B. (1961 [1949]) *Elmtown's Youth*, New York: Science Editions.

Irwin, John (1997) 'Notes on the status of the concept of subcultures', in K. Gelder and S. Thornton, *The Subcultures Reader*, London: Routledge.

Jameson, F. (1981) *The Political Unconscious*, London: Methuen.

Jordan, G. and Weedon, C. (1995) *Cultural Politics*, Oxford: Blackwell.

Keniston, K. (1965) *The Uncommitted: Alienated Youth in American Society*, New York: Harcourt Brace and World.

Kett, J. (1977) *Rites of Passage: Adolescence in America, 1790 to the Present*, New York: Harper Colophon.

Lewis, Jon (1992) *The Road to Romance and Ruin: Teen Films and Youth Culture*, London: Routledge.

Lipsitz, G. (1994) 'We Know What Time It Is: Race, Class and Youth Culture in the Nineties', in A. Ross and T. Rose, *Microphone Fiends: Youth Music and Youth*, London: Routledge.

McRobbie, Angela (1994) *Postmodernism and Popular Culture*, London: Routledge.

Matza, D. (1961) 'Subterranean traditions of youth', *Annals* 338: 102–18.

Meyer Spacks, P. (1981) *The Adolescent Idea*, New York: Harper Colophon.

Negus, K. (1995) *Popular Music and Society*, Oxford: Polity Press.

Plath, S. (1972) *The Bell Jar*, London: Faber and Faber.

Reich, C.A. (1972) *The Greening of America*, Harmondsworth: Penguin.

Remmers, H.H. and Radler, D.H. (1957) *The American Teenager*, New York: Charter Books.

Riesman, D., Glazer, N. and Denny, R. (1951) *The Lonely Crowd*, New Haven: Yale University Press.

Rose, Tricia (1994) *Black Noise: Rap Music and Black Culture in Contemporary America*, Hanover: Wesleyan University Press.

Ross, A. and Rose, T. (1994) *Microphone Fiends: Youth Music and Youth Culture*, London: Routledge.

Shuker, Roy (1994) *Understanding Popular Music*, London: Routledge.

Thornton, S. (1994) 'Moral Panic, the Media and Rave Culture', in A. Ross and T. Rose, *Microphone Fiends: Youth Music and Youth Culture*, London: Routledge.

Thrasher, F. (1927) *The Gang*, Chicago: University of Chicago Press.

Whyte, W. Foote (1947) *Street Corner Society: The Social Structure of an Italian Slum*, Chicago: University of Chicago Press.

Willis, Paul (1977) *Learning to Labour*, London: Saxon House.

ONE

*Fresh Contacts: Global Culture
and the Concept of Generation*

Charles R. Acland

'You have left your fingerprint on me'—*I hate my generation*—
Sloan (1994)

Generation X in Context

I remember the first time I encountered the term Generation X in its
contemporary form. It was in a photocopy of a short article Douglas
Coupland had written for a minor Canadian publication, now untraceable.
A younger brother handed the photocopy to me, saying something to the
effect of 'you've got to read this; it explains everything'. This was in 1990,
a year before the publication of Coupland's *Generation X: Tales for an
Accelerated Culture* (1991), which would become the largest selling book
for a first-time Canadian novelist. I would have recognized the term
initially as Billy Idol's 1970s punk band. This new use, however, typified
the tail-end of the post-World War II baby boom, roughly from 1961
to 1966—though the dates are a matter of contest—as cynical, over-
educated, underemployed, and as a demoralized population expecting only
a dwindling purchase on the currents of economic and cultural life.
Generation X, in this definition, would soon eclipse any memory of
other Xs, whether bands or references to various wayward generations,
including Hamblett and Deverson's (1965) investigation of British youth
and Coupland's own apparent source for the term, Paul Fussell's *Class*

(1983). And though my brother's exclamation may have been a bit too expansive, he wasn't wrong; Generation X explained a lot.

Or rather, it *felt* that way; it spoke to 'us'. The concept seemed to ground a set of ideas and experiences that had been hovering about without a perch. These include the context of an apparent permanent recession, 'belt-tightening', cutbacks, downsizing, and living in the cultural and demographic shadow of the bulk of Baby Boomers. Such conditions led to a sense of receding possibility, and hence, to a struggle to define one's own cohort. More broadly, Generation X referred to the experience of coming of age in the late twentieth century, but doing so with a certain lack of distinction. What is notable about being the second or third last generation of this century, of this millennium? While all generational delineations incorporate a degree of imprecision, Generation X is unusually ambiguous; it is in part about failure, which includes a failure to define a generational identity, except in negation to Boomer lifestyle and life-cycle. Jane Pilcher writes that one of Karl Mannheim's contributions to the study of generations is to propose that 'not every generation develops an original and distinctive consciousness' (Pilcher 1994: 491). Generation X may be thought of, somewhat paradoxically, as the designation of the inability, and struggle, to define just such a consciousness. It denotes a structure of feeling, describing the unavailability of satisfactory markers of youthfulness and maturity, announcing that prevailing models of 'growing up' did not suit the historical context. In this acknowledgement was the powerful mark of self-recognition, even as it expressed tales of the inability to assert such marks. Generation X was a sensation, that is, a bodily response of agreement and expression as much as a demographer's category, for it presented the thrill of hearing strangers tell stories of one's own life.

While there are abundant problems with the concept, I would suggest that many have to do with the selectivity of critics who have tended to see Generation X as evidence of white middle-class resentment only. Though in its reactionary forms Generation X is about the downward slide of a previously secure class faction, a point well documented by Sherry Orter (1998), it equally captures a pervasive sense of rootlessness among other young North American social factions. For example, it is not so far from what Cornel West (1988) described as the 'walking nihilism' of black America. The authors of *13th Gen* suggest that part of the distinctiveness of youth born between 1961 and 1981 is their experiences of and familiarity with a racially attuned discourse of civic life. However, they argue, this understanding of cultural and ethnic diversity is short-circuited by economic divisions. Ultimately, 'What they want, and what they fear others [that is, other generations] will not let them have, is a society as diverse and color-blind as common sense will allow' (Howe and Strauss 1993: 146). Douglas Coupland's (1991) original concept was to provide a description of a 'forgotten' youth culture living with the economic and cultural leftovers of the older boomers; this crosses formations of gender, class and ethnicity, and, as such, it is expressed and experienced variously.

It follows, in light of such a variety of experience, that we need to pay attention to the different registers of a generational formation. One register asks what does any specific conceptualization of 'generation' say and who is it taken to speak about; another asks who takes up this formation as a reasonable and resonant characterization. In this respect, generation has a multiple effectivity, circulating ideas about successions of populations and becoming a mode of identity, the two of which are not identical. Such a distinction is necessary given the prominent place 'generation' has in popular culture, appearing with regularity to explain everything from unemployment to shifts in musical styles, from voting patterns to fashion. Where youth has become more generalized, with some arguing that there has been a withering of the connection between 'youth' and age, by contrast, generational differences have become an obsession. In this respect—and this is the point I intend to elaborate throughout this chapter—the concept refers to particular manifestations of temporally designated communities, and might be best thought of as a form of *vernacular knowledge of historical location*, one that speaks to the role of novelty in contemporary capitalism.

For this reason, any examination of generation must be attuned to how it helps represent and verify a 'truth-value' of historical experience; studies of generation must extend beyond merely confirming or denying the authenticity of that truth. Designations of division and particularity in populations have a life and consequence beyond the segments identified and typified. Just as the notion of the Baby Boomer mobilizes a series of qualities and responses affecting those born far beyond the years following World War II, Generation X is as much about a cultural agreement as it is about self-recognition. Along these lines, Sherry Orter suggests that the 'public culture' of Generation X, that is, its life as a set of media texts, may in fact 'tell us as much about the anxieties of upper-middle-class parents as it does about some set of young people out there in the world' (Orter 1998: 434). We can extrapolate from this point to say that the concept of generation needs to be understood not only with respect to the experiential and material actuality it references, but also to its role as discourse, circulating ideas about work, status, familial relations, education, and historical situations. Glenn Wallach takes a similar approach in his sweeping history of American generations from 1630 to 1860. His study does not propose authentic generational units or experiences; instead, he identifies 'a powerful language of continuity shaping ideas about youth and generation,' focusing upon symbols and metaphors (Wallach 1997: 3). So, what cultural and significatory work does 'generation' do? How do ideas about the world and specific historical instances come to cohere around portions of a population? With what effect upon our thinking?

It seems that the concept of generation is especially important for cultural studies if only for the reason that it has not been explored with the same vigour and intensity as other terms related to youth cultures. Indeed, the important collection *Gender and Generation* (McRobbie and Nava 1984) does not even have its title's second key term included in the index. Instead, in cultural studies especially, 'youth' gets massively overplayed, as though it has some special semiotic slippiness, and as though it is a primary 'scandalous category,' as John Hartley (1984) puts it, that displays distinctive status as a destabilizing element in orders of meaning. In fact, the investment in an idea of 'youth'—and in particular, an image of the marginal *and* resistant young person—tells us quite a bit about the selectivity of cultural studies. Much of this research in British Cultural Studies emerged from an intersection with radical criminology in the early 1970s (see for instance, Cohen and Young 1973; Rock and McIntosh 1974), a meeting point that has been underplayed and often omitted from histories of cultural studies. The British Cultural Studies investment in youth culture resulted in a reworking of 'subculture theory' (Hebdige 1979; Hall and Jefferson, 1976), whose largely structuralist studies helped to challenge the imagined unity of youth by seeking out semi-autonomous cultures thriving in the shadow of parent cultures. Several groundbreaking studies explored the complexity of youth subcultures, including mods, Rastafarians and punks, by emphasizing the expressive coherence of such communities, though some criticized their implicit assumptions about authenticity. Revisions to this work have continued through the 1980s and 1990s, pointing out blind spots in the early research, and most importantly placing issues of gender and ethnicity at the forefront (cf. Thornton 1995; McRobbie 1980; Rose 1994). These revisions, however, did not push subsequent studies beyond a narrow age definition. One might ask, why is there not the same abundance of challenges to the semiotic stability of the adult, of the middle-aged, of the child, and of the senior?

Our attention should be drawn to the historical specificity of the many cultural analyses of youth, that is, to the fact that cultural studies work on youth is never about youth universally, but about particular manifestations. Though this argument of particularity is sometimes hidden and disguised, discussions of youth culture hold at their nucleus an argument about historical context; the expectations of the critic are such that the site of analysis for studies of youth are assumed to be transitory, to be new, to be different, to be contemporary. Historical context has many articulations, one of which is that of generations. As I will argue in what follows, the very notion of successive generations—one cohort being replaced by another—offers a way of talking about popular understandings of historical change. Put differently, historically specific interpretations of the nature of youth—many of which already treat it as a discursively and culturally constructed category—could usefully start by examining generational location.

Take for example a prominent argument about youth culture. The manner in which a Baby Boomer generation has been able to occupy the very idea of youth, with an associated set of styles and activities, even as its members push well along in the life-cycle, is a striking example of the non-essential articulation between age, 'youth' and cultural expression. Further, this linkage announces the power of demographic and economic determinants in the formation of specific articulations. By contrast, the notion of Generation X is not especially well articulated to a single population, often appearing as a way to describe any twentysomething group. Where John Gillis (1974) writes of the 'democratization' of youth as it lost its class-specific location of the nineteenth century, we have witnessed its powerful attachment to Baby Boomers, thus somewhat disarticulating 'youth' from any special age. Youth, now, is seemingly disconnected from 'adolescence'. Steve Redhead (1997) alludes to this development, claiming that the present 'lost generation' may be better thought of as the 'last generation'. Noting parallel trends across Europe, in England, Germany, Poland, Slovakia and the Czech Republic, he suggests that the increasingly 'permanent' quality of the supposedly transitional stage of youth is partly explained by increasing youth unemployment and a related lengthening of periods of education (Redhead 1997: 100–1). In an earlier work, Redhead (1990) understands the expansion of youth well into adulthood as, if not the end of youth culture, then at least a disarticulation of 'youth culture' and 'rock culture'. Thus, while the critical literature may point to a waning of the specificity of 'youth', it equally announces the historical context of this development. In actuality, the 'last generation' may be a symptom of one generation's overdetermination of 'youth', not that youth or generation *per se* are receding.

Such an argument should not be misunderstood as claiming that all studies of youth are in fact studies of generation. I am not so bold as to make a pronouncement as totalizing as that. Yet, generation does help us pay attention to the historical context in which we study youth and cultural change, or at least encourages us to pay attention to how cultural change is being understood in specific historical contexts. My treatment of discourses of generation as vernacular forms of understanding historical specificity, and as a related form of historically specific identity, is not without contest. For that reason, it is instructive to return to some earlier figurations of generation.

The Problem of Generations

Hans Jaeger characterizes two periods of abundant scholarly interest in generations in the twentieth century. In the first, 1920–1933, German intellectuals are most prominent, producing theoretical works on the concept. In the second, the post-WWII period, American empirical research is dominant (Jaeger 1987: 277). The two central approaches, for Jaeger, are '[t]he pulse-rate hypothesis which assumes a rhythm of historical generations', and is research that tends toward examinations of universal aspects, and 'the imprint hypothesis' which suggests that coming-of-age marks people with a particular view to the world, and whose research tends toward socio-historical studies (ibid.: 280). The latter has become the dominant view, one that has been easily appropriated by demography, whose statistical and functionalist view Jaeger wishes to critique. He hopes to refute 'the belief that an historical analysis of generations has to be without exception antimaterialist, antimarxist, or antisociological' (ibid.: 291), a position that is essential to extend.

A well known work that fits with this second approach is David Riesman, Nathan Glazer and Reuel Denny's (1950) expansive study *The Lonely Crowd*. Arguably, their analysis announced a heightened interest in one's cohorts during the post-WWII period of affluence in the US, the generational dimension of which Jaeger notes (1987: 279). In *The Lonely Crowd*, the accumulation of wealth and a related shift from modes of production to consumption results in an outer-directed character. For Riesman *et al.*, this leads to an increasing conformity, as our behaviour is continually guided by the actions, observed or imagined, of those that surround us. The veracity of the claims presented in this influential work is beside the point here; instead, *The Lonely Crowd* is emblematic of a critical discourse turning to emphasize temporally defined population segments, even proposing that generational frameworks have a special relation to advanced capitalism.

Daniel Bell makes a similar allusion in *The Cultural Contradictions of Capitalism*. He writes, 'Insofar as one makes one's *own* experience the touchstone of truth, one seeks out those with whom one has common experience in order to find common meanings. To this extent, the rise of generations, and the sense of generation, is the distinct focus of modern identity' (Bell 1976: 90). He continues by suggesting that this is equally an 'identity crisis', characterized by a loss of stable and traditional 'significant others' against which the self can be defined. In other words, noting a rise in the importance of generation as a source of identity was understood to be a rise in a certain brand of narcissism, a concern with one's own life, and an insecurity about how one was seen. Thus, once again, generation is taken as a mark of conformity.

The aforementioned authors offer glances into thinking about a relation between history, capitalism and generational sensibilities. Not all work deploying the concept concurs with this approach, especially (neo)functionalist sociological research. For example, David Kertzer has suggested that the problem of generation in sociological study is primarily definitional, that its 'multivocality, a virtue in popular discourse, [becomes] a liability in science' (Kertzer 1983: 125). His survey discusses scholarly literature that variously takes up the concept of generation as comprising groups ranging from three years to forty-four years in scope. He modifies a typology from Troll (1970), proposing four different uses of generation: as kinship descent, as cohort (deployed primarily by demographers), as life stage, and as historical period (ibid.: 126–7). He is especially critical of the imprecision of cohort, arguing that generation should be restricted to 'a relational concept bound to the realm of kinship and descent; it is not an appropriate tool for dividing societies into segments or populations into aggregates' (ibid.: 128). Kertzer points to Mannheim and Ortega y Gasset as sparking a contemporary confusion between the genealogical and cohort definitions. He makes a strong case for the analytical problems here, challenging research that begins describing the experiences of an aggregate, then slips to assure an argument of succession (ibid.: 127–9). Instead, Kertzer concludes by calling for a limited definition of generation as kinship descent, but placed in an historical context, 'analyzed in conjunction with the concepts of cohort, age, and historical period' (ibid.: 143).

While a reasonable suggestion and point of clarification for socio-logical work, Kertzer's critique cannot—nor does it wish to—account for the popular circulation of ideas about generation. It is fundamentally significant that this term has meaning beyond that of an analytic category; it is equally a nodal point for the organization of popular knowledge. And, importantly, this popular knowledge *does* conflate descent, cohort, age and history. The idea of loosely organized groups of successive populations that share an experience of cultural change runs rampant through contem-porary media. What is central, and what deserves special attention, is the way in which kinship and cohort are articulated in the popular imaginary. In this respect, Riesman and Bell are both evidence of contemporary views about generation, whose suggestions have been taken up and modified to become part of common sense. This includes a judgement that the concept of generation in the second half of the twentieth century bore the stamp of media-driven conformity, and that it was more prominent than it was in the past. The truth-value of these claims is not the issue; their effectivity stems from the fact that they are taken as true.

Mannheim's seminal 1927 discussion, 'The Problem of Generations', presents an invaluable contribution to just such an approach. Following a critique of the way generation has been used in positivist and romanticist studies, he nonetheless sees it as 'one of the indispensable guides to an understanding of the structure of social and intellectual movements' (Mannheim 1952: 286–7). His argument is consistent with his other proposals on the sociology of knowledge, convincingly submitting a bid for an historicized view to truth. Mannheim, in extending Marxist analysis, essentially treats generation as analogous to class, though the latter's determination by economic conditions becomes determination by patterns of experience. For Mannheim, generation is 'nothing more than a particular kind of identity of location' (ibid.: 292). But he goes beyond this to propose distinctions between location, actuality, status and unit, the latter of which will be discussed below. Jane Pilcher, for example, reads Mannheim's 'generation' as 'a key aspect of the existential determi-nation of knowledge', in which a 'dialectical, symbiotic relationship is characterized as fundamentally crucial to the constitution of individuals and society, to biography and history' (Pilcher 1994: 483, 490). She correctly indicates that he suggested that '[t]he likelihood of a genera-tion developing a distinctive consciousness is seen to be dependent on the tempo of social change' (ibid.: 483). Following this line of thought,

I want to highlight two of Mannheim's recommendations about generation.

According to Mannheim, generations mark an ongoing renewal of involvement in cultural processes. As he put it, there is a 'fresh contact' that occurs as yet another generation comes of age and from its historical position has its consciousness shaped to and by the world around. It is fairly standard to treat youth as a transitory stage, as something one moves through on the way to adulthood. A limitation of this view is that it cannot account for the way in which cohorts adhere and form groups of seemingly identifiable co-passengers through life. Youth may be left behind, but it is the period in which those imagined communities and alliances are forged, ones that mark a new view of the world, a 'fresh contact'. Such contacts let us assess what cultural knowledge can be discarded and what new knowledge is necessary (Mannheim 1952: 293–4).

The patterns of experience inscribed in fresh contacts accent the relationship between generation and change. Mannheim specifically identified 'generation-units' as the primary agents of change, which appear especially during periods of social upheaval. These subsets of a generation correlate to social positions of class, education and political commitments, and form the basis of generational identity and antagonism. While such units are always possible, they only become visible in times of turmoil. For this he offers the example of the absence of generation-units among agrarian populations in which 'the tempo of change is so gradual that new generations evolve away from their predecessor without any visible break, and all we can see is the purely biological differentiation and affinity based upon difference or identity of age' (ibid.: 309). Though this example would not work in the contemporary North American context, in which a farming crisis has indeed marked off generations of agricultural labourers, his point stands. Generation-units are smaller groups in an historical period produced in relation to senses of social change. They are focal points for organizing and comprehending responses to that change. One might think of this in these terms: not all people born between 1961 and 1966 are 'slackers'; and yet that imagined unit operates as a vehicle establishing a sense of historical location for and about that population. While Mannheim does imply that generational-units refer to a specific group, and his essay refers to 'actual generation' as marking those born during a certain time period, such claims are not his innovation. Instead, I would suggest that it is immaterial whether or not there is an actual population of slackers, but that it is alternatively an imagined unity; the sense of a generation-unit's appropriateness is a crucial mechanism in the ordering of the qualities of an historical era. This concept allows generation to be understood as consisting of heterogeneous identities and experiences, yet still organized around central terms and characteristics indicative of an historical moment.

To summarize, 'generation' is the marking of 'fresh contacts' of a population coming of age, producing particularly visible units in the context of change, ultimately providing an organizing structure to that population. The sense that novel subjectivities typify the process of maturation is frequently taken as a reason for studying youth cultures. For example, McRobbie suggests that merely acknowledging the high volume and turnover of cultural forms associated with youth reminds us 'of the extent to which young people tell us a good deal about the scale and the dynamics of social change itself' (McRobbie 1984: 179). Such a view is revealing, for it reiterates an understanding of youth as both product and measure of the 'tempo of change'; youth is a way of seeing change and making the novel visible, as much as it is an engine of change. A feeling of 'newness', a sense of difference from previous and subsequent populations, marks the distinctiveness of a generation. The point of an imagined mass fresh contact, then, is a struggle to negotiate new social demands and cultural locations, and not on the part of the young only. More broadly, generation is one articulation between an idea about historical change and its relation to configurations of cultural forms, practices and people. Further, this travels through popular media forms. Generation offers a loose idea of what it means to be part of a popularly conceived definition of an historical moment. As a result of this mediation generation presents an unstable claim about the coherence of successive populations and the specificity of their ideas and forms of expression. The concept tries to capture the experience of what it means to be of a particular time and place. Generation, then, refers to the making of a place in history for the understanding of one's feelings about uniqueness in light of social upheaval.

As Pilcher puts it, 'generations were conceptualized as one of the driving forces of social change and progression' (Pilcher 1994: 484). This might be revised to say that the notion of generations is one of the primary categories through which we think of social change. In this respect, generation operates as one organization of the dynamics of history, as it is acted upon and by a cohort. 'Generation', importantly, plays outside the 'legitimate' debates of sociology, becoming an everyday comprehension of age- and place-defined imagined communities, that is, a vernacular knowledge about history.

What is striking is the way in which this essentially epistemic force —for it organizes ways of knowing—is most frequently rendered as demographics for marketers, that is statistical portraits of populations designed to offer ways of selling. Currently, both the epistemological and demographic dimensions are intimately intertwined; however, it does not make sense to say that they are equal for the reason that one needs to understand the operations of generation as a lived category consisting of both experience and understanding. One may be tempted to see the popularity of generation as evidence of the powerful role marketers have in defining its particular characteristics, suggesting that what is most visible as the youth culture of the contemporary era is largely determined by the designations of specially attractive target markets. The lines connecting advertising plans and the everyday life of generational membership are amply evident but not direct. Popular, semi-scholarly books claiming to provide authoritative examinations of demographic trends, ultimately purporting to tender special advantage to marketers, are illustrations of this relationship. Indeed, in Canada there appears to be a resurgence of a popular faith in the form of empiricism advanced by demographers, a truth-value that tends to be taken as indisputable whether by journalists or policymakers. As the authors of the Canadian bestseller *Boom, Bust and Echo* put it, rather immodestly, 'Demographics explain about two-thirds of everything' (Foot and Stoffman 1996: 2). For them, demographics refers primarily to generational groupings whose buying patterns and careers appear to follow predictable paths. The groups they identify include the pre-World War I, World War I, the Roaring Twenties, the Depression Babies, World War II, the Baby Boom (whose tail end includes Generation X), the Baby Bust, the Baby-Boom Echo, and an unnamed 'future'. While Foot and Stoffman suggest the information they provide might be used for public policy, the focus is quite unambiguously on the identification of growth markets. The subtitle is an honest pronouncement that their data shows 'how to profit from the coming demographic shift'. This book does not stand alone, it is part of a recent slew, including *Teen Trends* (Bibby and Posterski 1992), *Marketing to Generation X* (Ritchie 1995), *Rocking the Ages* (Smith and Clurman 1997), *Generation X: The Young Adult Market* (Mitchell 1997) and *Chips and Pop* (Barnard *et al.* 1998), that display an emphasis on generational specificity. Their tenor is concern for the priming of new, young segments for future consumption, as well as alerting businesses to opportunities for exploitation.

These works perform a brand of intellectual labour, and their authors might be seen as contemporary substitutes for public intellectuals; such material helps to organize the reigning ideas of a society, presenting explanations of and understandings for the cultural changes that appear to abound. Regardless of what one thinks of these clearly consumer-invested analyses, or whatever contests to their veracity one might wish to mount, their theses circulate and function as conceptual organizations of daily life. With this theoretical framework in mind, I wish to now turn to an example of an emergent generational category, as identified and agreed upon in popular literature, to examine the discourse currently circulating. This formation concerns ideas about youth and globalization.

Globalized Youth

As early as 1992, popular media began to discuss the inappropriateness of Generation X. *Fortune*'s feature story on 'The Upbeat Generation' argued, drawing evidence from surveys, that 'twentysomethings' 'believe in the American dream—but an end-of-the-century version (Deutschman 1992: 42). Challenging Douglas Coupland directly, implying that his term 'Generation X' was itself cynical, the reporter wrote, 'But most twenty-somethings aren't suffering from diminished expectations . . . they confidently expect to garner a fair amount of wealth too' (ibid.: 42). Even when the term 'Generation X' was entering into popular language, doing so with astonishing speed, there was simultaneously a growing sense, especially among business journalists, that it ignored the entrepreneurship and optimism of contemporary young people.

A *Globe and Mail* article featured a demographic consulting company called D-Code that claims to give better readings of statistical data pertaining to young adults. Its founder states that the idea grew from a frustration with the ambiguities of Generation X, preferring instead Nexus Generation to connote the salient trait of 'a bridge or connection . . . between the industrial age and the birth of the information revolution' (MacDonald 1997: B11). As a set of lifestyle interests, Nexus members 'were nurtured on music, television, video games, computers and every other conceivable form of information. This generation rejects traditional institutions, marries late, travels around the globe and surfs across the Internet' (ibid.). D-Code employs young demographers to interpret the generation's interests for advertisers and government, arguing that this is a potentially massively profitable market for those who understand it.

Popular discourse of a new generation continues to accumulate, of which a *Business Week* cover-story, titled 'Generation Y', is exemplary. It presents an argument for a new generation of young consumers, born between 1979 and 1994, whose taste and consumer spending will require reorientations on the part of Boomer-focused marketers. These are not the terminally unprofitable and depressed Generation X; instead, Generation Y are described as massive in numbers, entrepreneurial in spirit, and heavily invested in media-defined branding, an argument David Foot (1996) also makes of the Baby-Boom Echo. Importantly, they are seen as globally attuned. As the article puts it, 'This generation is more racially diverse: One in three is not Caucasian' (Neuborne 1999: 82). This odd bit of evidence should not be taken as an accurate reading of an emerging multicultural US, nor that such diversity was not as pronounced in the past. Further, I would suggest that this figure underestimates the actual profusion of ethnic, gender, and sexual identities. Instead, it is a sign of diversity being articulated with the newness of this generation, and a sign that this quality is now on the radar screen of advertisers. An idea of ethnic diversity matches the apparent miniaturization of taste segments through internet commerce, which is also given credit for speeding up the turnover of fads and fashions.

Similarly, *Maclean's* offered the cover story 'How Teens got the Power' to describe both the demographic boom of Y or Echo members and their cultural predilections. For a staggering example of this purchasing and cultural power, the article notes that *Teen People* is among the fastest-growing magazines in the history of US publishing; it is read by 10 million readers per issue and its circulation is 1.2 million, growing from 500,000 at its 1998 launch (Clark 1999: 43). Yet, contrary to the impression of homogenizing points of cultural intersection, a notable metaphor in the report is the 'tribe', with demographers suggesting that the youth market has broken into smaller groups organized by taste and style, including 'ravers and boarders' (ibid.: 44). An overarching trait, again, is their 'multiculturalism'. As the reporter states, 'They are, by far, the most racially diverse generation in Canada's history' (ibid.). Further, this Y generation is taken as having a special relationship to the internet. Interestingly, it is not computers alone, but the image of 'gathering information and communicating on-line' that marks the distinctiveness of this cohort, with comparisons being drawn to the Baby Boom's presumed special relation to television (ibid.: 45).

The attributes emphasized as marking the newness of this emergent international generation are fragmentation, ethnic diversity and internet savvy. These qualities are familiar as the central ways in which globalization is understood, that is as a coterminous move to international connection and to local expression (cf. Hall 1991; Grossberg 1996; Appadurai 1996; and Ang 1996). Fluidity, flexibility and immediacy of capital, labour, services, markets, culture, and consumers are foundational concepts for global capitalism, its operations manifested as a hybrid of the local and the international. What interests me here is the circulation of a popular discourse about global culture as a way to characterize the specificity of our era and of the generation coming of age at this moment. We have lived through an era in which the distinctions between popular culture and youth culture appear to have vanished. Some point to the rise of the teenager as a catalyst to this collapse. As W.T. Lhamon puts it, youth culture of the 1950s 'became the atmosphere of American life' (Lhamon 1990: 8). This deserves extension; equally influential here is that Americanness became a mode of youthfulness internationally. This 'atmosphere of American life' did not stay bound by a single continent. Appadurai (1996) calls this 'the free-floating yearning for American style, even in the most intense contexts of opposition to the United States' (ibid.: 174). Michael Mitterauer (1992) argues that the contemporary history of youth has been one of 'deregionalization', where cultural forms and practices have forged a transnational and cosmopolitan youth sphere. Certainly, the decades of vociferous debate about the 'Americanization' of local and national cultures has had youth culture as its subtext, if not as its primary exemplar. The cry was often heard that teenagers' taste for US films, television and music was creating cultural homogeneity across the planet. The formation of a 'global teen' continues to include concerns about the loss of local and national cultural commitments as young people turn to an internationally circulating popular culture in order to construct forms of community and alliance. But an abundance of journalistic reports and books portraying global teens have taken to celebrating this aspect of a new, transnational generation.

Susan Ruddick (1997) has convincingly documented the manner in which youth are particularly situated in relation to forms of globalizing leisure and consumption. *National Geographic*'s special issue on 'Global Culture' (1999) is a case in point. The cover presents a traditionally attired woman from Mumbai, who is an affluent biochemist, sitting next to her catsuit-clad daughter, a model and former music video host. Though a portrait of successful, educated women, it is equally an image of contrasts between a parent world of cultural tradition and a youthful world of international fashion. For further illustration, one need only think of the numbers of television news reports and magazine features on China that use images of young people dancing in nightclubs as a metonymic sign of encroaching globalization, or the frequent appearance of images of young people secretly listening to the latest popular songs, congregating on streets, or talking about the underground traffic of contemporary videos in Asian and Eastern European countries. Such stock approaches to the journalistic depiction of currents in cultural life present the budding openness of a presumably closed society by drawing attention to how contemporary the fashion, dress and attitude of the young are; they are up to date, by a Western, and now international, standard. Over a decade ago, this was often used as a way to characterize a generation arising in Eastern bloc countries for whom communism was a waning ideology. Today, stories of bootleg popular music enhance depictions of the opening up of China; rollerblading and a sprinkling of young beauty culture captures the loosening of Iran. At times, this is an image of hedonism and of the disregard for heritage. At other times, this is a healthy resistance to tradition. But at all times, following Ruddick's observations, it is an image of fun and consumption. Pleasure, here, is the primary currency for an idea of transnational communities of young partiers and shoppers.

Thus, the supposed newness of this post-X generation appears in relation to other trends and concerns about globalization; further, this cohort is taken as the embodiment of the potentials of a global village and of the anxieties about the social change implied by international connection in general. From the IBM commercials of quaintly remote locations (a convent, a Middle Eastern desert, etc.) to Microsoft's 'Where do you want to go today?', from Benetton's racially obsessed images of diversity to Coke's vaguely neo-hippie multiculturalism and Pepsi's dance internationalism of 'Generation Next', a dominant representation is that of geographic and cultural borders being transcended by commodity forms that draw the interests of young people. Such images construct a form of fetishism—affixed to both commodities *and* young people—that carries a magical 'one worldness', in the end a pure ideological reverie of individual empowerment. 'One worldness' is seen as a determining characteristic of a unique generational phenomenon. Put differently, fragmentation, ethnic diversity and internet savvy are central terms in a popular discourse about the rate of social change and the definition of what it means to be part of this transnational time. These three are the topic of debate and evaluation, alternately taken as signs of some democratic potential or of the loss of certain important forms of communal life. Regardless of the assessment, fragmentation, ethnic diversity and internet savvy are understood as the signs of a 'fresh contact'.

It should not be surprising that an interest in *access*, that is, how one gets to participate, or how one comes to be part of this time, is the fourth term in the equation. Cell phones and pagers typify the mobile privatization of youth in the late 1990s, whose use and image is about being in touch, constructing connections and assuring safety. Even as businesses are in the process of developing models for 'e-commerce', a notion of access has its own life as a semiotic entity; it is an idea of contemporaneity evident in popular texts. Without a doubt, only a minority of teenagers and young people engage in these communication channels; nonetheless, the very sense of this mode of participation is powerful enough to be a quality of a generation-unit. This sense of participation, including individuals having access to people, commodities and information, as well as people and marketers having access to individuals, can be documented in popular media as a textual theme and a design conceit.

For example, MuchMusic and MusicPlus, the two main popular music video stations in Canada, have a programme on which special musical guests perform and are interviewed. 'Intimate and Interactive', whose guests have included Janet Jackson, Sloan, the Spice Girls, Alanis Morissette, Madonna and Beck, is a telling example of how an idea of the 'fresh contact' of a new generation is being understood in relation to new technology. This show carefully integrates live performance with audience participation. Avoiding a traditional dialogue between host and guest, the veejay takes questions not only from the studio audience but also from people gathering on the street outside, from phone-in callers, from faxes, from emails, from their 'Speaker's Corner' video booth, all in alternating order. Displaying an unambiguous obsession, 'access' by fans to guests is talked about and referred to again and again, with guests suitably impressed—or mystified. (Mel B said, 'Wow, you really do all this, all this "faxes-and-emails" stuff.') The MuchMusic studio in Toronto, tellingly described as an 'environment', boasts large street-level windows that open to expand the geography of their programmes out into the city. This is notably used in their popular dance music programme, 'Electric Circus', which occupies the interior and exterior of the studio with dancers, moving parts of the show through those large windows onto the sidewalk. A promotional loyalty initiative, giving fans discounts and information about music-related commodities, is called the MuchAccess Card. In other programmes, MuchMusic and MusicPlus veejays do hosting segments on hip streets around the world, from Argentina to the UK, as well as special shows devoted to eastern Canadian and western Canadian music scenes.

This apparent blurring of the lines between spectators and performers, between hosts and audience, between the 'environment' and the world outside is a mode of representation rather than an attitude of media activism (as it often gets talked about by Much's corporate representative, Moses Znaimer). The implicit statement is that this is your studio and your programming; and, significantly, this statement is the content as much as it is the form. In this context, access, control is a theme and a visual motif.

Other examples of the representation of access, control and inter-activity include the many television images that have opted for graphics of pull-down menus, and the vogue for advertisements with little cursor arrows floating across images, brightening as they seem to click on a desired hot spot. VH-1's 'Pop Up Video' presents balloons containing facts about the video, the performer or freely associated trivia that bubble up on top of popular clips. Forming a cluttered, information ridden screen—already familiar from programmes and channels that squeeze the image down so that running bands of weather, sports and stock market updates can fit into the frame—'Pop Up Video' presumes an audience that is always asking for more, and thus appears to be commanding the unearthing of data. It is a format that only makes sense in light of a reigning idea about hypertext, itself a techno-determinist's mythos of the collapse of the distinctions between reader and writer. In Calgary, the local independent station, the A-Channel, which presents itself as the young, hip station with its restless camerawork (no tripods!) and its style-conscious hosts, presents the weather segment of the local news with a close-up of the five-day forecast on the station's own website.

The image of access refers to being on-line, faster pace, being hooked up and in touch, and surfing the web. Access equally betrays concern and fear for the consequences of international culture. Panics about young people—especially children—having access to images of violence and sexuality on television, the internet, and in video games are prevalent. Such concerns range from learning how to make pipe bombs to meeting unfamiliar, unsavoury, people on-line. Nonetheless, access is, generally speaking, a commonsense good, an attribute associated with power, democracy and, now, youthfulness. Even in leftist critiques of new tech-nology, getting more access to disadvantaged groups is the easy, rapid conclusion, as though this is the path to the equalization of power relations. But can we be sure that this is always the most appropriate political action when access is already a dominant discourse? In the very least, the term harbours a subtle connotation of special status; its exnominated term is 'access denied', itself a familiar phrase from popular narratives involving security apparatuses or computer secrets. One only understands access in so much as it is not available freely; no one thinks of access to oxygen, except in circumstances of limited supply. The concept, then, confers a sense of privilege, even as an appended logic maintains that this privilege will vanish as the democratic potential it promises is realized.

What conclusions might be drawn from the identification of a popular discourse about a new generation? Most prominently, the presence of talk about new populations is an index of a sense that something is different today than it was yesterday, that some array of ideas about social upheaval has pointed to the requirement for a special diagram of a distinctive consciousness. Here is where the powerful relation between youth and new generations is fundamental, for it is youth that is taken as a transitory period of preparation for life. Its double signification as promise and threat stems from its inherent uncertainty; while youth hold a society's feeling of a future, it equally harbours a potential to fail (cf. Acland 1995). Thus, anxieties about youth are, in part, a way of expressing anxieties about the reproduction of a particular social order. The appearance of a discourse of a new generation, then, comprises a bid to organize for a specific historical instance what the nature of social continuity will be. Currently, nothing is more rife with uncertainty than the forces of globalization.

Simon During (1997) takes account of the implications of how cultural theory treats globalization. His project is to describe a Gramscian field of political agency—the popular—for international contexts, similar to what others have referred to as a transnational public (Appadurai 1996). Gramsci's popular has to do with the formation of an historical bloc, and with the 'take up' of cultural positions and alliances. Extending this, During characterizes cultural globalization, and the related possibilities for a global popular, as a pressing problem for many of the assumptions of cultural studies, ultimately contending that one brand of self-ethnography, a neo-liberal empowerment stance that finds resistance everywhere, is indeed a partner in the globalization process.

He makes a crucial point about a conflation, in much scholarship, between *signs in* and *signs of* the global popular, where cultural globalization, that is the internationalization of information and entertainment industries, is mistaken to be equivalent to other forms of transnationalism. The implication is that the many locations and instances of globalization do not run synchronously, hence posing a challenge to any impulse toward general models about the phenomenon. Such an impulse, in the end, only hampers our ability to respond politically, timely, and in a resonant fashion. Instead, as During reminds us, we require an analysis that pinpoints the specific articulation of different global hegemonies. For this reason, it does not make sense to be for or against globalization, an option which, by necessity, reads one site of critique into another. It is beyond a doubt that claims are being made in the name of a global popular, whether about genre, taste, identity, or political expression. While we may debate the possibilities of forming a transcultural popular or public, it is already being actively emptied of its politics in its descriptions as inevitable and desirable. *Globalization is being taken as the new end of ideology.*

In this, the working out of relations between local and global are partly a struggle between an imagined past and the reproduction of social relations tomorrow. Consequently, the young are a key site for a struggle of the meaning of the transnational circulation of culture and capital, in addition to the ongoing production of the new. The image of the young, escapist, cosmopolitan who seeks out international culture to the expulsion of national equivalences, so frequently appears alternately as the colonized victim of globalization or as its apolitical, hyper-consumerist, first citizen. This dynamic is amply evident in the representation promoting the individual lifestyle consumer as the dominant location for transnational sameness. But how can the minutiae of difference be the basis for transnational sameness? Is this not the foundational contradiction upon which the imagined 'one worldness' of the global teen is based? As Lawrence Grossberg convincingly puts it in his dissection of the processes of globalization, 'contemporary capitalism is powerfully articulated with the production of difference' (Grossberg 1999: 27). Implicated as a transnational cultural and representational operation, 'a particular set of media formations is producing new lived geographies organized around the very category of difference and a heterogeneity of produced locales as a new architecture of identity and individuality' (ibid.: 34). 'Generation' is one point of articulation for these 'new lived geographies', producing a popular intersection between kinship and cohort, and acting as a difference- and novelty-making machine that has become massively important to the circulation of capital.

While I have only taken a first run at mapping the contours of an emergent discourse of generation and the representation of its distinctive consciousness, the identification of inherent contradictions extends an advantage to critical analysis. Significantly, points of logical instability expose cracks in the reigning commonsense; it shows the contingencies of generational identity, as well as its ideological unpredictability. This is because the portrait above does not address how this image of generation is taken up, how this discourse is understood, is blended into quotidian existence, and becomes a sensation, or a feeling, for people. Dominant discourses of generations, especially their presumed 'newness,' are portraits of what a culture sees as important to being of a particular time and place. Fresh contacts and generation-units are ways of marking structures of feeling, but they are also have a conceptual and textual life as they help to order and regulate a sense of historical change.

Acknowledgements

Thanks goes to Keir Keightley for extensive comments and extended conversation on this topic, and to Larry Grossberg for suggested revisions to an early draft.

Bibliography

Acland, Charles R. (1995) *Youth, Murder, Spectacle: The Cultural Politics of 'Youth in Crisis'*, Boulder: Westview Press.

Ang, Ien (1996) *Living Room Wars: Rethinking Media Audiences for a Postmodern World*, New York: Routledge.

Appadurai, Arjun (1996) *Modernity at Large: Cultural Dimensions of Globalization*, Minneapolis: U. of Minnesota.

Barnard, R., Cosgrave, D. and Welsh, J. (1998) *Chips and Pop: Decoding the Nexus Generation*, Toronto: Malcolm Lester Books.

Bell, Daniel (1976) *The Cultural Contradictions of Capitalism*, New York: Basic Books.

Bibby, Reginald W. and Posterski, Douglas C. (1992) *Teen Trends: A Nation in Motion*, Toronto: Stoddart.

Clark, Andrew (1999) 'How teens got the power,' *Maclean's*, March 22: 42–6.

Cohen, Stanley (1972) *Folk Devils and Moral Panics: The Creation of the Mods and Rockers*, Oxford: Blackwell.

Cohen, Stanley and Young, Jack (eds) (1973) *The Manufacture of News: Social Problems, Device and the Mass Media*, London: Constable.

Côté, James E. and Allahar, Anton L. (1994) *Generation on Hold: Coming of Age in the Late Twentieth Century*, Toronto: Stoddart.

Coupland, Douglas (1991) *Generation X: Tales for an Accelerated Culture*, New York: St Martin's Press.

Deutschman, Alan (1992) 'The upbeat generation,' *Fortune*, July 13: 42–54.

During, Simon (1997) 'Popular culture on a global scale: a challenge for cultural studies?', *Critical Inquiry* 23, Summer: 808–33.

Foot, David K. with Stoffman Daniel (1996) *Boom, Bust, and Echo: How to Profit from the Coming Demographic Shift*, Toronto: Macfarlane Walter and Ross.

Fussell, Paul (1983) *Class: A Guide Through the American Status System*, New York: Summit Books.

Gillis, John (1974) *Youth and History: Tradition and Change in European Age Relations, 1770–Present*, New York: Academic Press.

Grossberg, Lawrence (1999) 'Speculations and articulations of globalization,' *Polygraph* 11: 11–48.

——(1996) 'The space of culture, the power of space,' in Iain Chambers and Lidia Curti (eds) *The Post-colonial Question: Common Skies/Divided Horizons*, New York: Routledge, pp. 169–88.

Hall, Stuart (1991) 'The local and the global: globalization and ethnicity,' in *Culture, Globalization and the World-System*, ed. Anthony D. King, London: Macmillan, pp. 19–39.

Hall, Stuart and Jefferson, Tony, (eds) (1976) *Resistance Through Rituals: Youth Subcultures in Post-War Britain*, London: Hutchinson.

Hamblett, Charles and Deverson, Jane (1965) *Generation X*, London: Tandem Books.

Hartley, John (1984) 'Encouraging signs: television and the power of dirt, speech and scandalous categories,' in William D. Rowland, Jr. and Bruce Watkins (eds), *Interpreting Television: Current Research Perspectives*, Beverly Hills: Sage Publications, pp. 119–41.

Hebdige, Dick (1988) *Hiding in the Light: On Images and Things*, New York: Comedia.

——(1979) *Subculture: The Meaning of Style*, London: Routledge.

Howe, Neil and Strauss, Bill (1993) *13th Gen: Abort, Retry, Ignore, Fail?* New York: Vintage.

Jaeger, Hans (1987) 'Generations in history: reflections on a controversial concept', *History and Theory* 24.3: 273–92.

Kertzer, David I. (1983) 'Generation as a sociological problem', *Annual Review of Sociology* 9: 125–49.

Lhamon, W.T., Jr (1990) *Deliberate Speed: The Origins of a Cultural Style in the American 1950s*, Washington: Smithsonian Institution Press.

MacDonald, Gayle (1997) 'Managing demographics: the eyes and ears of a generation,' *Globe and Mail*, February 4: B11.

McRobbie, Angela (1984) 'Dance and social fantasy,' in Angela McRobbie and Mica Nava (eds), *Gender and Generation*, London: Macmillan, pp. 130–61.

——(1980) 'Settling accounts with subcultures: a feminist critique', *Screen Education* 34: 37–49.

Mannheim, Karl (1952) *Essays on the Sociology of Knowledge*, ed. Paul Kecskemeti, London: Routledge and Kegan Paul.

52   The Radiant Hour

Mitchell, Susan (1997) *Generation X: The Young Adult Market*, Ithaca, N.Y.: New Strategist Publications.

Mitterauer, Michael (1992) *A History of Youth*, trans. Graeme Dunphy, Cambridge, USA: Blackwell.

Musgrove, Frank (1964) *Youth and the Social Order*, London: Routledge and Kegan Paul.

National Geographic (1999) Special Issue on 'Global Culture', no. 196.2 (August).

Neuborne, Ellen (1999) 'Generation Y', *Business Week*, February 15: 80–8.

Orter, Sherry (1998) 'Generation X: anthropology in a media-saturated world', *Cultural Anthropology* 13.3: 414–40.

Pilcher, Jane (1994) 'Mannheim's sociology of generations: an undervalued legacy', *British Journal of Sociology* 45.3: 481–95.

Redhead, Steve (1997) *Subculture to Clubcultures: An Introduction to Popular Cultural Studies*, Malden, Massachusetts: Blackwell.

——(1990) *The End-of-the-Century Party: Youth and Pop Towards 2000*, New York: Manchester University Press/St Martin's Press.

Riesman, David, Glazer, Nathan and Denny, Reuel (1950) *The Lonely Crowd: A Study of the Changing American Character*, Garden City: Doubleday Press.

Ritchie, Karen (1995) *Marketing to Generation X*, New York: Free Press.

Rock, Paul and McIntosh, Mary, (eds) (1974) *Deviance and Social Control*, London: Tavistock.

Rose, Tricia (1994) *Black Noise: Rap Music and Black Culture in Contemporary America*, Hanover: Wesleyan University.

Ruddick, Susan (1997) 'Youth and globalization', paper presented at the Inaugural International Conference in Critical Geography, Simon Fraser University/University of British Columbia, Vancouver, August.

Skelton, Tracey and Valentine, Gill (1998) *Cool Places: Geographies of Youth Cultures*, New York: Routledge.

Smith, J. Walker and Clurman, Ann S. (1997) *Rocking the Ages: The Yankelovich Report on Generational Marketing*, New York: HarperCollins.

Thornton, Sarah (1995) *Club Cultures: Youth, Media, Music*, Oxford: Polity Press.

Troll, L.E. (1970) 'Issues in the study of generations', *Aging and Human Development* 1.3: 199–218.

Wallach, Glenn (1997) *Obedient Sons: The Discourse of Youth and Generations in American Culture, 1630–1860*, Amherst: University of Massachusetts Press.

West, Cornel (1988) 'Interview with Cornel West', in Andrew Ross (ed.) *Universal Abandon?: The Politics of Postmodernism*, Minneapolis: University of Minnesota Press, pp. 269–86.

TWO

Children of the Revolution: Fiction Takes to the Streets

Elizabeth Young

> Now is the time of departure. The last
> streamer that ties us to what is known, parts.
> We drift into a sea of storms.
>
> (Derek Jarman, from the film *Jubilee*)

There used to be a very small, xeroxed, one-man magazine which appeared at irregular intervals in New York during the late seventies and early eighties. It was called *Sleazoid Express*. It devoted itself to appalling grind-house movies, urban street-life, interviews with dossers, winos and junkies and long rants by the editor and sole contributor, Bill Landis. At the beginning of the 1980s he wrote: 'Money and strange diseases . . . [are] the sexual signposts for the present decade' (Landis 1984: 7) Bill Landis was a man of some prescience. It took considerable foresight to perceive that during the ensuing decade the erotic and the financial would become inextricably intertwined and the mindless sexual libertarianism of the past twenty years would gradually assume the shrouded lineaments of the medieval Death or plague figure, skull, scythe and all. In retrospect, the eighties have much of the maddened frenzy of a millenarianist decade as if the Four Horsemen themselves had rounded Ludgate Hill and were thundering into the City.

Our images of the 1980s have already become fixed, homogenized. Looking back, a grotesque memorial tapestry streams past: the baying packs of yuppies and estate agents, an army of entrepreneurs in red braces and jelly-coloured spectacles. They are roaring right-wing platitudes; they are rigid with cocaine. Multitudes of blondes in black lycra jerk and steam in a million tiny clubs. No one sleeps; greed is good; the aristocrats have left the tumbrils, brushed off their voluminous satins and are throwing balls grander and madder than ever before. There are orgies of gross eating; a million pounds is nothing; the sky bristles with aeroplanes; giant glittering buildings spring up above the cityscapes, only to lie dark and tenantless. A constant confetti of dirty contracts, laundered money and drug profits falls like soiled snow; there is the stink of corruption and sickly blasts of insanely-priced couture fragrances. Above it all the gerontophilic courts of Thatcher and the Reagans kick up their legs in glee as buildings, trains and planes explode and endless showers of AIDS babies, homeless lunatics, murderers, beggars, homeboys and hookers, tearing at lesions and bullet wounds, tumble slowly past. This is the world we have already, mercifully lost. It was one wherein it was harder to have a social conscience than to pull up cosily around the roaring VCR and sink dully into the warm sensurround of total consumer dream.

The publishing industry was as little immune to the money madness as everything else during this period. Somnolent, gentlemanly English firms were sucked into American food conglomerates. There was the constant mighty crash of mergers, like icebergs in the night. Vast advances—a quarter of a million, half a million, a million yen, pounds, pesetas, rands were paid out for mountains of disposable airport rubbish. Forests were felled to produce door-stop paperbacks embossed with gold and stuffed with cotton-candy verbiage. *The Bonfire of the Vanities* was considered a serious book. Agents, once a fairly lowly form of life, became stars and were seen grinning like hyenas and clutching Andy Warhol's tweed jacket. No one knew—or cared—what art was any more. Feminist houses published accounts of menopausal distress from Denmark and Russia. Serious readers turned towards the Third World and started reading endless strange books about Islam and South American sorcerers.

It was against this background of publishing turmoil, of an industry divided between hysterical promotion of trash and obsequious worship of old-timers like Saul Bellow and John Updike that Bret Easton Ellis was to achieve such a notable success with his first book, *Less Than Zero*. It was successful, as were similar books by Jay McInerney and Tama Janowitz, for a very simple reason. It appealed straightforwardly to younger readers; it concerned a world they knew, one of drugs and clubs and MTV. Publishing houses had rather lost sight of the college-age readership and for complex and long-standing reasons. Since the sixties—and not for want of trying—there had been very little in mainstream publishing that appealed to that particular audience. The original Baby-Boom generation were known to have inexplicable and deviant reading tastes. They read Hermann Hesse and J.R.R. Tolkien. They liked political theory. They liked genre of all kinds—SF, horror, erotica, crime. (This was the generation that produced Stephen King and for whom he wrote. Interminably.) They read mountains of appallingly explicit comics. Serious readers from this period tended to swim towards the wilder shores of the *nouveau roman*, Pynchon, Burroughs, Black Mountain College and a lifetime of squinting at incomprehensible small press magazines. One trend from the late sixties was definitely towards this, the fringes of literature, the experimental, the avant-garde and increasingly towards postmodern theory. The other trend was probably more important. During the post-war period, the music industry has assumed a virtual total hegemony over the lives of adolescents, providing all that they need in terms of stimulus, nourishment and romance. The disaffected young intellectual of earlier generations would be likely to turn to bohemianism, art, politics and literature, or a combination thereof. After the early 1960s, when Bob Dylan demonstrated that a persuasive way with metaphor paid off, and with credibility, the same disaffected youth would almost certainly turn to the music business. And, as talented writers from Leonard Cohen to Morrissey have found, mass worship plus the fulfilment of whatever dreams of narcotic and sexual excess one might have is infinitely preferable to giving readings in deserted arts centres and grubbing along on miserly advances.

Throughout the Punk period young writers continued to hurl themselves at the microphone. The Clash song-writing team and a girl known as Poly Styrene were particularly effective lyricists, chronicling the whole day-glo urban nightmare in ways that novelists seemed quite unable to do. Poets such as John Cooper Clarke, Attila the Stockbroker and, in America, Patti Smith and Richard Hell decided that they were heirs to the oral tradition and promptly took to the stage as well.

Of course not all writers can sing, although they nearly all tried. If tone-deaf, however, they weren't going to be kept out of this vast playground of exotic delights. Many extremely good writers, particularly during the 1970s, became well known as music journalists. This was an astonishingly vague job description. Being a music critic enabled them to write about whatever they wanted, about whatever random enthusiasms might possess them, be it American automobiles, crime novels, occult history or semiotics; under the benign umbrella of 'music' papers such as

Rolling Stone in America or *New Musical Express* in Britain, the young writer had an intoxicating amount of space and freedom to hold forth on any aspect of contemporary culture or politics. Furthermore, one could stay in the life.[1] The playground widened year by year and a competent writer, if not felled by drugs, could carry on till retirement. One could specialize in something obscure, like jazz. If one was good enough, and willing to compromise, one could cross over to the straight press and become a real journalist. Or one could write for the many style magazines—*The Face* or *GQ*—which sprang up in the wake of the music press. One could become an editor, or write books about music or biographies of pop stars. 'Music publishing' became a growth area. As long as the good times kept rolling the possibilities were endless. Stay close to the life and you could retain the comforting illusion of credibility and integrity, however much money was pouring in. Thus, for two decades, by this strange route, the music business stole writers and readers. There were drawbacks, of course. It was a boys' barrio which did not extend much of a welcome to women in either role. And few people who sprang from the sixties counter-culture were writing serious fiction.

The youth culture of 1960–80 proved astonishingly resistant to the serious novelist. Tom Wolfe, an astute social commentator if indifferent novelist, remarks on this with wry bemusement in his introduction to *The New Journalism*. He describes: 'waiting for the novels I was sure would come pouring out the psychedelic experience . . . but they never came forth . . . I learned later that publishers had been waiting too. They had been practically crying for novels by the new writers who must be out there somewhere, the new writers who would do the big novels of the hippie life or campus life or radical movements or the war in Vietnam or dope or sex or black militancy or encounter groups or the whole whirlpool at once. They waited . . .' (Wolfe 1990: 45). Who did they get? Ken Kesey. Twenty years later Thomas Pynchon finally produced his great acid flash-back *Vineland*, the only novel to deal seriously with the rococo extravaganzas of the newly mediatized sixties. It was greeted with confusion and derision on account of its subject matter being uneasily poised between being an excruciatingly embarrassing memory and a newly fashionable phenomenon in the form of New Age neo-hippiedom. In any event, Tom Wolfe had been correct when he wrote: 'This whole side of American life that gushed forth when post-war American affluence finally blew the lid off—all this novelists simply turned away from, gave up by default.' One book, twenty years on, was no answer. Wolfe suggests that the problem lay in the fact of novelists seeming 'to shy away from the life of the great cities altogether. The thought of tackling such a subject seemed to terrify them, confuse them, make them doubt their own powers' (ibid.: 44–5).

In the early years of the sixties the culture shock was immense and no one, it seemed, could establish a language or tone to encompass the confluence of bohemianism, squalor, excess and black humour that comprised the counter-cultural world. Martin Amis, hampered by his own distance from that world and by his total ignorance of street talk, succeeded to some extent in *Dead Babies* by setting it in the future. Culturally it was a world dominated by fashion, and a writer, even if linguistically adept, could not hope to present a fictional portrait that would not have dated by the time the ink was dry. The entire confluence was dependent upon continual, tiny shifts in style nuance, cults, status and music. Furthermore, it seemed that if one took a serious, adult look at the whole status-crazy, drug-addled nexus, the cyber-spatial, nerve-shrivelling intensity of the urban megalopolis, one responded with horror. Hubert Selby, for example, wrote the best book ever about youthful, drug-addiction, *Requiem for a Dream*, but, deeply pessimistic, it is not a book that is ever introduced to young readers in school or college. Novelists, by and large, took a very long time to assimilate the profound societal shifts of the post-war world. They had to learn to handle a word-hoard, a Pandora's Box which, once opened, threatened to bury them alive in a shrieking ticker-tape of muzak print-out, sound-tracks, speeches, lyrics, talk-shows, and rap. It took twenty years before they could hope to produce anything other than a blast of brand-names, twenty years for Pynchon to write *Vineland,* for Paul Auster to produce his cityscapes and Seth Morgan the street-twang jive of *Homeboy*—or for a young author to write *American Psycho*. Happily there are indications that we are only now at the beginning of a fictional renaissance, with writers, who can handle the contemporary city. There was also in general, during that period, an actual shortage of creative writers. The ambitious money-hungry ones were in advertising, the neurotic boy poets were riding the swings and roundabouts of the music business, and the women were almost certainly grappling with feminism in one form or another. And so, Hunter S. Thompson, Tom Wolfe, and the other 'New Journalists' with Zola-esque pretensions had 'the whole crazed obscene uproarious Mammon-faced drug-soaked mau-mau lust-oozing modern world all to themselves' (Wolfe 1990: 45). For a while.

During the 1980s the younger readers and writers who concern us here[2] and those others who had remained largely alienated from mainstream publishing were to be involved in considerable changes. The readers from the original Baby-Boom generation had by now become middle-aged and they remained largely responsible for supporting a plethora of small, independent publishing houses including the feminist, gay and left-wing presses. The literary underground of experimentation and small presses had never quite gone away, even in Britain. (As Paul Valery had put it, 'Everything changes but the avant-garde'.) After William Burroughs, Kathy Acker was the only real inheritor of this bohemian tradition to cross over fully into the big-time publishing world. Acker, who lived for a long time in London, has commented on the lack of a literary 'underground' in Britain: 'I came out of a poetry tradition—the Black Mountain poets, the Language Poets. No such traditions exist over here. The underground just isn't known here. I mean, a huge network that's been there for years and years . . . there's no such thing here' (Acker 1991: 16–18). This is, of course one of the reasons why English critics are so ill-equipped to deal with much of contemporary fiction, why English writing remains so mired in a parochial backwater. Acker suffered from a degree of misunderstanding from the British press that, she said, amounted to 'slander' (ibid.) and that similarly stemmed from the lack of a strong British, counter-culture in writing. During the eighties the enormously diverse elements that comprised the American counter-culture seemed to gather strength and show some indications of producing new writers. This American underground which, as Acker points out, had never gone away over there, could be glimpsed by English readers in books and magazines like the Re/Search publications and Amok's Fourth Despatch catalogue. This latter offered all the books traditionally venerated by the 'underground' from de Sade and William Burroughs to Bakunin and Chomsky. The obsessions ranged through Mind-control, Occult Theory, Exotica, Psychedelia, Genetics, Cyberpunk, drugs, film and performance art. Fourth Despatch's books, they said, 'offer un-flinching looks at mayhem, virus and decay: dissections of the current global power structure; sexual impulses spinning out of control; psychiatric tyranny and schizophrenia; tribal rituals and ethnographic documents; psychedelic reality-maps; the tactics of individual subversion and autonomy; and other stark visions of our times.'[3] The stuff of fiction?—not in England. Despite a seemingly irreconcilable diversity of interests—from neo-Nazi, sado-masochistic body-fascism to New Age euphoria and smart drugs—the American art underground was (and is) an enormously eclectic and diverse community. Its sources reach far back into our century, into Modernism, Dada, Surrealism and the Beat generation. It has maintained the bohemian traditions of experimentation and artistic excess and has nourished generations of disaffected young artists. Britain has always maintained its philistine distance from the European avant-garde and its American off-shoots, which has guaranteed that the English novel has become increasingly limp and etiolated during this century. The American literary/artistic underground provides a sort of ongoing, slow-burning cultural revolution which has no parallel here.

Independent publishers, however, have tried to represent this. Semiotext(e) is one such. Hanuman Books in New York, which publish volumes looking like small pastel cakes of soap, have a list which is a roll-call of the international avant-garde from Jean Genet and Max Beckmann through Taylor Mead to John Ashbery, Gary Indiana and Cookie Mueller. A seminal New York fiction magazine, founded by Joel Rose and Catherine Texier in 1983, *Between C and D*, was published as a computer print-out with the words 'Sex, Drugs, Violence, Danger, Computers' on its covers. They nurtured a range of writers who included Texier and Rose themselves, Tama Janowitz, Patrick McGrath and Dennis Cooper. Some of their contributors were eventually identified as 'brat-pack' writers although this derisive term has little meaning beyond being a convenient media label. Most of the writers covered in *Shopping in Space* can be located, at least at the start of their careers, within the American art-underground, at a particular intersection of the artistic, literary and social worlds of New York. Ellis, McInerney and Janowitz might seem to English critics to have sprung from nowhere, writing incomprehensible froth, but although they may not hail from the deepest, maddest recesses of the underground as detailed above, they most certainly have links with a comprehensible literary and artistic culture closely associated with the fashionable New York art world of the eighties.

In literary terms, Britain did not remain completely static throughout the eighties, although there were those who would have it so. It had become fashionable to despair of young people as readers, to assume that they never read, that they were passive consumers of exclusively aural and visual entertainment. There was certainly little enough encouragement for them to read. They were neither inclined to the neo-fogey quibbling of the *Spectator* nor the hearty literary cliques of the Sunday press. English critic John Williams writes this of being a young reader of the time: 'Meanwhile I fancied myself something of a reader; this meant I would consume, at a rate of approximately one every three months, a book by the vogue serious novelist of the moment, Salman Rushdie, Milan

Kundera . . . global Booker prize types. These books I would read about, faithfully buy and faithfully get about half way through, admiring the wit and elegance and being too embarrassed to admit boredom' (Williams 1991: 8).

Williams at this time was representative of a youthful readership who found these, the rather academic texts of high postmodernism, more or less inaccessible, and indeed some of them were so devoid of life that they could be considered large-scale bluff or fraud. I happened to teach English to college students at this time. What did they read? They read, of course, the music press, the style magazines, the listings magazines. They stowed away great quantities of genre and pulp fiction: horror—Stephen King was first favourite—crime, fantasy, sword and sorcery. They had invariably been given *To Kill a Mockingbird* and *The Catcher in the Rye*, at school, just as I had been. Although they had no particular objection to these books, they certainly found them very quaint. A deep Southern childhood where adults were addressed as 'Ma'am', Twitchy fifties New York preppies drinking highballs (highballs?). What was this shit? To multicultural urban students these books were worlds away. There were few serious novels published at this time that held much appeal for young readers. Many of those that might have done (Truman Capote, Tennessee Williams's fiction, James Baldwin) were usually out of print. Colin MacInnes's *Absolute Beginners* was always an acquired taste, the element of authorial fantasy precluding that sureness of tone that can seduce the unsophisticated reader. Anyway, after the embarrassing failure of the film, the book became taboo. When *Less Than Zero* and *Bright Lights, Big City* were published, young people read them. Despite the high-handed tone of the critics and their sneering put-downs, they read these books. They were a relief. They described the known world.

They were also happy to read some of the books published by young London authors during this period. These—which included Michael Bracewell's *The Crypto-Amnesia Club*, Martin Millar's *Milk, Sulphate and Alby Starvation*, Robert Elms's *In Search of the Crack*, Oliver Simmons' touching *Delirium*, Geoff Dyer's *The Colour of Money* and Kate Pullinger's *Tiny Lies*—were at least recognizable. They dealt with young people in London, trying to survive, going to clubs and colleges, brooding a lot. These books may be extremely variable in quality but they were representative of a desire on the part of young British writers to deal with urban reality, commodity fetishism, status, love, sex and, in general, all the acne and the ecstasy of urban late adolescence. And to be fair, they were given a good deal of attention by the press. It is with this group that *Less*

Than Zero properly belongs, although it is by comparison—apart from the work of Michael Bracewell—frighteningly sophisticated.

In his book *Suburban Ambush: Downtown Writing and the Fiction of Insurgency*, Robert Siegle surveys the work of many of the American writers covered in *Shopping in Space*. Although he mentions Bret Easton Ellis, Jay McInerney and Tama Janowitz, Siegle prefers to focus on those he sees as most representative of a particularly East Village, grittily authentic postrealism: artists such as Lynne Tillman, Joel Rose and Catherine Texier. Despite their differences, however, he does see all these writers as being part of the same group, involved, he says, in 'the reinvention of American fiction' (Siegle 1988: 2). Siegle locates the mid-seventies—the very important Punk period, when, as Dennis Cooper describes it in his novel *Closer*, 'Punk's bluntness had edited tons of pretentious shit out of America'—as being the point when some of these writers first embarked upon 'a fiction of insurgency', a 'guerrilla campaign against the imminent transformation of American consciousness into a shopping-mall' (ibid.). He goes on to describe them as follows: 'This is the generation of writers about which the Right had been worrying. They schooled in the Velvet Underground, left their naivety on the streets . . . They scattered, reassembled, wrote for small presses and even smaller magazines, balanced jobs copy-editing or programming or typing and filing against their commitment to an art that did not comply with the gallery system's need for collectors' editions or the writing workshops' ideal of the "well-made story" ' (ibid.: 1).

There are obvious parallels here with the Beat Generation group of the fifties.[4] This hand-to-mouth creative striving that Siegle describes is admirably depicted in the work of Mary Gaitskill. Siegle feels that the works of these novelists 'corrode rather than conform to the commodity formulae toward which latter-day modernist fiction tends, just as the writers who create them have chosen not to live in the more comfortable academic and professional worlds in which late-modernist fiction still prevails' (ibid.: 2). The anti-academicism is correct; most of the writers we look at in *Shopping in Space* have an obvious distaste for the tired experimental strategies and resulting stasis of late, high postmodernist writing. They even have little patience with the writing that would seem to oppose all this, the 'Dirty Realism' newly beloved of Establishment critics who find hope in its drab, white-male 'writerly' qualities, so redolent of the Creative Writing Workshop. Siegle goes on to suggest that the post-Punk urban writers that concern us here are working in direct opposition to 'the great culture machine'—which includes academia, the literary establishment and the media—and that their writing has 'utopian' features, to the point where the authors are not trying to get rich 'unless they do it on their own terms' (ibid.: 2). Their work, Siegle says, 'opens space mentally, psychologically, semiotically—where simulation, repression and convention have converged to predetermine our Being.' The writing also, he says, 'shakes up reified relations—roles, genders, social structures' (ibid.: 3). Much of this is true, as any reading of the work of, say, Lynne Tillman or Dennis Cooper will confirm, but Siegle is writing about an extremely diverse group which, by his definition, would include writers as ill-assorted as Kathy Acker and Patrick McGrath, Jay McInerney and David Wojnarowicz. Some are hollow-eyed sixties survivors. Others are very young: Bret Easton Ellis was only twenty when he wrote *Less Than Zero*. Some are more obviously 'insurgent' than others. Some would appear to have less disdain for money and the commercial qualities of their work than Siegle might like. However, any attempts to define a literary 'group' or art movement are precarious and unstable and this applies as much to, say, Surrealism or Modernism as it does to these 'Downtown' writers. There are always mavericks, defectors, confusions about who participated and who didn't. Siegle is certainly able to locate common strands within the work of the urban postrealists. Ronald Sukenick wrote that, 'the form of the traditional novel is a metaphor for a society that no longer exists' (Sukenick 1985: 3) and Siegle is right to suggest that the artists in question are providing metaphors for the society that does exist now. Their work is what Raymond Federman hoped for when he envisaged: 'a kind of writing, a kind of discourse whose shape will be an interrogation, an endless interrogation of what it is doing while it is doing it, an endless denunciation of its fraudulence, of what it really is: an illusion (a fiction)' (Federman 1981: 11). Federman's words can be applied to many of the books discussed in *Shopping in Space*. He is describing a form of writing which is sometimes called, as noted, 'postrealist'. Fictional realism, its bare bones now exposed to reveal its wholly 'unreal' and illogic strategies, cannot hope to impose its conventions upon what Jean Baudrillard describes as the 'hyperreality', the heightened Disneyfied illusions of the modern city, so in literature a self-aware 'postrealism' has evolved which makes few concessions to the deceptions of classic realism. Siegle is also very illuminating in his account of the literary influences upon the Downtown authors. Although these can sometimes be hard to detect in the work itself they most certainly include, as he suggests, William Burroughs, Donald Barthelme, Robert Coover and Harry Mathews as well as, in Europe, Jean Genet and much poststructural theory including Michel Foucault, Jean Baudrillard and Roland Barthes. Last but not least, Siegle affirms the extent to which every single one of these writers has been influenced by *mass culture*. Nonetheless, even within Siegle's uncontentious list of influences and interests, there are qualifications to be made.

It is now generally accepted that postmodern fiction is, as Linda Hutcheon has suggested, 'a preferential forum for discussion of the postmodern' (Hutcheon 1988: 38) in that it reflects on what Fredric Jameson has described as 'the emergence of a new type of social life and a new economic order' (in Foster 1985: 113). When writing of post-modernism, both Hutcheon and Jameson are referring to life under consumer capitalism: the fun-house of desire ruled by spectacle, simu-lation and the media. The postmodern form in literature has come to challenge truths about fiction and about reality in response to the flow of images from this capitalist spectacle and at the same time to self-reflexively examine the ways in which fiction itself is constructed. This is now so well established that postmodernist fiction has already achieved a form of metafictional classicism known as 'high postmodernism'. Many of these writers, who include Umberto Eco, John Barth, Donald Bartheleme, Robert Coover, D.M. Thomas, E.L. Doctorow are, as Siegle points out, highly esteemed and very influential but they are all very theoretical writers, heavily dependent on what Eco has called 'the game of irony'. This kind of writing gradually tends towards a point where it has only the most minimal and self-conscious relation to anything that might be called 'reality'. It is so deeply involved in irony, pastiche, plays on fictional traditions and author games that, ultimately, it becomes mired in what has been termed 'post-modern paralysis'. At this point texts can often become extremely dull, or near-unreadable, as if the reader has been trapped by some hopelessly self-obsessed pub bore intent on relating the details of all his dreams. The writers whose work is analysed in *Shopping in Space*—Post-punk, Downtown or Blank Generation authors—have a very different engagement with postmodernism. Their fiction arises directly out of their own observations and experiences of postmodern culture, from out of the streets with no name; they are reporting from within a lived reality, not dissecting its constituents from the academic perimeters. In addition, their writing tends to close the gap between 'high' and 'low' art forms far more successfully than is ever possible in more theoretical metafiction, mainly because many of the younger urban writers genuinely cannot see such a gap. Their entire lives have been lived out within a milieu wherein art and pop music, advertising, films and fiction have always been inextricably intertwined, inseparable one from the other. This does not deny them critical insight but rather denotes an exceptionally sophisticated apprehension of these multifarious semiotic codes.

In much postmodern fiction the use of irony is commonly understood to be the way in which the distance between high art and contemporary mass culture is demolished. Irony, however, is a much more problematical discourse within the work of the young New York writers. This is because many such artists genuinely love aspects of the Disneyfied consumer culture. They do not secretly despise it, or feel alienated from it in the manner of older novelists or critical theorists. This may account for the blanded-out quality of some of the writing. An analogy can be drawn with the work of Pop and post-Pop visual artists. Although Andy Warhol was personally more or less unequivocally loving about consumer culture, his art-works were understood by the critical establishment to be seriously ironic and indeed they had that cutting edge to them. Some of the writing we are considering is closer in attitude to the work of Jeff Koons, whose detailed large-scale simulations of kitsch objects and totemic entertainment figures are both iconic and laudatory. Koons entirely lacks the 'distancing' effect of Warhol's work, that cool space where a range of quasi-ironic reaction is expected. He has frequently been accused of having himself been blandly 'consumed' by the consumer artefacts he portrays. It really is a question of distance. When one exists completely within a culture, as do the younger writers we are studying, who have no memory of the certainties and judgements of the pre-sixties world, even though that culture may be a self-conscious and 'ironic' one itself in many ways (look at advertising), it is impossible to sustain ironic comment about that culture as if one were writing, from without it. In *Shopping in Space* . . . we see a spectrum of relationships towards the dominant culture. Some authors are more obviously confrontational, damning and 'insurgent' than others, but even those writers actively engaged in the politics of gender, race and sex now find it hard to maintain, from deep within such a notably comfortable and privileged culture, any of the enraged revolutionary poses possible twenty years ago. In *Less Than Zero* the narrator says to a friend, Rip: 'But you don't need anything. You have everything.' There is a pause and then Rip goes for it: 'I don't have anything to lose' (Ellis 1986: 189). Whether this response is heartfelt, smart-ass or both doesn't really matter. The statement hangs there, inexorably. The American dream—'You have everything.'

Younger Blank Generation writers Douglas Coupland and Mark Leyner have commented on these issues. Coupland, author of *Generation*

X: Tales for an Accelerated Culture, describes his own generation as being over-educated, under-employed and unimpressed with the world they have inherited from previous generations 'like so much skid-marked under-wear'. He understands though that, 'A lot of the world would kill to have the problems this group has' (Coupland 1992: 27). Mark Leyner, author of *My Cousin, My Gastroenterologist* and *Steroids Made My Friend Jorge Kill His Speech Therapist* is more than articulate on his literary heritage: ' I never had to go through all that shit that postmodernists like Ron Sukenick and Steve Katz and Ray Federman had to go through back in the sixties. I came from the fictional womb like I am. The postmodern battles had already been fought and won.' He continues: 'I took off from the assumption that plot, character and setting were conventions to be manipulated and played with. Or abandoned. Or humiliated. Anarchy was my starting point . . . I vandalized the grave of narrative fiction. I've exhumed the corpse and eaten it. You know?' Talking of popular culture, Leyner says: 'That's as much a part of me as the colour of my eyes . . . I'm literally made of it. It is me,' and notes 'I think everybody in my literary generation feels this way . . . Most writing doesn't hold a candle to the exhilaration of being alive and media conscious' (Leyner 1992: 48). Hearing these young writers confirm what has become clear in studying the authors covered in the essays in *Shopping in Space* is odd in a way.

They know that, already, they are the successors to Bret Easton Ellis and Jay McInerney, that these writers are becoming settled and accepted. The entire consumer culture to which they are so happy to belong is proceeding at its usual furious overdrive pace, manically gobbling up new authors on the way. They too in their turn will be discarded.

There is no denying the precocity of *Less Than Zero*, written when the author was a twenty-year-old college student. Ellis was able to pare the book of all portentous adolescent fretting about identity and philosophical truths which, unless handled with J.D. Salinger's knowing assurance, dooms such efforts as unpublishable juvenilia. Bret Easton Ellis, Jay McInerney and Tama Janowitz were the original 'brat-pack' writers. In fact they were the only 'brat-pack' writers. All subsequent, similar books tended to be compared favourably to their work. They had become media stars far too quickly and as such, fell swiftly into disfavour. Initially, however, it was their technical skill that attracted the favourable critical notices as well as the fact that their work provided a heaven-sent opportunity for literary journalists to comment on such perennially inviting issues as youth, drugs and sex. There was an understandable urge to see in Ellis and his youthful confreres a new generation of scribes such as had not been seen since the emergence of the Beat writers. The fuss and froth was reminiscent of the music press's rapturous discovery of Punk in 1975. No matter that Ellis was apparently assisted in the writing of *Less Than Zero* by his mentor Joe McGinniss, known in Britain as the author of the true-crime bestseller *Fatal Vision* (1984). No matter that these writers had ambitious agents and powerful friends within the publishing industry, no matter that their success was somewhat orchestrated. The press always need an angle and these bright young things with their dead-pan tales of life in the urban fast lane seemed perfect, regardless of the fact that literary movements do not happen like that but come about piecemeal, slowly, over many years. No matter. These were postmodern writers for a postmodern media, quick, easy, disposable—one-hit wonders. But writers are just not like rock singers, and in the end, although they certainly couldn't quarrel with the money, these three were far more wounded and hurt than helped by the build 'em up, tear 'em down tactics of the press. In Britain, of course, the blizzard of hype that accompanied them ensured that no one gave them any serious critical attention at all. The name of Bret Easton Ellis is now, at the time of writing [1992], virtually synonymous with hype. There is a vague feeling that his entire career has been artificially foisted upon us, against our will, and it is hard to regain sight of the initial enthusiasm that greeted the arrival of his first book in America.

If Bret Easton Ellis and Jay McInerney had a literary forerunner, it is surely F. Scott Fitzgerald. Fitzgerald is a more complex, a more lyrical writer than either, but he too was successful very young and became the literary pin-up for the Jazz Babies of his generation. His early work was also understood to have a quasi-autobiographical element and he too felt impelled to chart the behaviour of the young people around him. In Fitzgerald's elegiac paeon to his youth, 'Echoes of the Jazz Age', in *The Crack Up*, he recalls the nervous syncopated pleasures of the twenties and the maddened roller-coaster joy-ride of the Bright Young Things, the first significant Teen generation. 'An age of miracles . . . an age of excess . . . and an age of satire . . . This was the generation that corrupted its elders and eventually overreached itself less through lack of morals than lack of taste. A whole race going hedonistic, deciding on pleasure . . . and it seemed only a question of a few years before the older people would step aside and let the world be run by those who saw things as they were' (Fitzgerald 1988: 10–11, 19). He could be writing of the sixties, if not the eighties. Fitzgerald and his wife, the pouting, gin-crazed Zelda, were media darlings. They were idolized by glamour-hungry wannabees. They lived fast and died young, sad and worn-out. Fitzgerald is particularly interesting in the context of *Shopping in Space*; he is probably closer to the ambitious young New York writers of the eighties such as Ellis than any of the other writers—Kerouac, Salinger—associated with youth culture in the intervening years. The twenties were, like the eighties, a decade of extremely conspicuous consumption for moneyed, status-conscious pleasure-seekers and there was an enormous gulf between them and the underprivileged masses in American society. The bums, beggars and hobos that return to haunt the pages of the eighties novel were just outside the periphery of Fitzgerald's world. While desperate to represent the flaming youth of his time, Fitzgerald was also sufficiently astute and puritanical to write critically of that same moneyed high society which so drew him. Eventually, like Gatsby, he was wrecked. The snobbish, luxury-loving, night-clubbing aspects of his persona took over to the point where the serious artist was awash in drink and self-loathing. There are unmistakable parallels with the 'brat-pack' writers' own experience of literary stardom in the 1980s, which helps to account for the very slight traces of Fitzgerald discernible in their books.

Bret Easton Ellis was similarly catapulted, virtually overnight, into the full glare of the American publicity machine and, indeed, appeared to relish his position. He could be seen, peering out, sullen and slightly petulant from countless photographs in the company of fatuous celebrities at chic locations and indeed was shortly to be castigated for having so swiftly adopted such a highly visible and notoriously empty public life. The stresses of literary fame in America must be very great—Fitzgerald, Truman Capote and Norman Mailer all had to be soothed by high society as well. However, there are still significant differences between Ellis's success as a representative voice of the younger generation and the careers of previous youth chroniclers. Writers who had previously captured a youthful readership, Fitzgerald to some extent but certainly Salinger and Kerouac, all had years of serious literary endeavour and disappointment behind them, as well as other adult rites of passage, whereas Ellis seemed to exist solely in the light entertainment industry, as if his early career were indeed that of a rock star. It has become a truism to observe that the gap between endeavour and success for talented rock stars—and by extension today, writers—is now so brief as to allow them no time for development, meaning that they run down quickly and are soon stranded, rich, hungry for further adulation and lacking the material with which to achieve it. This is in itself merely an aspect of the post-war consumer spectacle and the furious pace at which it must transform experience into financially viable entertainment. Young artists such as Ellis or the late Jean-Michel Basquiat are grist to fine-grinding mills. Furthermore, whether it is the sheer speed of the dream machine that produces a somewhat listless response outside of the obsessive rock-music arena, or whether serious writing is now just too negligible a part of the cultural carnival, it is certain that Ellis did not command the devotion and loyalty of his youthful readers in the way that Fitzgerald, Salinger and Kerouac most certainly did. It was as if the more present he was in the media the more insubstantial he became as a writer; a ghost in the machine— the same deinvigoration that has caused Mailer to roar like a bull at his own increasing perplexing insubstantiality.

There has been an inevitable erosion of the 'real' in terms of authentic connections and relationships between artist, audience and work. Ellis, in particular, may have suffered from that eighties Zeitgeist which produced a mean-minded and resentful response to success, which meant that the emotions between the fan and the star were, basically, comprised of hatred and aggression rather than love and affection. But, ultimately, and most importantly in the literary sense, the reason why Ellis had no hope of inspiring his audience was inextricably involved with the nature of his writing. He would not, could not, could never create a Jay Gatsby, a Holden Caulfield or a Dean Moriarty. The characters in his books, by very dint of their lack of individuality in a homogenized society, cannot be 'created', cannot be born as personalities in the old sense, because as Ellis suggests, personality in the manner of individuals can no longer exist. Ellis is describing a world where even the most extreme attempts at individuality are doomed because personality itself has become commodity. For Ellis's characters, and for ourselves, the shadow always falls between the person and the personality. Even to be 'natural' is to decode and assume the elements of a consumer crux. Additionally, it is impossible in fictional terms nowadays to unselfconsciously create 'character' as it existed in the traditional novel or what Jean-Francois Lyotard called 'Grand Narrative'. The world in which Dickens could 'write' a Fagin is gone. We are in another country, where the author is dead and 'character' comes to us in wraiths, projections, pastiche, mutating entities, archetypes, comic cut-outs and intertextual refugees from history, film, fiction and myth.

And so, against this background of consumer frenzy and a fragmented fictional landscape, Ellis and his literary peers took fiction to the streets of America. They hoped, as authors always do, to tell the truth as they saw it, although it had become increasingly difficult to 'see' anything, let alone render it in text through the blizzard of fall-out from an uncertain, nervously apocalyptic world which seemed constantly poised, like a psychotic at bay with no hostages, on the brink of shooting itself in the head.

Notes

1   The phrase 'the life', meaning the underground or counter-culture, was first used by Tom Wolfe in his essay 'The Pump House Gang', reprinted in *The Purple Decades* (London: Cape, 1983).
2   Editor's note—as this chapter was originally published in 1992 as part of the book *Shopping in Space: Essays on American 'Blank Generation' Fiction* (London: Serpent's Tail), references in this essay are made to the fiction discussed elsewhere in the same book.
3   Amok Bookstore Fourth Despatch Catalogue 1991 (PO Box 86/867, Terminal Annexe, Los Angeles, CA 90086-1867).
4   Editor's note—there are parallels too with Generation X, as explored by Douglas Coupland in his novel of that name. See the essays by Acland, Lewis and Philo in this volume.

Bibliography

Acker, Kathy (1991) Interview in *Gargoyle* 37/38: 16–18.

Coupland, Douglas (1992) Interview in *Time Out* magazine, 1–8 April 1992: 27.

Ellis, Bret Easton (1987) *Less Than Zero*, London: Picador.

Federman, Raymond (ed.) (1981) *Surfiction: Fiction Now and Tomorrow*, Chicago: Swallow Press.

Fitzgerald, Scott, F. (1988) *The Crack-Up*, London: Penguin.

Foster, Hal (ed.) (1985) *The Anti-Aesthetic: Essays on Postmodern Culture*, London: Pluto Press.

Hutcheon, Linda (1988) *A Poetics of Postmodernism: History, Theory, Fiction*, London: Routledge.

Jameson, Fredric (1985) 'Postmodernism and consumer society', in Hal Foster (ed.) *The Anti-Aesthetic: Essays on Postmodern Culture*, London: Pluto Press.

Landis, Bill (1984) *Sleazoid Express* 4(1): 7.

Leyner, Mark (1992) Interview in *Mondo 2000*, March: 48.

Siegle, Robert (1988) *Suburban Ambush: Downtown Writing and the Fiction of Insurgency*, Baltimore and London: Johns Hopkins University Press.

Sukenick, Ronald (1985) *In For: Digressions on the Art of Fiction*, Carbondale: Southern Illinois University Press.
Williams, John (1991) *Into the Badlands: A Journey Through the American Dream*, London: Paladin.
Wolfe, Tom (ed.) (1990) *The New Journalism*, London: Picador.

THREE

Disposable Youth/Disposable Futures:
The Crisis of Politics and Public Life

Henry A. Giroux

Framing Youth

Lauded as both a symbol of hope for the future and a threat to the existing society, youth occupy increasingly unstable and politically disadvantaged positions within the diverse public spheres that constitute contemporary social order. Increasingly denied opportunities for self-definition and political interaction, youth are transfigured by discourses and practices that subordinate and contain the language of individual freedom, social power and critical agency. Symbols of a declining democracy, youth are located within a range of signifiers that largely deny their representational status as active citizens. Associated with coming-of-age rebellion, youth become a metaphor for trivializing resistance. At the same time, youth attract serious attention as both a site of commodification and a profitable market. For many aging Baby Boomers, youth represent an invigorated referent for a mid-life consciousness aggressively in search of acquiring a more 'youthful' state of mind and lifestyle.

At stake in such representations is not only how American culture is redefining the meaning of youth, but also how it constructs children in relation to a future devoid of the moral and political obligations of citizenship, social responsibility, and democracy. Caught up in an age of increasing despair, youth no longer appear to inspire adults to reaffirm their commitment to a public discourse that envisions a future in which human suffering is diminished while the general welfare of society is increased. Constructed largely within the language of the market and the increasingly conservative politics of media culture, contemporary youth appear unable to constitute themselves through a defining generational referent that gives them a sense of distinctiveness and vision, as did the generation of youth in the 1960s. The relations between youth and adults have always been marked by strained generational and ideological struggles, but the new economic and social conditions that youth face today, along with a callous indifference to their spiritual and material needs, suggest a qualitatively different attitude on the part of many adults toward American youth—one that indicates that the young have become our lowest national priority. Put bluntly, American society at present exudes both a deep rooted hostility and chilling indifference toward youth, reinforcing the dismal conditions that young people are increasingly living under.

Commentators such as Mike Males argue that the current historical juncture represents 'the most anti-youth period in American history' (Males 1999: 8–9). James Wagoner, the president of the social service organization Advocates for Youth, claims that 'Young people have been portrayed almost universally as a set of problems to be managed by society: juvenile crime, teen-age pregnancy, drug use'(in Powers 1998: 8). Both of these commentaries suggest that American society has undergone a profound change in the last two decades, both in terms of how it views youth and how it treats them.[1] Underlying this shift are a number of social problems such as racism, poverty, unemployment, and the dismantling of childcare services that are rarely discussed or analysed. What appears as an underlying feature of these public discussions is that many adults appear obsessed with young people but not with the idea of either listening to their needs or addressing the problems they face. In fact, many adults exhibit what Annette Fuentes calls a 'sour, almost hateful view of young people' (Fuentes 1998: 21). For example, growing adult fear and disdain for young people is echoed in a 1997 Public Agenda report, 'Kids These Days: What Americans Really Think About the Next Generation'.[2] The report found that two-thirds of the adults surveyed thought that kids today were rude, irresponsible, and wild. Another 58 per cent thought that young people would make the world either a worse place or no different when they became adults. Unfortunately, such views are not limited to the findings of conservative research institutes. Former Senator Bill Bradley, a prominent liberal spokesperson, reinforces the ongoing demonization of youth by claiming that the United States is 'in danger of losing a generation of young people to a self-indulgent, self-destructive lifestyle' (in Males 1999: 341). Within this discourse, there appears to be a limited number of categories available to examine what Henry Jenkins calls 'the power dynamic between children and adults' (Jenkins 1998: 23).

One of the most incessant and insidious attacks waged by the media has been on poor and urban black youth in the United States. Represented through a celluloid haze of drugs, crime and sex, black youth—as in a slew of 1990s Hollywood films including *Boyz N the Hood* (1991), *Sugar Hill* (1993), *Menace II Society* (1993), *Clockers* (1995), and *187* (1997)—are viewed as menacing and dangerous. In addition, popular representations of youth in the music press take on a decidedly racial register as they move between celebrating the politics of cynicism and rage of white singers such as Alanis Morrisette and Courtney Love, on the one hand, and giving high visibility to the violence-laden lyrics and exploits of black rappers such as Snoop Doggy Dog and the recently deceased Tupac Amaru Shakur and Notorious B.I.G.

Caught between representations that view them as either slackers, gangsters, or sell-outs, youth increasingly are defined through the lens of contempt or criminality. If not demonized, youth are either commodified or constructed as consuming subjects. For instance, in the world of media advertising, prurient images of youth are paraded across high-gloss magazines, pushing ethical boundaries by appropriating the seedy world of drug abuse to produce an aesthetic that might be termed 'heroin chic'. Capitalizing on the popularity of heroin use in films such as *Trainspotting* (1996), fashion designers such as Calvin Klein portray barely dressed, emaciated youthful models with dark circles under their eyes as part of an advertising campaign that combines the lure of fashion and addiction with an image of danger and chic bohemianism.

Yet, the corporate exploitation of youth does not account for the insurgent racism that breeds a different register of violence against young people. Racism feeds the attack on teens by targeting black youths as criminals while convincing working-class white youth that blacks and immigrants are responsible for the poverty, despair, and violence that have become a growing part of everyday life in American society. Racism is once again readily embraced within mainstream society. This is evident, in part, in the celebration in the popular press of overtly racist books by authors such as Denise D'Souza, Charles Murray, and their increasingly colour-blind liberal cohorts such as Jim Sleeper and Randall Kennedy, but also in the more overt acts of police brutality and daily violence being waged against young black and brown Americans who are filling up America's prisons at an alarming rate.

The institutional and cultural spheres bearing the brunt of the racialization of the social order are increasingly located in the criminal justice system, the urban public schools, in retrograde anti-immigrant policy legislation, and in the state's ongoing attempts to force welfare recipients into workfare programmes. Moreover, as I previously suggested, the popular imagination is being fed a steady diet of racial panic and right-wing extremism through a host of 'new' Hollywood films that suggest that urban kids who are black, brown and poor are not simply dangerous and pathological but disposable, subject to attacks by vigilantes and 'night riders'. These cultural texts constitute a public pedagogy that links issues of representation with various underlying political and economic forces that point to where life and death struggles are taking place over the politics of difference. It is precisely these popular cultural texts that academics should be paying attention to less as ways to breathe life into clever modes of formalistic, abstract theorizing than as a cultural politics that takes issues of power and political intervention seriously.

In what follows, I want to focus on a recent Hollywood blockbuster, *187*, illustrating how such texts might be taken up as a public project designed to integrate representations of cultural and racial difference with material relations of power that animate the dynamics of racially exclusive practices and policies in sites that often appear too far removed from the privileged security of the university to be included in the discourse of academic enquiry.

Beyond the Racial Politics of Demonization

During the last five years, a number of Hollywood films such as *Dangerous Minds* (1995), *The Substitute I* (1996) and *High School High* (1996) have cashed in on the prevailing racially coded popular 'wisdom' that public schools are out of control, largely inhabited by illiterate, unmotivated, and violent urban youth who are economically and racially marginalized. The increasingly familiar script suggests a correlation between urban public space, rampant drug use, daily assaults, broken teachers, and schools that do nothing more than contain deviants who are a threat to themselves and everybody else. The film *187* is a recent addition to this genre, but takes the pathologizing of poor, urban students of colour so far beyond existing cinematic conventions that it stands out as a public testimony to broader social and cultural formations within American society that makes the very existence of this blatantly racist film possible.

Directed by Kevin Reynolds and written by former school teacher, Scott Yagemann, *187* narrates the story of Trevor Garfield (Samuel L. Jackson), a science teacher who rides to school on a bike in order to teach at a high school in Bedford-Stuyvesant, in New York city. Garfield is portrayed as an idealistic teacher who against all odds is trying to make his classes interesting and do his best to battle daily against the ignorance, chaos and indifference that characterizes the urban public school in the Hollywood imagination.

In the film's opening scenes, students move through metal detectors under the watchful eyes of security guards—props that have become all too familiar to urban high school settings. Clearly, the students in *187* are far removed from the squeaky clean, high-tech classrooms of white suburbia. On the contrary, the school looks more like a prison, and the students, with their rap music blaring in the background, look more like inmates being herded into their cells. The threat of violence is palpable in this school and Garfield confronts it as soon as he enters his classroom and picks up his textbook, which has the figure '187' scrawled all over it. Recognizing that the number is the police code for homicide, Garfield goes to the principal to report what he believes is a threat on his life. The principal tells Garfield he is overreacting, dismissing him with 'You know what your problem is? On the one hand, you think someone is going to kill you, and on the other hand, you actually think kids are paying attention in your class.' But Garfield hasn't left before the principal confirms his worse fears by revealing that he has told a student in Garfield's class that he has flunked the course. Not only has the principal violated Garfield's privacy, but the student who he has flunked is on probation and, as a result of the failing grade, will now be sent back to prison. The threat of violence and administrative ineptitude set the stage for a hazardous series of confrontations between Garfield and the public school system. Terrified, Garfield leaves the principal's office and walks back to his classroom. Each black male student he now sees appears menacing and poised to attack. Shot in slow motion, the scene is genuinely disturbing. And before Garfield reaches his classroom, he is viciously and repeatedly stabbed with a nine-inch nail in the hallway by the black male student he has flunked.

Fifteen months later, Garfield has relocated and finds a job as a substitute teacher at John Quincy Adams High School in Los Angeles. The students in this school are mostly Latino. They wear oversized pants and torn shirts, carry boom boxes blaring rap music, and appear as menacing as the African-American students Garfield taught in

Brooklyn. As the camera pans their bodies and expressions, it becomes clear that what unites these inner-city students of colour is a culture that is dangerous, crime-ridden and violent. Assigned to teach his class in a bungalow, Garfield's first day is a nightmare as students taunt him, throw paper wads at him, and call him 'bitch'. Garfield has moved from New York to California only to find himself in a public high school setting that has the look and feel of hell. Images of heat rising from the pavement, pulsating rap music, shots of graffiti, and oversized shadows of gang members playing basketball filtering through the classroom window paint an ominous picture of what Garfield is about to experience.

Ellen Henry (Kelly Rowan), a perky, blonde computer science teacher, tries to befriend Garfield, but he is too battered and isolated, telling Ellen at one point that when he was assaulted in New York, it robbed him of his 'passion, my spark, my unguarded self—I miss them'. Garfield's descent into madness begins when his bungalow is completely trashed by the gang members in his class. He becomes edgy, living his life in a shadow of fear heightened by his past. Ellen then tells Garfield that Benny, a particularly vicious gang member in his class, has threatened to hurt her, and indicates to Garfield that she doesn't know what to do. Soon afterwards Benny disappears, but her troubles are not over, as Benny's sidekick, Cesar, and his friends kill her dog. As a result, Cesar becomes the object of vigilante justice. Roaming drunk near the LA freeway, he is stalked, shot with a spiked arrow, and while unconscious his finger is cut off. The tension mounts as Ellen finds Benny's rosary beads in Garfield's apartment and confronts him with the evidence that he might be the killer. Garfield is immune to her reproach, arguing that someone has to take responsibility since the system will not protect 'us' from 'them'. Ellen tells Garfield she doesn't know him anymore, and Garfield replies, 'I am a teacher just like you.' As the word circulates that Garfield may be the vigilante killer and assailant, the principal moves fast to protect the school from a lawsuit and fires him. Garfield, now completely broken, goes home and is soon visited by Cesar and his gang, who, inspired by the film *The Deer Hunter*, force Garfield into a game of Russian roulette. With little to lose, Garfield tells Cesar he is not really a man, and ups the stakes of the game by taking Cesar's turn. Garfield pulls the trigger and kills himself. Forced into questioning his own manhood, Cesar decides to take his turn, puts the gun to his head, and fatally shoots himself as well. In the final scene of the film, a student is reading a graduation speech about how teachers rarely get any respect, the shot switches to Ellen who is in her classroom. Ellen takes her framed teaching certificate off the wall, throws it into the wastebasket, and walks out of the school.

The conditions that produce such denigrating images of inner-city public schools—poverty, family turmoil, violent neighbourhoods, un-employment, crumbling school buildings, lack of material resources, or iniquitous tax structures—are, of course, absent from *187* and all other films in this rising genre. Decontextualized and depoliticized, Hollywood portrays public schools as not only dysfunctional, but also as an imminent threat to the dominant society. Students represent a criminalized under-class that must be watched and contained through the heavy-handed use of high-tech monitoring systems and military-style authority. Instead of smaller class sizes, inspiring teachers, visionary administrators and ample learning resources, the children of the urban poor are treated to the latest 'security' techniques. Hence, urban schools are increasingly subject to electronic surveillance, private police forces, padlocks and alarms more suggestive of prisons or 'war zones'. Films like *187* carry the logic of racial stereotyping to a new level and represent one of the most egregious examples of how popular cultural texts can be used to demonize black and Latino youth while reproducing a consensus of common sense that legitimates racist policies of either containment or abandonment in the inner cities. The depictions of urban youth as dangerous, pathological and violent, in turn, finds its counterpart in the growth of a highly visible criminal justice system whose get-tough policies fall disproportionately on poor black and brown youth. Such policies represent more than the celebrated 'war on drugs'; they threaten to wipe out a whole generation of young black males who are increasingly incarcerated in prisons and jails, and whose populations are growing at the rate of about 7 per cent a year and cost more than \$30 billion annually to operate. The figures are disturbing:

Between 1983 and 1998 the number of prisoners in the U.S. increased from 650,000 to more than 1.7 million. About 60 percent of that number are African-Americans and Latinos. More than one-third of all young black men in their 20s are currently in jail, on probation or parole, or awaiting trial. We are now adding 1,200 new inmates to U.S. jails and prisons each week, and adding about 260 new prison beds each day.

(Marable 1998: 31)

This state of affairs is compounded by the disturbing fact that as a result of serving time nearly half of the next generation of black males will forfeit their right to vote in several states. How can a cultural text such as *187* be used to engage students in addressing their own views on race and the politics of difference? At the very least, educators can address *187* not merely in terms of what such a text might mean but how it functions within a set of complex social relations that create the conditions of which it is a part and from which it stems.

Engaging the potential discursive effects of films such as *187* might mean discussing the implication of this Hollywood film in appropriating the name of the controversial California proposition to deny mostly non-white students access to public schools. Or engaging how *187* contributes to a public discourse that rationalizes both the demonization of minority youth and the defunding of public and higher education at a time when in states such as California 'approximately 22,555 African Americans attend a four-year public university . . . while 44,792 (almost twice as many) African Americans are in prison [and] this figure does not include all the African Americans who are in county jails or the California Youth authority or those on probation or parole.'[3]

Hollywood films such as *187* must be addressed and understood within a broader set of policy debates about education and crime which often serve to legitimate policies that disempower poor and racially marginalized youth. For example, nationwide state spending for corrections has increased 95 per cent over the last decade, while spending on higher education decreased 6 per cent. Similarly, 'over a ten year period, the number of correctional officers increased four times the rate of public higher education faculty.' Again, it is not surprising that the chosen setting for *187* is primarily California, a state that now 'spends more on corrections (9.4% of the General Fund) than on higher education.'[4] While it would be absurd to suggest to students that films such as *187* are responsible for recent government spending allocations, they do take part in a public pedagogy and representational politics that cannot be separated from a growing racial panic and fear over minorities, the urban poor and immigrants.

As public discourses, films such as *187*, *The Substitute I and II*, *Dangerous Minds*, and *Belly* fail to rupture the racial stereotypes that support harsh, discriminatory crime policies and growing incidents of police brutality, such as the highly publicized torture of Abner Louima by Brooklyn patrolmen or the recent shooting death of Amadou Diallo by four New York City plainclothes policemen who riddled his body in an apartment building vestibule with forty-one bullets, in spite of the fact that Diallo was unarmed. Such films also have little to say about police assaults on poor black neighbourhoods such as those conducted by former LA police Chief Daryl Gates against South-Central Los Angeles.

What is unique about *187* is that it explores cinematically what the logical conclusion might be when dealing with urban youth for whom reform is no longer on the national agenda, for which containment or the militarization of school space seem both inadequate and too compromising. Carried to the extreme, *187* flirts with the ultimate white supremacist logic, i.e. extermination and genocide of those others deemed inhuman, despicable, and beyond the pale of social reform. *187* capitalizes on the popular conception reported endlessly in the media that public education is not safe for white, middle-class children, that racial violence is rampant in the public schools, that minority students have turned classroom discipline into a joke, that administrators are paralysed by insensitive bureaucracies, and the only thing that teachers and students share is the desire to survive the day. But the implications of cultural texts such as *187* become meaningful not just as strategies of understanding and critical engagement that raise questions about related discourses, texts, and social issues, they also become meaningful in probing what it might mean to move beyond the sutured institutional space of the classroom to address social issues in related spheres marked by racial injustices and unequal relations of power.

The popularity of such films as *187* in the heyday of academic multiculturalism points to the need, in light of such representations, for educators to expand their understanding of politics as part of a broader project designed to address major social issues in the name of a multiracial democracy. This suggests getting beyond reducing the politics of difference and cultural politics more broadly to simply the study of texts or discourse in order to address the politics of difference and youth studies as part of the struggle over power and resources in a variety of public spheres. In what follows, I want to make some suggestions regarding how academics in higher education might think through the limits of the spaces they inhabit in order to address some of most serious problems youth face within the boundaries and traditional limits of university politics.

Public Politics and the Responsibility of Intellectuals

What do we represent? Whom do we represent? Are we responsible? For what and to whom? If there is a university responsibility, it at least begins with the moment when a need to hear these questions, to take them upon oneself and respond, is imposed. This imperative for responding is the initial form and minimal requirement of responsibility.

(Derrida in Rand 1992: 3)

The last few decades have been a time of general crisis in university life. Issues regarding the meaning and purpose of higher education, the changing nature of what counts as knowledge in a multicultural society, growing dissent among large numbers of underpaid adjunct faculty and graduate assistants, the increasing vocationalization of university life, battles over affirmative action, and intensifying struggles over the place of politics in teaching have exacerbated the traditional tensions both within the university community and between the university and the broader society. In the above quotation, the French philosopher Jacques Derrida raises timely fundamental questions not only for university teachers but for all educators and cultural workers who work in the public realm. In response to the ongoing crisis in the university, to the crisis of university responsibility, I have been concerned with interrogating the fundamental link between knowledge and power, pedagogical practices and effects, authority and civic responsibility. I have argued elsewhere that the question of what educators teach is inseparable from what it means to invest in public life, to locate oneself in a public discourse (see Giroux 1997, 1988). Implicit in this argument is the assumption that the responsibility of educators cannot be separated from the consequences of the knowledge they produce, the social relations they legitimate, and the ideologies they transmit to society. Educational work at its best represents a response to questions and issues posed by the tensions and contradictions of public life and attempts to understand and intervene in specific problems that emanate from the material contexts of everyday existence.

Educational work is both inseparable from and a participant in cultural politics because it is in the realm of culture that identities are forged, citizenship rights are enacted, and possibilities are developed for translating acts of interpretation into forms of intervention. Pedagogy in this discourse is about linking the construction of knowledge to issues of ethics, politics and power. It suggests making the political more pedagogical by addressing how agency unfolds within power-infused relations; that is, how the very processes of learning constitute the political mechanisms through which identities are produced, desires mobilized, and experiences take on specific forms and meanings. This broad definition of pedagogy is not limited to institutionalized forms of schooling, but points to all those cultural sites where youth imagine their relationship to the world, where social agency is both enabled and constrained across multiple sites, and where meanings enter the realm of power and function as public discourses. The assault on youth today, that I spoke about earlier, suggests that educators need to rethink the interrelated dynamics of politics, culture, power and responsibility. This implies the need for a critical language in order to both redefine the political role of educators at all levels of schooling but also to rethink the relationship between culture and politics, theory and practice, and text and context.

Educators and others must begin to recognize that the political, economic and social forces that demonize young people in the cultural sphere and defund the public services youth rely upon are also at work in the public schools and universities. The increasing influence of corporate power to commodify youth culture and eliminate the decommodifed spheres where youth meet and develop a sense of agency and autonomy is not unrelated to attempts on the part of corporate culture to vocationalize all aspects of public and higher education by turning such institutions over to the imperatives of the market, devaluing notions of social betterment, and radically deskilling academic labour. Schools have become crucial battlegrounds for disciplining and regulating youth, particularly poor urban youth of colour. Moreover, the continued devaluation of education as a public good points to the need for educators to struggle collectively to reclaim such sites as democratic public spheres. But crucial to such a struggle is the recognition that the necessity to reclaim schools as sites of democratic learning cannot be removed from broader economic, cultural and social struggles that affect the lives of many young people. This is not meant to suggest that educators should split the academic and the political, or the performance of institutional politics from cultural politics, but rather find ways to connect the politics of schooling with political struggles that take place across multiple social spheres and institutions (see Giroux 1992). In this context, cultural politics constructs itself in response to the demands of both the institutional contexts of schooling—in all of its differences—and the broader demands and practical commitments that point to change and resistance in ideological and institutional structures that oppress young people on a daily level.

Cultural politics challenges the priority of corporate culture's exclusive emphasis on the private good and reconnects educational theory and criticism to a notion of the public good that links democracy in the sphere of culture with democracy in the wider domain of public history and ordinary life. Broadly defined, culture in this perspective collapses the divide between high and low culture and extends the reach of what counts as a serious object of learning from the library and the museum to the mass media and popular culture. Similarly, the politics of culture not only reconstitutes and maps how meaning is produced, it also investigates the connections between discourses and structures of material power, the production of knowledge and the effects it has when translated into daily life. But before educators can retheorize what it means to make connections to popular formations outside of the walls of public education and the university, they will have to analyse the institutional and ideological structures that shape their own academic lives.

Critical educators need to address what it means to exercise authority from their own academic locations and experiences while assuming the challenge of putting knowledge in the service of a more substantive democracy. This requires redefining the relationship between theory and practice in order to challenge its formalist legacy, one that often abstracts theory from concrete problems and the dynamics of power. Theory in this sense is reduced to a form of theoreticism, an indulgence in which the production of theoretical discourse becomes an end in itself, an expression of language that removes itself from the possibility of challenging strategies of domination. Rather than performing the bridging work between public practices and intellectual debates or implementing political projects that merge strategies of understanding and social engagement, theory often becomes less a means for social amelioration than an end for professional advancement. Cut off from concrete struggles and broader public debates, theory assumes a reactionary posture in privileging rhetorical mastery, playfulness and cleverness over the politically responsible task of challenging the inertia of commonsense understandings of the world, opening up possibilities for new approaches to social reform for youth, or addressing the most pressing social problems that young people have to face.

Similarly, within many liberal and critical approaches to education, the politics of meaning becomes relevant only to the degree that it is separated from a broader politics of engagement. Reading texts becomes a hermetic process, removed from larger social and political contexts, that engages questions of power exclusively within a politics of representation. Such readings largely function to celebrate a textuality that has been diminished to a bloodless formalism and the non-threatening, if not accommodating, affirmation of indeterminacy as a transgressive aesthetic. Lost here is any semblance of a radical political project that 'grounds itself in the study of concrete cultural practices and . . . understands that struggles over meaning are inevitably struggles over resources' (Lipsitz 1990: 621). By failing to connect the study of texts to the interests of a project that expand the goals of economic justice, children's rights campaigns, radical democratic visions, and the opposition to anti-welfare and immigration policies, many educators conceive politics as largely representational or abstractly theoretical.[5] Also missing in this perspective is the crucial opportunity to develop connections between analyses of representations and strategies of political engagement, that is, the occasion for educators and others to do critical readings of texts as 'routes to a larger analysis of historical formations' (Johnson in Long 1997: 465).

Addressing the problems of youth suggests that rigorous educational work needs to respond to the dilemmas of the outside world by focusing on how young people make sense of their possibilities for agency within the power-regulated relations of everyday life. The motivation for scholarly work cannot be narrowly academic; such work must connect with 'real life social and political issues in the wider society' (Bennett 1998: 538). This requires, in part, that educators and other cultural workers must address the practical consequences of their work in the broader society while simultaneously making connections to those too often ignored institutional forms and cultural spheres that position and influence young people within unequal relations of power. Moreover, it is crucial for critical educators to recognize that the forms of domination that bear down on young people are both institutional and cultural, and one cannot be separated from the other. Within this approach to cultural politics, the effects of domination cannot be removed from the pedagogical conditions in which such behaviour is learned, appropriated, or challenged.

Analyzing the relationship between culture and politics in addressing the problems of youth also requires that critical educators and cultural workers engage both the symbolic and material conditions that construct the various social formations in which young people experience themselves and their relations to others. That is, any viable form of cultural politics must address the institutional machineries of power that promote child poverty, violence, unemployment, police brutality, rape, sexual abuse and racism. But this is not enough. In addition, educators must also interrogate those cultural pedagogies that produce specific meanings, affective investments, and desires that legitimate and secure specific acts of domination aimed at young people. This suggests that educators do more than simply interview young people through the convenience of academic-based research methods. It also suggests that educators become border crossers (without passports), willing to examine the multiple sites and cultural forms that young people produce to create their own means of being heard. Ann Powers, a writer for the *New York Times*, has insightfully pointed out that as young people have been shut out of the larger society, they have created their own web sites, alternative radio programmes, 'published their own manifestoes in photocopied fanzines, made their own music and shared it on cassette, designed their own fashions and arranged to have them sold in boutiques' (Powers 1998: 8). Moreover, Powers has argued that many young women have not sat passively by as they see themselves misrepresented in the American cultural landscape as lazy, shiftless, dangerous and pathological. In response, they have produced a 'far-ranging girls' culture, which includes bold young athletes, musicians, film makers and writers [which] is invigorating the discourse of women's liberation. [In addition], activist groups like YELL, an ACT Up youth division . . . have devised new approaches to safe sex education' (ibid.). The presence of today's diverse youth culture suggest that educators and others need to become attentive to the cultural formations that young people inhabit while making a serious effort to read, listen and learn from the specific languages, social relations and diverse types of symbolic expression that young people produce.

But if educators are to take seriously what it means to link academic criticism to public knowledge and strategies of intervention, they will have to re-evaluate the relationship between culture and power as a starting point for bearing witness to the ethical and political dilemmas that connect the university to other spheres within the broader social land-scape. In doing so, educators must consider becoming more attentive to how politics gets worked out in urban spaces and cultural formations that are currently experiencing the full force of the attack on youth. At issue is the need for critical educators to give meaning to the belief that academic work matters in its relationship to broader public practices and policies. Such work holds the possibility for understanding not just how power operates in particular contexts, but also how such knowledge 'will better enable people to change the contexts and hence the relations of power' (Grossberg 1997: 252–3) that inform the inequalities that undermine any viable notion of democratic participation in a wide variety of cultural spheres, including those that play a powerful role in shaping children's culture.

In the new millennium, educators, parents and others need to re-evaluate what it means for children to grow up in a world that has been radically altered by corporations and new electronic technologies. At the very least, we need to assess how the impact of new modes of symbolic and social practice affect the way we think about power, social agency and youth, and what such changes mean for expanding and deepening the process of democratic education, social relations and public life. In part, such a challenge points to the need for educators to develop a reinvigorated notion of cultural politics in order to reassess the relationship between texts and contexts, meaning and institutional power, critical reflection and informed action. Progressives need new theoretical tools for addressing how knowledge and power can be analysed within particular spaces and places, especially as such contexts frame the intersection of language and bodies as they become 'part of the process of forming and disrupting power relations' (Patton 1993: 183). At the same time, critical educators and cultural workers need to develop notions of cultural politics that provide an opportunity for parents, educators, and others to better understand how public discourses regarding youth have been transformed into the discourses of control, surveillance and demonization. Interrogating how power works through such discourses and implicates particular social formations provides opportunities for progressives to challenge the endless stereotypes and myths that provide a rationale for regressive legislative policies that serve to contain youth and undermine much needed social investments in their future. Such an approach cannot be addressed through the ritualistic condemnation of young people, but through a critical attentiveness to the historical, social and institutional conditions that produce those structures of power and ideologies that bear down on youth at the level of their everyday existence.

Notes

1   One index measuring the quality of children's lives claims that the social health of children is at its lowest point in twenty-five years. See 1996 *Index of Social Health* (New York: Fordham Institute for Innovation in Social Policy, 1996). p. 6. See also, Sylvia Ann Hewlett and Cornell West, *The War Against Parents* (New York: Houghton Mifflin, 1998).
2   Steve Farkas and Jean Johnson, *Kids These Days: What Americans Really Think About the Next Generation*, a report from Public Agenda, sponsored by Ronald McDonald House Charities and the Advertising Council, 1997, pp. 1–13.
3   Figures cited in The Justice Policy Institute/Center on Juvenile and Criminal Justice Policy Report, *From Classrooms to Cell Blocks: How Prison Building Affects*

Higher Education and African American Enrollment in California (San Francisco, CA: October 1996), p. 2.

4 Cited in 'From Classrooms to Cell Blocks: A National Perspective,' The Justice Policy Institute (February 1997), p. 2.

5 Larry Grossberg argues that Edward Said's *Orientalism* is a classic example of a text that focuses on questions of difference almost entirely in terms of identity and subjectivity while ignoring the related issues of materialism and power. See Lawrence Grossberg, 'Identity and Cultural Studies. Is That All There Is?' in Stuart Hall and Paul Du Gay, (eds) *Questions of Cultural Identity* (Thousand Oaks: Sage, 1996), pp. 87–107.

Bibliography

Bennett, T. (1998) 'Cultural studies: a reluctant discipline', in *Cultural Studies*, 12(4).

Derrida, J. (1992) 'Mochlos; or the conflict of the faculties', in Rand, R. *Logomachia: The Conflict of the Faculties*, Lincoln: University of Nebraska Press.

Giroux, H. A. (1988) *Schooling and the Struggle for Public Life*, Minneapolis: University of Minnesota Press.

——(1992) *Pedagogy and the Politics of Hope*, Boulder: Westview Press.

——(1992) *Border Crossings*, London and New York: Routledge.

——(1997) *Channel Surfing: Race talk and the Destruction of Today's Youth*, Basingstoke: MacMillan.

Grossberg, L. (1997) *Bringing It All Back Home: Essays on Cultural Studies*, Durham: Duke University Press.

Jenkins, H. (ed.) (1998) *The Children's Culture Reader*, New York: New York University Press.

Johnson, R. (1997) 'Reinventing cultural studies: remembering for the best version', in Elizabeth Long (ed.) *From Sociology to Cultural Studies*, Malden: Basil Blackwell.

Lipsitz, G. (1990) 'Listening to Learn and Learning to Listen: Popular Culture, Cultural Theory, and American Studies, in *American Quarterly*, 42, 4 (December).

Males, Mike (1999) *Framing Youth*, Monroe: Common Courage.

Marable, M. (1998) 'Beyond color-blindness' in *The Nation* (December).

Patton, C. (1993) 'Performativity and spatial distinction', in Eve Kosofsky Sedgewick and Andrew Parker (eds) *Performativity and Performance*, New York: Routledge.

Powers, Ann (1998) 'Who are these people, anyway?' in *The New York Times*, April 29.

Filmography

Belly (1998), directed by Hype Williams, Artisan Entertainment.
Dangerous Minds (1995), directed by John N. Smith, Buena Vista Pictures.
Clockers (1995), directed by Spike Lee, 40 Acres and a Mule/MCA/Universal.
187 (1997), directed by Kevin Reynolds, Warner Brothers.
High School High (1996), directed by Hart Bouchner, Columbia Tristar.
The Substitute I (1996), directed by Robert Mandel, Orion Pictures.
The Substitute II (1998), directed by Steven Pearl, Live Film and Mediaworks.

FOUR

How Katy Lied: Pictures of Joy and Pain in
What Katy Did *and Other American Girls' Stories*

Jenny Robinson

With love from Mummy and Daddy, Christmas 1953

This was the inscription inside my copy of Susan Coolidge's *What Katy Did*, first published in 1872. Other girls' stories were similarly inscribed in subsequent years. I was far from alone in this; many girls of my generation received such gifts, inscribed with parental love, as perhaps younger generations of girls still do, judging from present publication lists. Why were these stories, so gladly received and eagerly devoured, so treasured that, decades later, many of us still retain our original copies? What was the 'meaning', the joy and pleasure to us of the textual treasures that we stored in our chests? What messages, 'gifts' from parents and storytellers, did we, in devouring our textual food, digest and internalize?

The most fundamental 'gift' from parents is the defining of identity; this is the most precious gem in a child's treasury. It is the gift not only of parents, but of all those powerful 'parental' voices which interpret for the growing child the discursive messages of the parent culture. All those with such powerfully defining voices are in this sense founding fathers and mothers; they are authors of the child's subjectivity, the girl's foundation in life. As one such founding mother, the powerful authorial voice of the narrator, speaking *in loco parentis* as gift-giver of identity, suggests answers often enciphered in the cryptic clues of metaphor to the girl's question 'Who am I?'

In patriarchal societies, which both Coolidge's America in the 1870s and my Britain of the 1950s were,[1] socially constructed identities are gendered. In such societies, stories for children not only reflect gendered images of identity, but also, as discourses, 'generate sexual difference . . . they are [in] the logic that drives writing' (Laqueur 1990: 17). Girls' stories, then, as cultural texts, answer the girl's question 'Who am I?' with a cryptically enciphered message that suggests who she can or should be, as a social construct of young femininity in her society. As a genre, girls' stories work as an example of a 'literary institution or social contract . . . whose function is to specify the proper use of a particular cultural artefact' (Jameson 1981: 106–7). The 'proper use' of the girls' story is that it constructs for girls a map of socially constructed female identity and the metaphoric path of female destiny is made manifest in the plot. It is part of the general schooling process teaching a young girl what it 'means' to be female in her society.

What Katy Did, then, suggests answers to such questions as 'Who am I, as a girl?' 'What do I do?' 'What, as a woman, will I do next?' The past historic of what Katy did, first as a girl and next as a woman, suggests a conditional future of what may be for the girl reader, connected in the present by what the girl does now in the act of reading and of constructing 'meaning' in her interactive dialogue with the text. In this way, the language of girls' stories is one 'place where social identity is constructed' (Howarth 1995: 165). Such stories, as a set of linguistic practices, work like threads in a spider's web, together with interconnected discourses, as part of a 'specific language game' (Rorty 1980: 10). This language game for girls shows them where they are positioned in the cultural labyrinth of power relations. The plot is a textual treasure trail, with clues enciphered in metaphor to signpost the 'right' way to the finish; here the closure of the text indicates the X-marked spot on the cultural map where the treasure-chest of socially constructed female identity is located.

In discussing the 'meaning' and the value of the treasure-trove I discovered hidden in the text of *What Katy Did*, I can speak only for myself. Other readers no doubt made their own discoveries of differently inscribed valuables at the X-marked spot. Each reader constructs her own meaning in her interactive dialogue with texts; every reader's subjectivity is created 'through a dynamic exchange with another's discourse' (Pearce 1986: 89) and therefore every reader's interpretation of texts is another one than mine. Similarly, cultural messages are interactively interpreted differently for children by different 'parental' authorities. The resulting cacophony means that the messages passed on to the child are a 'specific language game' of Chinese Whispers; their voices often sound ambiguous, contradictory and in conflict, not only with other voices, but with themselves; 'we' speak in a plurality of voices. In texts of identity this is also the case because the signposts on the textual trail are expressed cryptically in the allusive language of metaphor, the richness of which allows for a multiplicity of reading. It is small wonder that, even with the narrator as our guide and map reader, different girl readers deciphered the sign posts differently and followed manifold paths on the textual map. Negotiating the treasure-trail of identity can be a twisted and tortuous journey through sites which cause great anxiety; the maze-like paths can lead different explorers through different territory and end in a different cultural space, at a different X-marked spot.

What Coolidge did with her authorial, authoritative founding-mother's voice was to create, in the opening chapters of the text, a different route to female subjectivity from that with which I was already familiar, growing up as I was in a society in which social constructs of identity were deeply rooted in gender. In the patriarchal bourgeois societies of America and Britain gender identities were polarized and oppositional;[2] this was still recognizably so in my childhood, even if the oppositional images of male and female identities were not so starkly contrastive as in 1872, when *What Katy Did* was first published. As Nead points out (1988: 27), building on Foucault's arguments, these societies constructed an image of femininity which, although 'artwork' designed to ensure gender and class hegemony, was made to seem 'natural and universal, the way things inevitably are'. It was 'naturally' assumed that, while men's place was in the public sphere, women's allotted cultural space was that of the private domestic sphere. Since men were active, articulate and powerful, then women, as 'the empty category . . . based on difference between sexes in which the standard has always been man' (Laqueur 1990: 94), were in contrast passive, silent and submissive. Little girls, then, were often represented in cultural texts as, for example, playing quietly in homes and gardens with their dolls, while their brothers noisily climbed trees and rode bicycles. Enid Blyton's books, so popular with many of my generation, presented many such didactic images; and even if the girls did go out with their brothers, they were never leaders but followers. Alternative images of identity were, quite literally, written out of the text. These gaps in the text spoke volumes to girl readers.

Socially defined identities work as much by exclusion as by inclusion; femininity is defined by what the female subject cannot be and do, as much as by what she can, or should, be and do. That is, she is defined, not only by her script, but by the gaps within it too. As maps of identity, cultural texts are full of 'Keep Out' signs, the prohibitions of culture which warn subjects to keep within the boundaries of their allotted territory, inside their cultural reservation. What twelve-year-old Katy did, in the opening chapters of the text, suggested how, as girls, we readers could trangress the boundaries of female social identity; she showed how we could leave the cultural reservation of enclosed domestic space and, flouting the prohibitory 'Keep Out' signs, occupy a different cultural space which was altogether wilder and more open. Opening the book, then, was to open a door which revealed to me a new path, promising to lead the way to all sorts of unaccustomed delights; it was a textual feast. Katy, as protagonist, was a textual friend to lead the reader along the track with fun and games along the way; she was a joy to meet. What Katy did became what I did too, in the joyful imaginary space created by the text. The trail we blazed together through the opening chapters was the storyteller's gift to me, created by a narrative voice which, far from sounding 'parental', had the power of a fairy godmother: Katy and I did, indeed, have a ball.

What Katy did, more specifically, was defined by Coolidge's naming of her protagonist, which is in itself illustrative of the 'naming' authority of the 'parental' narrative voice. Coolidge (1995: 2) tells her readers that the title of her book is a word-play on a North American grasshopper-like insect, which seems to say 'Katy did'. Katy is, in the early chapters of the book, very grasshopper-like: she leaps across the page on her long legs and is ceaselessly active and vocal in all that she does. In defiance of the conventional nineteenth-century image of femininity, she 'hated sewing and didn't care a button about being good' (ibid.: 4). She tears her dresses every day and gets into all sorts of mischief, particularly in the chapter entitled 'The Day of Scrapes'. Despite the warnings of Aunt Izzie, the moral lectures of her kind papa, and her frequent decisions to mend her ways as well as her clothes, she continues to do what she has done since the first chapter, much to the delight of many readers as they follow her trail of escapades. Coolidge vividly depicts what Katy does when adults are absent and therefore not in control; she initiates wild games in which she is usually the leader. When Aunt Izzie is out, for example, Katy and her friends play 'Kikeri', an energetic version of hide-and-seek played in the dark. The players try to evade the nominated catcher and reach the hall, significantly designated 'Freedom Castle'; this clearly represents the free space which absence of adult control creates for Katy and her siblings.

After reading *What Katy Did*, my ur-text of girls' stories, I read similar stories written by other North American women, whose protagonists did, broadly speaking, what Katy did. Anne in L.M. Montgomery's *Anne of Green Gables*, in addition to dying her hair green, gives her friend Diana home-made wine to drink; the latter's drunkenness so horrifies her mother that she declares Anne to be 'not a fit friend for Diana to associate with' (Montgomery 1977: 111). Rebecca, eponymous heroine of *Rebecca of Sunnybrook Farm* by Kate Douglas Wiggin, so outrages her Aunt Miranda with her activities that she is declared to be not only 'into every nameable thing in the neighbourhood . . . but generally at the head and front of it, especially when it's mischief' (Douglas Wiggin 1955: 130). Both Rebecca and Anne are colourful illustrations of active girlhood; each eleven years old, they 'make a vivid contrast to the cramped and colourless adults around them' (Scott Macleod 1994: 23). So does Jo, in Louisa M. Alcott's *Little Women*; despite her resolution to be 'prim as a dish and not get into any scrapes' (Alcott 1989: 24), she has many mishaps, not only burning her clothes, but burning off Meg's hair with the curling tongs. All these girls seemed to me to act in defiance of powerful adult voices, and in the phrase I would have used at the time, they 'got away with it'. Their activities constructed an escape route out of domestic confinement into 'Freedom Castle' where, I felt, they acted just as they pleased. These subversive images of rebel girls performing carnivalesque[3] handstands acted as signposts, pointing out a most tempting textual trail; they seemed to indicate an anarchic, joyful route which stood the usual adult/child power relationship on its head. They were indeed a treat, delightful illustrations on which to feast the eye; as food for thought, they were the stuff of fantasy.

What Katy did also stood patriarchal ideology on its head; in the carnivalesque, topsy-turvy territory of the text she was more powerful, more articulate, more active and more inventive than any of the boys. In what was a subversive delight for many girl readers, Katy did what boys traditionally did and perhaps did it better. The language of the text makes this clear; at times it borrows imagery more typical of American male genres. When Katy loses her sun bonnet in the schoolyard of a rival school, she refuses to let her 'enemies' from the rival school 'dance war dances around [it], pinning it on a pole . . . treating it as Indians treat a captive taken in the war. Was it to be endured? Never! Better die first'; she retrieves it, despite her enemies who 'with a howl of fury precipitated themselves upon Katy' (Coolidge 1995: 29). Here the metaphor of Katy bravely battling with an Indian warband clearly borrows from and parodies the language of American pioneer narrative; Coolidge's writing here exemplifies language appropriation as a parodic act which creates a polyphonic text,[4] enabling the writer to 'challenge the dominant ideological codes by pluralizing [dialogizing] meaning' (Morris 1997: 155). As a child, of course, I knew nothing of such concepts, but I knew I found the episode 'funny' because what Katy does here was nothing like what girls were supposed to do. Katy appears as an illustration on the textual map of female identity in her war bonnet, dancing a war dance—what could be more subversive fun? At school, Katy invents a new game named 'The Game of Rivers'. She selects girls to enact the roles of American rivers, instructing them to run violently into each other, 'because, as Katy said, rivers do' (Coolidge 1995: 31). Katy saved for herself the part of 'Father Ocean', sometimes crying for 'a meeting of the waters', while 'Father Ocean . . . roared loader than all of them put together' (ibid.). In this game, it is not merely that Katy's boisterous, noisy activity contests the traditional image of quiet, sedentary girlhood; as game inventor, definer, initiator and leader, she acts out a series of traditional 'male' roles, signified in her title as 'Father' Ocean. In such episodes, Coolidge challenges the male prerogative to name which is so entrenched in patriarchal theories of language. Katy and others like her 'produce their own world of meaning by ordering and naming, creating identities opposed to the pre-existing ones offered them in the Symbolic order' of language (Foster 1995: 30).

In *Little Women*, Jo enacts a range of male roles; she whistles, stands with her hands in her pockets, and uses slang. In an episode which, since I met her on the textual trail after I met Katy, reminded me of 'Father Ocean', Jo acts in her play 'The Witch's Curse', the title of which I will discuss later. Jo literally enacts the male roles of hero and villain, initiating and directing the action both on and off stage. Alcott's language as she describes these activities is humorous, parodying melodrama and the male roles within this genre, much as Coolidge parodies male roles in American frontier narratives. Rebecca and Anne are protagonists created a quarter of a century after Katy and Jo, by which time patriarchal discourses were not so repressive. Rather than their leisure activities posing a covert, parodic threat to patriarchy, as Katy's and Jo's do, they compete with boys in the open arena of education, and both win prizes in the academic competition. In the nineteenth-century maps of female identity which all of these girls' stories create, then, Coolidge and Alcott paint illustrations of girls in their war bonnets covertly ambushing patriarchy's little soldiers; Montgomery's and Douglas Wiggin's girl leaders charge into action in more open territory, brandishing those trophies of war, their school prizes. There is, then, the possibility of much subversive laughter for the girl reader as she negotiates her way through the text; this is part of the carnivalesque fun of the textual fair.

Those little soldiers, the boys in the text, are in comparison with vivid Katy and her allies, pale manifestations of identity. Katy's brother, greedy Dorrie, repeatedly writes in his journal that, except what he ate, he 'forgit what did' (Coolidge 195: 28). His sisters and possibly the reader laugh at this; yet the comparison between a boy who 'forgits' and a girl who did the exciting deeds that Katy did is a striking one. In *Little Women*, Laurie commonly appears on the periphery of the action, looking in through the window of the March girls' house, in a subversive metaphor which reverses the image of female exclusion. In a variety of ways, then, boys and girls in these texts are so delineated 'as to suggest, if not to recommend, gender roles and codes of behaviour which subvert con-temporary hegemonies' (Foster 1995: 125). In these girls' stories it is boys who are marginal notes, while the girls occupy the centre of the text; they are centre stage and the spotlight is on them. There is another textual game being played with the picture clues of metaphor. The many androgynous qualities of sensitive Laurie, who is 'quick to see and feel beauty of any kind' (Alcott 1989: 141) constitute another challenge to traditional assumptions of gendered identities.[5] This is also the case with the presentation of Katy's brothers. 'Pretty little' Phil is a baby to be looked after, while Dorrie 'seemed like a girl who had got into boy's clothes by mistake' (Coolidge 1995: 7). These two 'girlish' boys are oppositional images, not only to Katy, but also to her sister, significantly called Johnnie by the children, who is 'like a boy, who in a fit of fun, has borrowed his sister's frock' (ibid.: 8–9). The textual maps of identity, then, have as illustrations boys who look like girls and girls who look like boys. This narrative act of subversive reversal seemed, to me as a girl reader, a playful, topsy-turvy game.

It was not only boys who paled into insignificance when compared with the protagonists; their more conventional, traditional friends and sisters appear as insipid pale faces when compared with Katy on the war-path. Katy's sister Clover is, as her name suggests, a modest little flower, 'a fair sweet dumpling of a girl . . . those eyes and her soft cooing voice always made people feel like petting her' (ibid.: 6), but this little pet is rarely active, never imaginative or interesting, and I, for one, was bored by her. These conventional, cooing pets are often enciphered in metaphor as dolls. Jo's sister Meg is likened to a doll when she is dressed for a party. Rebecca's friend Emma Jane is a 'little fat doll of a girl' (Douglas Wiggin 1952: 265). The narrative voice, as Cipher[6] of the textual map of identity, explains the doll's significance: Emma Jane is so characterless that her 'blue eyes said nothing; [she had] red lips from between which no word worth listening to had ever issued' (ibid. 1955: 127). Indeed, none of these 'dolls' is very interesting, compared to the active, self-assertive protagonists. It is their passivity that is the defining feature of the patriarchal social construct of the 'good' woman; it is this same insipidly pretty passivity which makes the 'doll' image such a resonant cultural signifier. There were, however, warning signs next to the pictures of the dolls, as the narrative voice, acting as key to the map of female identity, directs us to see that these 'good' girls can be deceitful, plausible manipulators. Katy is blamed for stealing Clover's doll, when in fact the 'innocently' tearful Clover, good at making people feel like 'taking her part' (Coolidge 1995: 6), has stolen Katy's doll. The rebel girl, then, can be blamed for the misdeeds of the 'good' girl, who 'purred in triumph like a satisfied kitten' (ibid.). The little pet, then, has claws. Jo's sister Amy, as a 'most important person, in her own opinion at least' (Alcott 1989: 4), cultivates her lady-like image so that, 'when the opportunity came, she might be ready to take the place from which poverty excluded her' (ibid.: 257). Rebecca recognizes the corruption of these self-important little ladies, commenting 'they can . . . cheat in lessons, tell lies, be sulky and lazy, but all these can be conducted quite lady-like and genteel' (Douglas Wiggin 1952: 82). These insipid young ladies were not to be trusted; speaking with forked tongue, they might turn out, beneath their smiling, pretty masks,[7] to be snakes in the grass.

Beside other illustrations of girlhood in *What Katy Did*, there were mocking warning signs, cryptically enciphered in metaphoric pictograms. These were parodic pictures of the heroines of popular nineteenth-century fiction which, even in the 1950s, were not entirely unfamiliar to me. They were certainly familiar to Katy and the other protagonists, as textual examples of what they read make clear.[8] One of Katy's favourite books, for example, is Warner's *The Wide, Wide World*; her brother Dorry asks for Maria Edgeworth's *Harry and Lucy* for Christmas. Such didactic books feature 'good' children as protagonists, with the emphasis on selfless suffering. Similarly, Jo favours Charlotte Younge's *The Heir of Redcliffe*, in which the hero dies while nursing his worst enemy. Such literary references abound, filling these girls' stories with intertextuality, so that the 'text is a mosaic of quotations; any text is the absorption and transformation of another' (Kristeva 1981: 66). Since in *What Katy Did* this 'absorption and transformation' is parodic, the replica prints of fictional heroines appear in the text as music-hall burlesques of the originals.

In the intertextual 'mirage of citations' (Barthes 1976: 16) which constitutes *What Katy Did*, one of these burlesque caricatures is, as a 'mirage' of young ladyhood, a very shady lady indeed. Imogen Clarke is a grotesque parody of a fictional romantic heroine; she tells a web of ridiculous lies about her relationship with a Brigand, who has fallen in love with her beauty. This 'mirage' is a blot on the textual map, as the narrator's deciphering of the pictogram makes clear; although Katy at first thinks Imogen looks 'like a lady in a story', her 'satin slippers' and 'yellow gloves' are 'dirty' and her 'fine clothes' are 'old and darned' (Coolidge 1995: 82). This is a threadbare, shabby identity to be discarded by active, intelligent girls, as Katy eventually learns. Her papa takes on the narrator's deciphering role here, explaining that 'make-ups are all very well as long as people don't try to make you believe they are true' (ibid.: 89). Made-up young girls may try to make up to you, then, but one should not let their showy masks disguise the reality beneath. Katy learns later that Imogen is self-obsessed and superficial; she is a travesty of a friend. In polarized opposition to this shady lady is Cecy, who in her fantasies is a picture of the fictional self-renunciatory saint. Although in life 'a pink-and-white' girl, she imagines herself in a 'black silk dress . . . always teaching in Sunday school and visiting the poor' (ibid. 17–18), so perfectly selfless that although 'young gentlemen' will want to ride with her, she will refuse them all. The self-delusion and false humility of this is mocked by the unfolding narrative trail as Cecy turns out to be the most wordly of the girls, the first to have a 'beau' and the first to marry. The black dressed saint, then, is another parodic mirage; behind this burlesque is the 'pink-and-white' of a bride. Either 'mirage' is, of course, a patriarchal construct of the 'good' female, just as shady Imogen is a junior version of that patriarchal construct of a 'bad' woman, the 'femme fatale'. Both are ridiculed and rejected: they are fake gems, forgeries in a patriarchal treasure-chest.

As a child I had no problem in recognizing the worthlessness of the dolls, the 'femme fatale' and the saint/bride; they all seemed pastiche compared to those priceless pearls, the protagonists. Certainly, these self-assertive girls were not beautiful: Katy's mouth, and indeed her voice, was 'quite too large at present to suit the part of a heroine'; she was 'very awkward', too tall, and her hair was 'forever in a tangle' (Coolidge 1995: 9). Of the other girls, Anne has red hair, freckles and a 'small, plain face' (Montgomery 1977: 13); Rebecca's face 'was without colour and sharp in outline' (Douglas Wiggin: 1995: 12); Jo is 'tall, thin, and brown' with a 'comical nose . . . round shoulders . . . [and] big hands and feet' (Alcott

1989: 4). Their eyes, however, show their real worth: Rebecca's eyes carry 'such messages, such suggestions, such hints of sleeping power and insight that one never tired of looking into their shining depths' (Douglas Wiggin 1955: 13). Jo has 'sharp, grey eyes which seemed to see everything and were by turns fierce, funny, or thoughtful' (Alcott 1989: 4). Behind these protagonists' eyes, there were 'delightful schemes rioting' in their 'active brains' which they all used to build 'castles in the air' (Coolidge 1995: 10). It was hardly surprising that I felt of Katy and the other protagonists that, as Aunt Miranda says of Anne, 'I never saw anything in my life to equal' them (Montgomery 1977: 35). Their eyes represent what they are behind the masks of their otherwise plain faces: not only active, but imaginative and creative. It was not only what Katy did that fascinated me; it was also what she thought and imagined.

What Katy did and what she imagined became one in the act of writing. The female writer is a resonant cultural signifier; the act of writing alone proclaims Katy, Rebecca, Jo and Anne to be rebels against patriarchal ideology. Since writing asserts the self as being worthy of recognition, in patriarchal discourses it is 'naturally' what 'man' does; for 'woman', oppositionally constructed as silent and passive, writing is a 'step out of silence' and passivity (Smith 1993: 24). In the nineteenth century, women who wrote were often perceived as 'anomalous [and] freakish because as a "male" characteristic it is essentially unfeminine' (Gilbert and Gubar 1984: 10). However, the authors and protagonists of these girls' stories write a self for themselves which is very different to the 'self' given to them by dominant discourses; they may have seemed 'anomalous' and 'freakish' under the surveillance of the patriarchal eye,[9] but their self-willed act of self-creation is their 'chief treasure' (Alcott 1977: 17). These stories carry a powerfully double picture of the female writer, for the protagonists represent the narrator inside the textual space. These female authors were contesting fixed, hierarchical constructs of gender identity, just as their protagonists do. Indeed, Coolidge's relish in recounting Katy's adventures, her parodic reversal of gender roles and male writing genres, and the mocking, ironic laughter which suffuses the text, all suggest a humorously subversive narrative voice. Moreover, just as Jo's taste for writing Gothic novels reflects Alcott's similar taste, so Katy's stories replicate Coolidge's authorial tastes. Although Katy's stories are influenced by popular literature of the time, her humorous creations, such as 'The Blue Wizard or Edwitha of the Hebrides', depict active, interesting heroines, much like Katy herself. In contrast, Cecy's stories are of limp, romantic heroines who meet tragic fates, providing like Cecy herself mocking intertextual parodies. Katy as a writer is a junior version of Coolidge as writer, presenting for many girl readers a stunning double vision of 'mother' and 'daughter' writers.[10]

A cluster of spatial metaphors further emphasize female creativity: Katy reads her stories to the other children in the loft; Rebecca writes in a loft, while Jo's writing space is an attic. The 'heights' that Rebecca feels she is gaining, as she ascends the ladder to the loft (Douglas Wiggin 1952: 60), suggest the 'lofty' forbidden 'heights' of female literary ambition and creative imagination, the girl's escape from domestic confinement to the imaginative space of 'golden dreams' (ibid.). The loft/garret signifies the imagined space created by the act of writing, the X-marked spot where the hidden treasure of self-willed, self-written identity is to be found. Katy's 'Freedom Castle' signifies the inner space of creativity, seen as a fortified stronghold of a freely willed self. The 'golden dreams' of this inner space are represented by the protagonists' 'castles in the air'. Rebecca thinks she might storm 'some minor citadel of Mohammedanism' (ibid.: 40). In its use of military metaphor, this is markedly similar to Katy's vision that she might 'head a crusade and . . . Carry a sacred flag' (Coolidge 1995: 20). These 'castles' are also peopled by creative figures: Katy wishes to 'paint pictures . . . or make figures in marble' (ibid.: 21); Jo wishes to write out of 'a magic inkstand'. All these activities, whether militaristic or creative, were culturally defined as 'male', and therefore when the protagonists of girls' stories envision themselves as active and creative, they can only imagine themselves as 'male'; the pictures of knights, soldiers, writers, sculptors and other 'men' encipher this message. The narrator provides us with a verbal key to decipher such pictograms, which is also the key to the titles of the first three of the 'Katy' series: it is the verb 'to do'. In the chapter 'Castles in the Air' in *Little Women*, Jo says that she wants to 'do something splendid' that will be remembered after her death (Alcott 1989: 143). Katy wishes to *do* something grand, but realizes that what she will *be* is 'quite different' (Coolidge 1995: 20). When Jo imagines 'going into' her castle after performing great deeds, she refers, the context makes clear, to a life of domesticity as a grown woman. Thus while the earthly castle in which a woman must 'be' represents culturally defined enclosed female space, the 'castle in the air' signifies imagined space in which she can 'do' rather than exist in stasis.

In trespassing the boundaries of male territory and claiming an active identity for themselves, such girls would indeed be 'head of a crusade', carrying 'the sacred flag' of female desire for a dynamic, creative life outside the cultural reservation of domestic enclosure. The active, vocal nature of such 'crusaders' positions them in patriarchal discourses as 'bad' women, often represented in cultural texts as witches. The title of Jo's play is significant here; 'The Witch's Curse' is the war-cry of these dynamic, creative girls. It is a powerful medicine woman's curse on patriarchy.

At this point in *What Katy Did*, with the narrator leading the way, signalling and signing as guide and interpreter, the textual trail of identity seemed to lead on to vast open prairies with far horizons, full of opportunities for leading a self-chosen, self-willed, creative life. This was the land of opportunities, the land of Rebecca's 'golden dreams' and Jo's 'chief treasures', in which Katy could 'do' as she wished. For me, it was a utopian vision of an earthly Paradise, and this is the image at the centre of the hermeneutic circle, the focal point at the cluster of images signalling female creative identity. Rebecca in her loft thinks herself in an 'ever new Paradise' (Douglas Wiggin 1952: 60); Katy's happiest times of freedom were spent in a thicket, which the children called Paradise, because to them it seemed 'as wide and endless and full of adventure as any forest in fairyland' (Coolidge 1995: 13). Here Coolidge creates intertextual space by appropriating and mixing genres. The children's Paradise is a transformed mixture of the biblical garden of Eden and the land of children's fairytale, in which the 'wild roses' (ibid.) signify the flowering of the children's identities, beyond the control of the patriarchal gardener. As a girl reader, 'the "I" which approach[ed] the text' was 'already a plurality of other texts' (Barthes 1976: 16); I was familiar with both textual territories. Katy's version of Paradise, however, was more tempting in the treasures it offered. In it the children ate all sorts of childhood delicacies, but the greatest treat was the metaphoric eating of the Tree of Knowledge, in the form of storytelling and shared fantasies. Such a banquet, in the enciphered message of metaphor, signifies that the eating of the forbidden fruit of creativity is permitted for the young daughters of Eve in this Paradise.[11] The eating of forbidden fruit is, of course, always delicious.

Jo's eating of apples has a similar resonance, as Elaine Showalter (1989: x) points out, representing female defiance of patriarchal prohibition in the same way that writing enables women to gain authority over experience and 'author' themselves (see Gilbert and Gubar 1984: 10). In writing the word, and in writing the self, female writers disobeyed the word of patriarchal prohibition; Coolidge is thus being subversive in many ways when, in writing, she 'authors' a girl to write and locates her in Paradise. As a girl reader, unaware of some of these resonances, I nevertheless recognized girls' rebellion when I saw it. I 'enjoyed myself a treat' in Paradise with Katy, and thought it much better fun than the Paradise I learned about in Sunday school. These images of creative space, with Paradise at the centre, are a child's illustration of 'the wild zone' of adult female creativity beyond the borders of patriarchal control, 'literally no-man's-land, a place forbidden to men' in which female writing can 'make the invisible visible . . . make the silent speak' (Showalter 1993: 262). This 'wild zone' is similar to the Dark Continent[12] of which Cixous writes; the girls' version of the wilderness, of life beyond the frontier, is not dark, but is a child's treasury of bright opportunities to be explored. It is also sociable, because the wilderness of Paradise can be shared: Katy shares her stories with other children, both in the loft and in Paradise; Anne forms a story club; Jo and her sisters have the Pickwick Club. Here they share their readings and writings in the assumed personae of Dickens' male club members, in a many-faceted act of intertextual subversion by Alcott. In all these girls' stories, many parodic voices signal messages of rebellion in the imagined 'wild zone'.

The wilderness was, as I well understood, located very firmly in America. The images of Paradise in these girls' stories reflect and create myths of the American wilderness as a new Eden, suggesting that 'America is "the fountain of youth" . . . a place of youth. . . of new beginnings' (Robertson 1980: 348). As a 'youthful' nation, America was as preoccupied with questions of national identity[13] as the young girl protagonists were preoccupied with personal identity. As a textual trail of identity, the girls' stories present cryptic clues which suggest answers to both questions: the American Dream is a national mythic version of Rebecca's 'golden dreams'. Just as the loft/garret is the girl's imagined free space, the Edenic territory where dreams come true as she writes herself a self-chosen identity, so America is that Edenic free space in which Americans can realize themselves in a land of golden opportunities. The presentation of Katy and the others as free, independent, and at times wild, is a metaphoric expression of the vision Americans had of themselves as republican, hardy, self-reliant pioneers. Douglas Wiggin (1955: 27), for example, tells us that 'whatever else there was or was not, there was freedom at Randall's farm. The children grew, worked, fought, ate what and where they could.' This is similar to the more middle-class message of Katy's papa, who 'wished to have the children hardy and bold, and encouraged climbing and rough play' (Coolidge 1995: 4–5). The discursive message is summed up in *Little Women* by John Brooke, who informs 'patronizing' English visitors that 'Young ladies in America love independence as much as their ancestors did and are admired and respected for supporting themselves' (Alcott 1989: 133). Not only Jo as a writer, but also Anne as a teacher and writer, exemplify this self-supporting, independent female spirit, just as their narrators do, in their own lives as writers. The textual map of American girls' stories was, therefore, a colourfully fascinating 'place' to me as a girl, quite another place than 1950s Britain, which at times seemed to me drab and grey; in oppositional contrast, the 'map' of America was bright and golden, a promised land across the horizon; like the conquistadors, I longed to discover this Eldorado.

In writing stories about self-willed, independent-minded girls, the narrators were 'writing the self' in more ways than one. All these stories were autobiographical fiction, as the journals of some of them make clear;[14] the protagonists were images of themselves projected into text. In re-writing their own scripts as fiction, they expressed the same discursive messages about American girlhood as did more clearly autobiographical accounts.[15] In the face of such accounts 'any image of prim and proper little girls . . . dissolves . . . these American girls climbed trees, fell into rain barrels and fished in the horse troughs' (Scott Macleod 1994: 7). In rewriting their own scripts in autobiography and fiction, these narrators not only wrote their protagonists' stories; they were writing another story for me, a creative, alterior life sited in the 'otherness' of mythic America. My dialogic interpretation of the American Dream had been made manifest destiny in the unwinding of the textual trail; here, at the X-marked spot, the 'golden dream' of dynamic, creative, self-chosen identity could be realized. The narrator promised that, 'without any fear of an angel with flaming sword to stop the way' we could enter and 'take possession of . . . Eden' (Coolidge 1995: 23). This, then, was the 'meaning' to me of the 'gift' of parents and culture, wrapped in text by the narrator. Of the banquet I ate with Katy in Paradise, 'each mouthful was a pleasure' (ibid.: 16); but the juicy apple of the text I eagerly devoured was more than ordinary pleasure. It was sheer bliss.[16]

I looked forward to several more chapters of joyful exploration of the text. At this point, two-thirds of the way along the textual trail, Katy falls from a swing and spends four years in painful paralysis. I write this so starkly, because to me it *was* shockingly stark; it was, I felt, a deep betrayal of the promise, implicit in the text, that Katy and I could continue our joyful, anarchic journey through free territory as the textual trail unwound. Katy had not, in the 'end' been allowed her self-willed, self-defined identity as a lively, creative rebel; she was not to be allowed a destiny in which she independently, actively 'did' what she chose to do.

Contrary to the narrator's promise, she could no longer enter Paradise. Neither could I. The swing's 'violent twist', which 'tossed Katy into the air' (Coolidge 1995: 117), twisted not only Katy's back, but the textual trail, and for me too 'all grew dark'. Quite simply, I felt I had been deceived and betrayed; the text had lied. There was, then, no X-marked spot on the map where the treasure-trove of autonomous, dynamic female identity was to be found; this had been a false trail which came to a dead-end with Katy's paralysing fall. To what destiny would this new twisted textual trail lead? What, if any, treasure of identity would be hidden at the X-marked spot where it ended? What, finally, would the parental/cultural 'gift' confer upon the girl reader? And why did Katy fall?

What Katy did next in falling was, most obviously, get punished by the narrator for being 'naughty'; this was immediately apparent to me when reading the text for the first time. She had disobeyed Aunt Izzie's prohibition of using the swing and the moral is that 'young children must obey their orders without explanation' (ibid.: 113). In punishing Katy by 'breaking' her spine, the plot is punishing her by breaking her will; metaphorically she has no 'spine' left. From the vantage point of this part of the textual trail, looking back along it with hindsight, I now saw that many narrative signposts had pointed this way. The structure of chapters such as 'The Day of Scrapes' is a dire warning of this: there is a prohibition from Aunt Izzie near the beginning; Katy breaks the prohibition with sometimes calamitous, if humorous, results; the chapter ends with kind papa spelling out the moral lesson to be learnt, and Katy thereupon promises to mend her ways. The very night before her fall, she had thought 'tomorrow I will begin', but had woken up feeling 'quite differently' (ibid.: 110). That she yet again disobeys instructions and is punished seems, then, inevitable; indeed, children's literature often has such a 'cruel and coercive streak . . . which produced books that relied on brutal intimidation to frighten children into complying with parental demands' (Tartar 1992: 8). However, I had not 'picked up' the 'right' clues, for the path to Paradise had been misleading. As an inexperienced, 'innocent' map reader, I had not read the 'Danger' signs beside the illustration of the rebel girl; but I was fast learning the brutal and intimidatory message, just as Katy did.

Other discourses also pointed out the error of the way Katy and I had taken; while I did not yet realize that every concept implies the existence of its opposite, since language implies meaning through a system of difference,[17] yet I dimly realized that if there was Paradise there could also be Paradise lost. Not yet familiar with Milton's version, I knew the Bible story, and although I was unfamiliar with the Calvinist doctrine of original sin, I knew that our first parents, like Katy, were disobedient. Neither had I heard of panoptic surveillance,[18] but I knew, both from God's role in the Bible story and from experiential evidence nearer to home, about being watched and 'found out', as Katy was watched and 'found out' by her narrator. Similarly, I was unaware that in American discourses Paradise is located in the socio-psychological state of childhood, so that 'Americans sought their lost innocence increasingly in their children' (Sanford 1961: 112) and allowed them a certain licence in childhood, as rebels 'sanctioned' by society. Stories that I read later, of Mark Twain's boy heroes, Tom Sawyer and Huckleberry Finn, made this clear.[19] While girls never had the same licence, even they had a certain latitude on the map of identity as long as they were small children. As children grow up, how-ever, they lose their Paradise in losing their innocence and are expected to become responsible members of society. For this reason, and because in nineteenth-century America there was 'absence of a fixed social order, lightness of the Law [and] fluidity of economic and social life' (Scott Macleod 1994: 97), the internal restraints of conscience and guilt needed to de developed. These lessons in 'growing up' and 'being your age', becoming responsible, and developing an active conscience and a weight of guilt were all too familiar as discourses in my own life, so that I did not need to understand the underpinning American discourses to make 'sense' of the lesson I was being taught. That is, since 'the "self" is always an intertextual patchwork of all second-hand language that has constructed us' (Morris 1997: 156), my 'self', already a patchwork of discursive and lived experiences, was able to piece together the chart of the rebel girl's destiny and make 'sense' of it.

Having been granted a certain amount of licence as a child, twelve-year-old Katy is now expected to become more responsible; since she does not, horrific punishment must follow. Her just dessert was not to be the banquet in Paradise, but the medicine of the sickroom, as I realized when I looked in horror into the textual abyss where Katy lay twisted and in pain. That is the punitively vicious script that the text hands out as a 'gift' to child renegades. This was a bitter textual pill to swallow, but I was about to have it rammed down my throat in 'the schooling process' of this cultural text, just as Katy learned to swallow her medicine in her 'School of Pain'. The 'lesson' Katy had to learn was not only about growing up, but about growing up *female* in a patriarchal society. Just as a cluster of pictograms depict the child's Paradise, in opposition to this there are a montage of picture clues which signify the woman's Paradise lost. At the centre, as focal point of this different hermeneutic circle of dominant discourses, lies the crippled body of Katy herself; beside her lies the permanently crippled body of her Cousin Helen. After her accident, Helen 'gave up' her fiancé so that he could marry a 'healthy' woman and have children. She also 'gave up' her self-willed identity and became the self-less, renunciatory 'good' woman beloved by patriarchy. She is, there-fore, a role model for Katy, who must give up what she wanted to 'do' because this is in opposition to what she must 'be' as a woman: she must be submissive, silent and passive, renouncing activity, creativity and self-willed identity. For dynamic, imaginative, 'self-willed' girls like the protagonists of these stories this is indeed crippling. Her schooling in 'submissiveness and selflessness' will be experienced as sickening, because 'to be trained in renunciation is almost necessarily to be trained in ill-health' (Gilbert and Guber 1984: 54). Sickness, then, can be a manifes-tation of 'inner' sickness, an extreme discontent with the social construct of femininity that women are required to 'be'; the female 'body' revolts against digesting this poisonous 'medicine', which is prescribed for her by the patriarchal 'doctor' of women, just as Katy's doctor papa prescribes her medicine after her fall.

Katy's 'sick', paralysed body, then, is an enciphered cryptic clue on the textual trail, signifying the sick 'body' of female identity. Since 'the "body" is actively produced by the junction and dysfunction of symbolic domains' (Stallybrass and White 1992: 192), the 'broken' female body is a diagram representing 'broken' self-will and, therefore, a broken, fragmented sense of identity. In her fall out of the Paradise of childhood and into the abyss of womanhood, Katy has been broken, just as a young horse is broken by training; she has been pulled apart, not only physically by her fall from the swing, but also psychologically by the fragmenting of her active, creative identity as she reaches womanhood. As a passive construct of femininity, Katy as subject no longer 'did' anything; she was 'done to'. The violence done to her broken body pained and sickened me. There are equally violent illustrations in *Little Women*. Jo, when asked by patriarchal figures such as Dr Bhaer and her publisher to change what she wrote, felt like a parent 'being asked to cut off her baby's legs' (Alcott 1989: 347). All the protagonists are, in effect, told to 'kill' their creativity and give up writing. Later, as a mother, Jo 'told no stories' except to her own boys and those of her school (ibid.: 487). Anne, at a similar stage of her life, describes her children as 'living epistles' (Montgomery 1994: 362). Women, the textual clues suggest, should express their creativity physically by giving birth; all other creativity is to be renounced. Their writing, as offspring of this creativity, is to be killed in an act of bloody infanticide.

The montage of illustrations on the socially constructed trail of female identity is a grisly one: there are pictures of broken women and chopped up babies. This part of the textual trail is through the Valley of Death, closed in by the oppressive cliffs of patriarchy, which allow no breathing space, and in this confined textual place, the reader as traveller discovers not treasure, but dead bones. The textual illustration of dead women is a cryptic clue to the position the 'good' woman is required to assume, that of the death-in-life state of self-denial and self-lessness. One cannot be more self-less than in death. For this reason, nineteenth-century cultural texts are littered with dead women's bones, since there was 'an inability to realise woman . . . in terms other than death' (Pearce: 1991: 54). In these girls' stories, Katy's and Anne's mothers are dead before the text opens, and Rebecca's mother, being far away, is 'dead' to her. Jo's sister Beth, an extreme example of the child-like dependency of passive women, also dies, thinking 'it was never intended that I should live long . . . I never made any plans about what I'd do when I grew up' (Alcott 1989: 374). These dead women are held up to the living, growing protagonists as role-models of 'good' femininity. Katy is asked by her papa to remember her dying mother's wish that she should be 'a Mamma to the little ones when she grows up' and he indicates it is about time for her 'to take this dear place towards the children' (Coolidge 1995: 52). Similarly, on Beth's death Jo 'renounced her old ambition' and 'pledged herself to a new and better one' (Alcott 1989: 419). These protagonists, in taking the place of deadly passive women, must as an act of renunciation kill their self-willed, creative selves. It is small wonder that Anne, after she is married, writes only obituaries; all of the protagonists, in assuming the 'dead' identity of the self-less woman, write their own obituaries. No longer writing the self, and denying themselves a story, their textual trail comes to a stifling dead-end.

Instead of enjoying the blissfully juicy apples of Paradise, these protagonists had eaten culturally poisoned apples of identity. As a child reader, I was familiar with the 'lost codes'[21] of fairy tales; I had seen the picture of Snow White, comatose in her coffin, poisoned by the gift of such an apple. What the texts of these girls' stories offered me, as part of the 'circular memory of reading' (Barthes 1975: 36), were similar 'gifts' of poisoned apples of identity. I was familiar, too, with that icon of female passivity, Sleeping Beauty. Paralysed in a death-like coma, these comatose heroines were silenced, just as the loss of their writing silenced the protagonists of the girls' stories. The violence done to Katy, however, is more like that done to another fairytale heroine, the Little Mermaid, who was silenced by the cutting out of her tongue. The mutilation of female identity does not stop there; the Little Mermaid is mutilated below the waist by the loss of her tail, just as Katy is crippled below the waist after her fall. It is below the waist, then, that women are mutilated, suggesting that not only their voices but also their sexuality must be curtailed; just as the Little Mermaid's story is one of self-sacrifice, so is that of Katy. The sacrifices of voice and sexuality, in order to become a 'good' woman, are lessons to be learned in the cultural School of Pain; this is the violent self-obliteration that is enciphered in pictures of crippled and dead women.

The cryptic picture clues in girls' stories and fairy stories form a montage which signifies another message: Katy is crippled below the waist from the age of twelve to that of sixteen; Sleeping Beauty bleeds when she pricks her finger on a spindle at the age of sixteen; the Little Mermaid 'surrenders' her powerful siren identity when she 'becomes bifurcated and bleeds as if, once the innocence of childhood has passed, that very sexuality turns against its possessor and make the young woman a victim' (Warner 1994: 378). The young woman becomes, that is, a 'victim' of menstruation as part of the crippling nature of her sexuality. This 'chilling message' (ibid.) is the cultural diet absorbed by reading girls. Since 'images are more direct than words, and closer to the unconscious' (Anzaldua 1987: 69), the message is digested on a subconscious level through the enciphered clues of metaphoric pictures and assimilated as part of the process of identity formation; since we become what we eat, we internalize this 'unhealthy' sense of self, with 'unwholesome' results.

In this sense, the 'gift' of *What Katy Did* was similar to another 'gift' that girls of my generation received; with titles such as 'What Every Girl Should Know', they informed girls about the 'curse' of menstruation. The text of girls' stories told every girl what she should know about the wider patriarchal 'curse', which is 'the myth of power, a representation, which keeps [the female] subject' (Armstrong 1996: 85), and keeps her in her proper, passive place. The curse is, then, a patriarchal taboo; it forbids women to be active, vocal or creative. As a prohibition sign, it is an intimidatingly huge structure built of interlocking ideological practices, blocking out light and warmth for female travellers along the textual trail of identity. Girls' stories worked together with other cultural texts in 'transmitting and enforcing the norm of the silent woman . . . power-fully symbolizing and codifying the status quo, they served as paralysis for the powerless' (Bottigheimer 1986: 130). In a self-mutilating act of 'vraisemblance' (Culler 1975: 139), as a girl reader I put together my assorted cryptic clues and subconsciously made a 'sick' sense of it all. Two and two made an unwholesome four, in a lesson taught with gruesome visual aids in cultural set texts. An innocent, inexperienced reader, however, I still hoped that Katy would 'get better', recover her self-willed self, and that the textual trail would wind its way back to the lost treasure of Eldorado.

Where I found myself was in Katy's School of Pain. Here Katy has her father as doctor and Cousin Helen as teacher, to show her the lessons to be learned before she assumes her socially constructed identity as a grown-up woman. The main lessons are those of 'Patience . . . Cheerfulness . . . Making the Best of Things . . . Hopefulness . . . Neatness' (Coolidge 1995: 134–5). Katy is told that God is a friend to help her and in a dream he appears to help her read a difficult text. The hand which, in pointing, makes the text legible, acts as a cryptic clue: God the father, like doctor/father, will help the daughter understand her identity text. Helen passes on another lesson from her own father; he taught her that she must always look pretty for him, because otherwise a sick woman is a 'slattern'. Once she had learned this lesson, he thought that his 'active, healthy girl' was 'never such comfort as his sick one lying there in bed'. This School of Pain is, particularly in its connections with religious discourse, a female version of *Pilgrim's Progress*. As a child reader, I had not 'read' the ominous cryptic clue of the Hill of Difficulty which lies just outside Paradise. Neither did I initially understand that *Pilgrim's Progress* is, as well as being a parental Christmas gift to the girls, a structuring device in *Little Women*, with Marmee and the absent father teaching the girls lessons in good womanhood, much as Helen and Katy's papa teach Katy. I did not, however, need to be familiar with these discourses to 'get the message' of the harsh School of Pain. The lesson I learnt, together with Katy, was that becoming a woman would be a harsh and painful experience. This was sickness-inducing poison, not, as it was presented, medicine to help Katy recover.

The focal image which pictures what Katy must become as a woman is that of an angel. Katy is told by her father that Helen is 'half an angel already . . . I couldn't ask anything better than to have my little girl take pattern after her' (ibid.: 105). As angel in the house, however, she will have her wings clipped; although Katy's father teaches her, after years of paralysis, to walk again as a socially constructed woman, this is painful for her, just as the Little Mermaid finds that every step she takes on her alien legs is like walking on broken glass. For previously active, dynamic girls like Katy, living as a woman in a society which constrains women is as restricting as the corsets many of them wore. After flying as a free child spirit through Paradise, she falls to earth as a broken woman and must learn to move in an environment which is alien to her. After 'flying' on the swing, she never 'flies' again; as a domestic angel she is flightless. Similarly, Rebecca appears in a different yet similar guise. As she grows up, she decides that 'if she could not sing in the orchard like the wild bird she was, she could still sing in the cage like a canary' (Douglas Wiggin 1952: 65). Caged birds and flightless angels, then, as metaphoric pictograms along the textual trail of identity, represent women 'caged' in their socially constructed identities, in the 'body' of the text and in domestic confinement.

Katy first walks downstairs on her mother's birthday, and takes her mother's place, with approving Helen telling her that she has 'won the place . . . of being to everybody "the Heart of the house" '. (Coolidge 1995: 211) At the closure of the text, in the chapter aptly enough called 'At Last', Katy has become the 'living', if selflessly passive, image of her dead mother. This is her destiny, made manifest in the plot. The final picture clue at the end of the textual trail is the deciphering key to the 'good' woman's identity: superimposed on the image of the dead mother is an image of her daughter, who is only a shadowy travesty of her former, colourful self; and shimmering above this lies a doll-like pastiche of a woman. For Katy, at the end of the trail, is hardly distinguishable from Clover; this is the final irony, the final grotesque injury done to her. The 'real' Katy, the original 'self-willed' girl, had of course been killed in the fall. The X-marked spot did not locate the hidden treasure-trove of active, creative identity; it was the site of the red-spotted patriarchal curse on self-willed girls. I could not have expressed this at the time, of course. However, I knew bitter disappointment when I felt it. I had read on to the end in the forlorn hope that, when Katy walked again, she and I could resume our precious adventures in the wilderness beyond the frontier. I hated, loathed with a passion, what had happened to Katy; I was bored by the born-again Katy. How could this limp rag doll be presented to me as the same vibrant girl whom I had met at the trail's beginning? I was confused and hurt. I felt, as I had felt when she fell, betrayed: the text had lied again.

As for the narrator, she no longer seemed to me the powerful medicine woman who made all things possible in the Edenic wilderness. Instead, she seemed to be a combination of Aunt Izzie and Helen. She had told me a tale about a girl who was 'broken' in punishment for being a 'self-willed' girl, just as Aunt Izzie told the children stories 'about children who broke their bones' (Coolidge 1995: 57) in order to frighten them into submission and obedience. Since Katy was not frightened, but kept on her 'self-willed' way (ibid.), the narrator made it happen that she broke her back and her spirit. Just as Cousin Helen makes Katy learn in the School of Pain, the narrator makes the female reader learn similarly painful lessons in identity; she is the nurse of the patriarchal doctor, making the girl swallow bitter textual medicine which will poison her as an autonomous being. She had deceived and tricked me. I did not know then that the authors of these texts were themselves conflicted in their identity, as both women and writers in a patriarchal society; nor that what they wrote had to conform to the demands of publishers; nor that their lives were at odds with what they wrote,[22] just as surely as were those of the protagonists, their 'selves' pictured in text. However, I could tell that they liked their wayward heroines and they clearly knew that growing up as a woman was a tortuous process. I did not know consciously that the overt narrative and its didactic lessons were subverted by the enciphered cryptic clues of metaphor. I did not realize that the cryptically enciphered picture clues in the texts might be 'a coherent feminized framework which stands in opposition to a dominant order' (Foster 1995: 29). But I knew that I was appalled by it. My reaction, like the text of female identity, was conflicted and ambiguous.

The 'gift' the author, as founding mother of identity, had wrapped up in text and presented to me as the 'gift' of parents and my parent culture was, finally, an ambivalent one. It encouraged me to be active and creative with an androgynous, fluid, plural sense of my own identity: this was the treasure I locked in my chest. At the same time it showed me, in a viciously violent way, how I would be punitively cursed if I continued to do what Katy first did: this was the painful lesson of the cultural text. What do I do with this 'gift' now? What 'gifts' of identity do we, graduates of the school of our culture, pass on to our children? I read *What Katy Did* now as an act of 'rememory', as Toni Morrison (1981) describes this in *Beloved*; more than an act of remembering, it is an act of revisiting the past, reliving it, and interpreting it differently so that one can redefine the relationship of the past to the present. Otherwise, as *Beloved* shows, the past is a ghost which haunts the present. Not for nothing does Anne, nostalgic for the Paradise of childhood, think of the woodland where she played as a Haunted Wood, full of phantoms. In rememory, one works to lay the past to rest so that the present can be fully lived. This time, in the re-written text in the 'wild zone' of my imagination, Katy does not fall, die, and undergo reconstruction as a rag doll, a flightless angel of a good woman; she continues to live on into adulthood as the person she was as a child: active, creative, dynamic and a joy to 'do' with as a friend.

This is, of course, an androgynous identity, unrestricted by gender. After all, 'the feminine is a myth' and I do not wish 'to fall into the patriarchal trap of failing to question male/female dichotomy' (Cameron 1992: 179). This would be to encounter the pit-falls of essentialist traps, just as Katy did. The key to a healthy identity, whether we are men or women, it seems to me, is to 'do' for ourselves as adults what Katy did as a child, as an act of self-creation. There is, of course, no Paradise to be regained, no fixed X-marked spot of identity to reach; there is only the onward journey along the trail, across the frontier, and into the wilderness of unexplored territory. What Katy did first is what we can do next, not as an act of rebellion, but as what we can 'naturally' do. The text is never closed; each time we 'read' its 'meaning' we each interpret it dialogically and differently, in a kind of 'playful pluralism, responsive to the possibilities of multiple critical schools and methods, but captive of none' (Kolodny 1993: 161). This is the blissful, juicy *jouissance* of authoring our own stories and writing the texts of ourselves. This is the most precious 'gift' we can give to our children to store in their treasure chests; this is the treasure we alone can create for ourselves.

Notes

A general note should be made about the context of Susan Coolidge's work, whose real name was Sarah Chauncey Woolsey (1835–1905). She was born in Cleveland, but lived in Connecticut and Rhode Island. She was a contemporary of Louisa May Alcott whose most famous novel *Little Women* was published in 1868–9, and like Alcott, never married. Coolidge was related to both Puritan preacher Jonathan Edwards and Governor Winthrop. Coolidge's *What Katy Did* appeared in 1872 and formed part of a 5-book series published between 1872–1891. A reading survey in Britain in the 1990s found that the 'Katy' books were in the top ten for 12-year-old girls.

1   For a discussion of the 'cult of domesticity' see N.F. Cott, *The Bonds of Womanhood: 'Women's Sphere' in New England 1780–1835* (New Haven: Yale University Press, 1977).

2   There are many studies of these polarized identities which build on the theories of M. Foucault, *The History of Sexuality* (London: Penguin, 1981).

3   I use 'carnivalesque' in the Bakhtinian sense of carnival being, for medieval society, a time when normal power relations in a society were disrupted. See M.M. Bakhtin, *The Dialogic Imagination: Four Essays*, ed. M. Holquist, (Austin: University of Texas Press, 1986).

4   For discussion of the polyphonic text as the heteroglossia of many voices, see M.M. Bakhtin, 'The Problem of Speech Genres', in C. Emerson and M. Holquist (eds) *Speech Genres and Other Late Essays* (Austin: University of Texas Press 1966).

5   For a discussion of Laurie's androgyny and of how the text was changed to meet the publisher's demands, see Elaine Showalter's introduction to *Little Women* (London: Penguin, 1989).

6   Several writers discuss the female storyteller as Cipher or Sibyl; see, for example, M. Warner, *From the Beast to the Blonde* (London: Chatto and Windus, 1994).

7   For an illuminating study of the masks and deceptions of the 'good' woman, see S.S. Gilbert and S. Gubar, *The Madwoman in the Attic: The Woman Writer and the Nineteenth Century Imagination* (New Haven: Yale University Press, 1984).

8   Romantic heroines in nineteenth-century girls' books are studied in K. Flint, [1994] *The Woman Reader 1837–1914* (Oxford: Clarendon Press), Chapter 6.

9   See M. Foucault, *The History of Sexuality* (London: Penguin, 1981).

10   In her autobiography *Memoirs of a Dutiful Daughter* (London: Penguin, 1963), Simone de Beauvoir wrote that Jo as writer had been an inspirational role model.

11   For a discussion of Eve's eating of the apple and its links with authority and power, see H. Mitchie, *The Flesh Made Word* (New York: Oxford University Press, 1986).

12   For related ideas, see H. Cixous and C. Clement, *The Newly Born Woman* tr. B. Wing (Manchester: Manchester University Press, 1986 [1975]).

13   See N. Campbell and A. Kean, *American Cultural Studies: An Introduction to American Culture* (London: Routledge, 1997), Chapter 1.

14   See M. Rubio and E. Waterston (eds) *The Selected Journals of L.M. Montgomery* (Toronto: Oxford University Press, 1985) and J. Simons, *Diaries and Journals of Literary Women From Fanny Burney to Virginia Woolf* (London: Macmillan, 1996), Chapter 6.

15   See Laura Ingalls Wilder's accounts of her life as a junior pioneer in the 'Little House' series.

16   For the distinctions between bliss (*jouissance*) and pleasure (*plaisir*), see R. Barthes, *The Pleasure of the Text*, tr. R. Miller (London: Cape, 1976).

17   One useful discussion of structural linguistics is in T. Hawkes, *Structuralism and Semiotics* (London: Methuen, 1977).

18 M. Foucault, 'Preface to Transgression', in D.F. Bouchard (ed.) *Language, Counter-Memory, Practice: Selected Essays and Interviews* (New York: Cornell University Press, 1977).
19 See J. Fetterley, 'The Sanctioned Rebel', in D. Kesterson (ed.) *Critics on Mark Twain* (Carol Gables: University of Miami Press, 1973).
20 See A.M. Estes and K.M. Lant, 'Dismembering the Text: the Horror of Louisa May Alcott's *Little Women*', in H. Bloom (ed.) *Women Writers of Children's Literature* (Philadelphia: Chelsea House Publishers, 1998).
21 This notion of 'Lost Codes' and its implications is discussed by Roland Barthes; see R. Barthes, *S/Z* (London: Cape, 1975) and R. Barthes, *The Pleasure of the Text* (London: Cape, 1976).
22 See note 14. Very little has been written about Susan Coolidge; see S. Foster, *What Katy Read: feminist re-readings of 'classic' stories for girls* (Basingstoke: Macmillan, 1995).

Bibliography

Primary Texts

Alcott, L.M. (1989) *Little Women*, London: Penguin, first published 1868–9.
Coolidge, S. (1995) *What Katy Did*, London: Puffin, first published 1872.
Douglas Wiggin, K. (1952) *More About Rebecca*, London: Black, first published 1904.
Douglas Wiggin, K. (1955) *Rebecca of Sunnybrook Farm*, London: Black, first published 1903.
Montgomery, L.M. (1977) *Anne of Green Gables*, London: Puffin, first published 1908.
Montgomery, L.M. (1994) *Anne of Ingleside*, London: Puffin, first published 1939.

Secondary Texts

Anzaldua, G. (1987) *Borderlands/La Frontera*, San Francisco: Aunt Lute Book Company.
Armstrong, I. (1993) *Victorian Poetry: Poetry, Poetics and Politics*, London: Routledge.
Bakhtin, M.M. (1986a) *The Dialogic Imagination: Four Essays*, M. Holquist, ed., Austin: University of Texas Press.
——(1986b) 'The problem of speech genres', in C. Emerson and M. Holquist (eds) *Speech Genres and other Late Essays*, Austin: University of Texas Press.
Barthes, R. (1975) *S/Z*, tr. R. Miller, London: Cape.
——(1976) *The Pleasure of the Text*, tr. R. Miller, London: Cape.
De Beauvior, S. (1963) *Memoirs of a Dutiful Daughter*, London: Penguin.

Bloom, H. (ed.) (1989) *Women Writers of Children's Literature*, Philadelphia: Chelsea House Publishers.

Bottigheimer, R. (1986) *Fairy Tales and Society*, Philadephia: University of Philadelphia Press.

Cameron, D. (1992) *Feminism and Linguistic Theory*, London: Methuen.

Campbell, N. and Kean, A. (1997) *American Cultural Studies: An Introduction to American Culture*, London: Routledge.

Cixous, H. and Clement, C. (1975) *The Newly Born Woman*, B. Wing, Manchester: Manchester University Press.

Cott, N.F. (1977) *The Bonds of Womanhood: 'Women's Sphere' in New England 1780–1835*, New Haven: Yale University Press.

Culler, J. (1975) *Structuralist Poetics: Structuralism, Linguistics and the Study of Literature*, London: Routledge and Kegan Paul.

Estes, A.M. and Lant, K.M. (1989) 'Dismembering the text: the horror of Louisa May Alcott's Little Women', in H. Bloom (ed.) *Women Writers of Children's Literature*, Philadelphia: Chelsea House Publishers.

Fetterley, J. (1973) 'The sanctioned rebel', in D. Kesterson (ed.) *Critics on Mark Twain*, Coral Gables: University of Miami Press.

Flint, K. (1994) *The Woman Reader 1837–1914*, Oxford: Clarendon Press.

Foster, S. (1995) *What Katy Read: Feminist Rereadings of 'Classic' Stories for Girls*, Basingstoke: Macmillan.

Foucault, M. (1977) 'Preface to transgression', in D.F. Bouchard, *Language, Counter-Memory, Practice: Selected Essays and Interviews*, New York: Cornell University Press.

——(1981) *The History of Sexuality*, London: Penguin.

Gilbert, S.M. and Gubar, S. (1984) *The Madwoman in the Attic: The Woman Writer and Nineteenth Century Literary Imagination*, New Haven: Yale University Press. First published in 1979.

Hawkes, T. (1977) *Structuralism and Semiotics*, London: Methuen.

Howarth, D. (1995) 'Discourse Theory', in D. Marsh and G. Stoker (eds) *Theories and Methods of Political Science*, London: Macmillan.

Hunt, P. (ed.) (1999) *Understanding Children's Literature*, London: Routledge.

Jameson, F. (1981) *The Political Unconscious*, New York, Ithaca: Cornell University Press.

Kolodny, A. (1980) 'Dancing through the minefield: some observations on theory, practice and politics of a feminist literary criticism', in E. Showalter [1993] *The New Feminist Criticism: Essays on Women, Literature and Theory*, London: Virago.

Kristeva, J. (1981) *Desire in Language: A Semiotic Approach to Literature and the Arts*, ed. L. Roudiez, Oxford: Blackwell.

Laqueur, T. (1990) *Making Sex*, Cambridge Mass.: Harvard Press.

MacCannell, J.F. (1986) *Figuring Lacan: Criticism and the Cultural Unconscious*, London: Croom Helm.

Mitchie, H. (1986) *The Flesh Made Word*, New York: Oxford University Press.

Morris, P. (1997) *Literature and Feminism*, Oxford: Blackwell Publishers Ltd.

Nead, L. (1991) *Myths of Sexuality*, London: Blacko.

Pearce, L. (1991) *Woman/Image/Text*, London: Harvester.

Robertson, J. (1980) *American Myth, American Reality*, New York: Hill and Wang.

Rorty, R. (1980) *Philosophy and the Mirror of Nature*, Oxford, Blackwell.

Rubio, M. and Waterston, E. (eds) (1985) *The Selected Journals of L.M. Montgomery*, Toronto: Oxford University Press.

Sanford, C.L. (1961) *The Quest for Paradise: Europe and the American Moral Imagination*, New York: AMS Press.

Scott MacLeod, A. (1994) *American Childhood: Essays on Children's Literature of the Nineteenth and Twentieth Centuries*, Athens: University of Georgia Press.

Showalter, E. (1993) 'Feminist criticism in the wilderness', in *The New Feminist Criticism: Essays on Women, Literature and Theory*, London: Virago.

Simons, J. (1990) *Diaries and Literary Journals of Literary Women from Fanny Burney to Virginia Woolf*, London: Macmillan Press.

Smith, S. (1993) *Subjectivity, Identity and the Body*, Bloomington: Indiana University Press.

Stallybrass P. and White A. (1996) *The Politics and Poetics of Transgression*, Ithaca NY: Cornell University Press.

Tartar, M. (1992) *Off with Their Heads!*, New Jersey: Princeton University Press.

Warner, M. (1994) *From the Beast to the Blonde*, London, Chatto and Windus.

FIVE

Ideologies of Youth and the Bildungsromane of S.E. Hinton

David Holloway

Embedded in the national mythography of secession from the 'Old', new beginnings and perennial rebirth, the American ideology of youth presents us with several peculiarly American problems, principal among which is the ideology's fetishizing character, its tendency to define the 'new' in ideal or essentially abstract terms. This tendency may appear, for example, in the robbing of history of its historical content, in the rendition of America as a metaphysical condition that is simply 'discovered' one day in its divinely ordained Adamic form. Youth's privileging of the new may appear as a metaphor for universal progress, where universal comes to mean American and vice versa, and where the *idea* of perpetual regeneration and self-renewal stands as a quasi-spiritual value around which the nation might gather as a unified 'whole'. It may appear in the less affirmative but equally Hegelian experience of what Toffler called 'future shock', where US history becomes a technologically driven but more or less supernatural energy, a force that simply happens to people without their needing or consenting to it. Or it may figure as it does in certain modernisms, where the new is valorized precisely for its intangible or other-wordly relation to the 'common sense' of extant things, the experimental or the avant-garde acquiring cultural and political value by the very distance it places between the world and itself in the moment where 'the new' is conjured up in aesthetic form. Indeed, if modernism in the broadest sense of the word has always lain deep in the American grain, one reason for this might be the rarefied attachment to the new as process, as means in itself, which the discourses of modernism and Americanism have at times had in common. When Whitman enjoins his countrymen to assert themselves as Americans and as moderns, to 'Unscrew the locks from the doors! / Unscrew the doors themselves from their jambs!', when he launches 'all men and women forward with me into the Unknown' (Whitman 1977a: 86, 115), it is the launching and the unscrewing itself, the 'original energy', the 'ever-push'd elasticity' (ibid.: 63, 116) that he celebrates, not the objective consequences or material derivations of that original energy. Just as when Clinton uses his first inaugural address to 'celebrate the mystery of American renewal', to 'force the spring—a spring reborn in . . . the vision and courage to reinvent America', the 'mission' of which he speaks is 'timeless', an organic thing liberated rhetorically from the inauthentic taint of History (Maidment and Dawson 1994: 197). Doubtless it is this boundlessness of 'youth', its all-encompassing but open-ended quality, which fits it to those great rituals of bourgeois democracy which are *Leaves of Grass* and the Presidential inaugural. But Whitman's 'span of youth' (Whitman 1977a: 116) and Clinton's 'spring reborn' are things to be experienced ultimately by their rhetorical absence or incompletion in the material world: by their status as qualities or things that lie beyond what is currently known, things which are only just coming into being, things which are forever just around the corner, and which are therefore properly inconceivable as such.[1]

The first thing we must do, then, is flesh out this abstraction with a more material content. For if, in its emphasis upon abstract process or the act of separation from history, the ideology of youth effects a drawing away of the eye from the tangible world of human affairs, it is important to establish that this ideology, like all ideologies, has its roots in the objective social relations of life as they are actually lived. This becomes doubly important in an American context where youth (*viz* Clinton) is institutionalized as a state ideology, and so belongs to that far broader ideological apparatus of the liberal-democratic tradition, where the realm of freedom is defined in wholly abstract terms as rights, or as representation, or as the social contract, but not as a genuinely egalitarian distribution of material wealth or equalizing of class interests. This is not to say that youth, as an ideological category, has historically had nothing to do with the problem of class or of competing class agendas. On the contrary, as Joyce Appleby has demonstrated, at that moment in modern American history when the rhetoric of the new first emerges as an ideological force capable of galvanizing public opinion and influencing the national political process, its presence is closely linked to a challenging of the elite Federalist political class, and to the strength of American agricultural production in the international marketplace which acts as a catalyst in this overturning of the older order. Driven on by the rising price of grain exported to Europe, the protracted ideological struggles of the 1790s are underwritten by the new prominence of bourgeois (or petty bourgeois) traders on the American scene, for whom the old Federalist assumptions about a politically active elite and a compliant or deferential electorate now appear as fetters on the new productive energies of the rising class. In the eventual triumph of the Jeffersonians in the election of 1800, the rhetoric of the new figures as a political springboard from which a wholesale transformation of state ideology might then flow. For attached to (and impacting back upon) these economic shifts, what we find in the Jeffersonian rejection of the old is nothing less than a redrawing of the meaning of American republicanism itself: the classical theory of the colonial/Federalist position (where property is that which binds the citizen to the republican structure of virtue, freeing him to concentrate on the common weal) giving way to a more recognizably bourgeois position, where property is that which produces a surplus, and where virtue 'attached itself instead to the private rectitude essential to a system of individual bargains' (Appleby 1984: 96).

In an American context, the rhetoric of youth, the ideology of the new beginning or perennial rebirth, then begins to look less like one bourgeois ideology among others, and more like an ur-ideology of some kind, a rhetoric from which other ideologies are spun, and to which these others might turn for their own validation at particular historical junctures. As we have seen, the repudiation of the past which features so prominently in the Jeffersonian republican writings of the 1790s, is inextricable from a further conjunctural ideology which arises to meet the needs of a particular class or class strata at a specific time (the privatizing of virtue, where the classical notion of the common weal becomes loosened, and the market itself is now defined as the guarantor of social harmony and individual liberty). Just as Whitman's 'tan-faced children' and 'youthful sinewy races', who 'debouch upon a newer mightier world', '[c]onquering, holding, daring' their way across 'the virgin soil' of the American West during the heroic bourgeois expansionism of the mid-nineteenth century (Whitman 1977b: 257-8), find the meaning of their 'youth' reinscribed within the ideology of manifest destiny. Just as the youth paintings of Winslow Homer, and the novels of Alcott or Twain, are caught up in the sense of new beginnings for the Union which surfaces in the childhood cult of the late 1860s and 1870s: a sense of newness which flows from the unifying of the mode of production in the Civil War, and from the need to bury or forget the embedded class tensions out of which this 'unifying' is magically built. At crucial moments in the twentieth century too, notably during the great expansion of the market and the new 'disciplining' of labour either side of the First World War, and in the first decades of 'the third technological revolution' (the so called 'golden age' of American capitalism in the permanent arms economy of the 1950s and 1960s), shiftings in the pattern of American class relations have been accompanied by youth cults of whatever affirmative or oppositional kind.[2] As a metaphor which continually reinscribes the nation within a timeless, original or authentic condition at each successive moment of transformation in the economic order, youth may indeed function as a powerful ideology in the properly 'negative' sense of the word: such that structural adjustments within the mode of production itself become over-lain by a special kind of cultural rhetoric, whose idealist language of 'natural' rebirth and 'organic' new growth tends to appear at precisely those moments when the very human dynamics of modern capitalism have been most vigorously at work, in the very historical destruction and reforming of productive forces and relations. The ideological implications of this rhetoric are surely clear enough. For if the crisis prone system which requires this constant revolutionizing of the instruments of produc-tion actually brings capitalist society ever *closer* to those authentic laws of nature invoked by Jefferson, then the cure for the problems of that (now global) society—overproduction and unemployment, progressive de-skilling and the slow death of the public sector, endemic socio-economic instability, chronic levels of poverty and ill health in First and Third Worlds, international military confrontation, class domination in all its forms—will always be more of what causes the problems in the first place.

But if we take the American ideology of youth on its own terms, as an abstract thing whose orientation toward the future means that America (and the world now fashioned in America's image) is always unfinished or incomplete, then the meaning of youth can never be just this one-dimensional thing. For if youth forces upon us the inkling of another, currently inconceivable condition of things, one that is potential in what is extant, then it is by definition a leaky ideology: an ideology that might fail in its role as a containing agent whose function is to limit what is politically thinkable at any given time. While a constant looking or thinking beyond what currently exists may deflect the eye from the way things actually are, an institutionally sponsored ideology which directs the attention toward an order which has not yet come into being might equally function as an insurgent counter-ideology: the drive to think in terms of the future and its possible contents establishing a fluid set of hypothetical standards against which the current state of things might then be judged. By virtue of the weight of contradictions it is forced to carry, it may then be that the ideology of the perpetual 'new beginning' is always susceptible to its own dialectical implosion, and its conversion into a more progressive or transparent perspective on the workings of a world it is otherwise programmed to conceal.

It is just such a definition of youth ideology that we find in the work of Randolph Bourne, where youth appears as a trope for the struggle of the intellectual to embed herself fully in the world upon which she reports, while simultaneously preserving a relatively autonomous or objective critical 'space' within which the act of social criticism might take shape. The meaning of 'youth' for Bourne, in other words, lies precisely in its ideological duality. To experience youth is to be both fully contained within the extant order of things, while simultaneously 'going beyond' (Sartre) the ideological strictures which secure and reproduce that order. Writing in the years immediately before the First World War, Bourne figures youth as the 'drastic antiseptic' inserted between the festering 'certainties' of childhood and adulthood (Bourne 1977a: 100), that moment of radical indeterminacy where the normative and the fixed are suspended within the flux of life, and where a willed openness to the new exposes the self to the relationality of all things. Describing this shift from child to adult as 'the time of contradictions and anomalies', the time of 'tearings and . . . grindings and . . . wrenchings' when '[t]he atoms of things seem to be disintegrating' (ibid.: 93, 95), youth becomes for Bourne the moment in which personality, detached from the bourgeois moorings of ego or selfhood issuing from a sovereign centre, is instead defined as an immersion of the self within contradictory experience. Glorying in this 'sudden servitude' to contradictions, youth 'is content to let the new master lead wherever he will; and is as surprised as any one at the momentous and startling results' that accrue. Youth, Bourne suggests, 'is vulnerable at every point. . . . Youth at its best is this constant suscepti- bility to the new, this constant eagerness to try experiments' (ibid.: 96).

For Bourne, youth then becomes a metaphor for what he elsewhere called 'the life of irony', a continual juxtaposition of multiple points of view, an 'insistent judging of experience', with 'all the little parts of one's world being constantly set off against each other, and made intelligible only by being translated into and defined in each others' terms' (Bourne 1977b: 134). Privileging the relational over the determinate, this youthful life of irony is 'not fixed in predestined formulas', is not 'measurable by fixed, immutable standards', and 'has no citadel of truth to defend' (ibid.: 136). As a modernist category (rather than a postmodernism), the life of irony constructs for Bourne a nodal point around which the relationality of all things is ultimately centripetal, providing a model for the *production* rather than the negation of 'values'. Irony, he argues, 'compares things not with an established standard but with each other, and the values that slowly emerge from the process, values that emerge from one's own vivid reactions, are constantly revised, corrected, and refined by that sense of contrast' (ibid.: 136).

Most important, therefore, when assessing Bourne's contribution to American intellectual history, is the way in which this youthful life of irony then unlocks the political potential implicit in modernism's repudiation of the normative and the determinate.[3] For the production of values implied in the ironic stance effectively preserves the possibility for the articulation of collective truths, upon which any model of truly radical or revolutionary politics must finally depend. In the ironic taking of another's stance, the limitations of one's own position, and the possibilities inherent in those alternative positions which confront it, are brought to light. Like 'a judge on the bench, giving men a public hearing', the ironic spirit of youth 'tests ideals by their social validity, by their general interchangeability among all sorts of people and the world', And 'if it leaves the foundations of many in a shaky condition and renders more simply provisional, those that it does leave standing are imperishably founded in the common democratic experience of all men' (ibid.: 142, 138). Too many 'outworn ideas', Bourne tells us, 'are skulking in dark retreats, sequestered from the light; every man has great sunless stretches in his soul where base prejudices lurk and flourish. On these the white light of irony is needed to play. And it delights the ironist to watch them shrivel and decay under that light' (ibid.: 137). Offered as a metaphor for Bourne's life of irony, 'youth' is therefore defined as a mechanism whose function is the denunciation of 'values' which purport a commonality, but whose 'dark retreats' conceal their status as partial things; ideas, for instance, which may masquerade as properly universal human values, but which are objectively subordinate in the final instance to the reproduction of a given social system, and to the power of a particular social class whose interests that system is constructed to serve.

Another way of putting this in more conventionally Marxian language would be to say that youth's very openness to the existence of 'contradictions and anomalies', as the bedrock of all existing social relations, allows it to expose the workings of ideology as a dynamic force in bourgeois life.

To live the life of youthful irony means to live as a political animal in a world where bourgeois ideology is robbed of its persuasive power, laying bare in the process the very contradictions which it seeks to conceal. 'The deadliest way to annihilate the unoriginal and the insincere,' Bourne suggests, 'is to let it speak for itself', and the ironic discourse of youth is precisely 'this letting things speak for themselves and hang themselves by their own rope'. Like 'the acid that develops a photographic plate', youthful irony 'does not distort the image, but merely brings clearly to light all that was implicit in the plate before' (ibid.: 138). As a modernist metaphor for that moment in which the occluded content of things becomes suddenly transparent, we might say that the juxtaposition of alternative values in youth then *embodies* ideology, but only so as to undo or 'neutralize' it, leaving the ideology standing, but in a new hollowed out form which simultaneously exposes the limitations of the argument it forces upon us.[4]

What we can do now is test this characterization of youth discourse as a formal mechanism for the production *and* negation of ideology, by applying Bourne's ideas to the *bildungsromane* (or 'novels of education') of S.E. Hinton, a series of short novels which exemplify the ideological duality of 'youth' in striking ways, in part because they are written from both sides of the adolescent divide. Hinton's first novel, *The Outsiders* (1967), was 'apparently inspired by social injustices at her high school in Tulsa, Oklahoma' (Rees 1984: 126), and was written when she was only seventeen years old. Her second, *That was Then This is Now* (1971), followed four years later, after her graduation from the University of Tulsa, and her third, *Rumble Fish* (1975), four years after that. Although these novels are told by different narrators, their similarity in plot and theme, and their tendency to reintroduce the same protagonists from one story to the next, creates in the novels a fictive world whose anxieties and ideologies arise and develop over time with a certain coherence. Each novel is told in the first person by an adolescent male protagonist, who details to the reader a violent (but decidedly moralistic) teenage world from which adults are either absent, or are tangentially present as failed role models or guardians. The three novels, as Rees suggests, are pretty much 'the same book . . . The characters may have different names, but they are similar stereotypes; the language, the . . . narration, the events, the attitudes are more or less identical' (ibid.: 126). This general similarity of Hinton's fictive world over time is particularly useful to us here, because while she begins as a teenage writer of teen stories, by the time of her second and third novels she has herself become an adult writer of teen stories, and so is able to juxtapose in her fiction a double perspective on the 'fall' out of adolescence and into adulthood which the *bildungsroman* has traditionally detailed. Grounded in this double perspective, the novels are notable, in Bourne's terms, for the range of different sources for social identity that they propose. The teenage gang, social class, loyalty to family or friends, the public good, private conscience, the possibility of class mobility for the 'private' individual under bourgeois social relations: all of these things figure in Hinton's fiction as competing models upon which the maturing personality might be built, as the novels mediate between and among the models on view. As the writer and her young protagonists move from adolescence to adulthood, youth narrative emerges in these novels in more or less the way that Bourne implies it might, as a writing which sets those various possible choices off one against the other, sifting the available options in an open field from which a 'mature' voice then emerges to assess its own possible futures in the 'adult' world. In examining Hinton's 'ironic' juxtaposition of different models of social identity in these stories, we can draw upon the critical vocabulary provided by Bourne, and read the multiple perspectives of her fiction within a specifically ideological frame of reference. We can look for the ways in which each of Hinton's 'youth' texts may be read as a self-conflicted thing. We can look for ways in which the findings of one novel in the series may damage the findings of another, and for ways in which this whole cycle of 'contradictions and anomalies', 'tearings and . . . grindings and . . . wrenchings', then shapes itself into a set of new 'values' which can be scrutinized under Bourne's 'white light of irony' for their ideological and counter-ideological content.

In examining what Bourne would term the production of these 'values' in Hinton's fiction, we will be concerned with a number of different things. We will need to consider how the adult world looks to the young writer and her young protagonists, and conversely how the world of adolescence then appears to the more 'mature' voices in the fiction. We will need to identify the motor forces of the adult world which awaits Hinton's young protagonists like fate itself, and we will need to look at the outer limits of this 'fate,' the ideological parameters of adulthood beyond which none of her protagonists are finally able to go. At some stage we will also need to historicize the contradictions which this cycle of novels offers as its central thesis: the 'lesson' we are taught being that while the fall into adulthood and the class-boundedness of that fall are inevitable things, the central problem of collective or class identity is that it promises/portends diametrically opposed things for different protagonists. On the one hand, ciphered through the central motif of the teen gang and its unspoken codes of class solidarity and communal belonging, the social collective appears in these novels as a thing of strength, a platform for resistance to those other hermetic 'gang' groupings which populate Hinton's teen scene, and a way of life in which the gang as a unified entity becomes something more than the sum of its individual parts. 'It was great,' one character tells us in *That was Then This is Now*, 'we were like a bunch of people makin' up one big person, like we totalled up to somethin' when we were together' (Hinton 1975: 53). Cutting against this proposition, however, we also find a more properly ideological insistence that the gains of collective life are essentially illusory: that the behaviour of one collective at war with other collectives merely perpetuates outdated conflicts (gangs we are told at one point, are 'out of style' (Hinton 1977: 24)); that collective commitments as such tend to stunt the potential for individual growth and self-fulfilment, and that in the end it is to the bourgeois self alone that one must turn for 'authentic' experience or knowledge when entering the 'mature' world of adulthood. Compounding this initial contradiction there is then a further problem in these novels, in that the authentic narrator who is liberated from the 'gang' will subsequently find himself locked into a new kind of existential alienation, both from himself as an 'centred' agency in the world, and from those other characters around him who share the same socio-economic conditions (none of whom, with the internal fragmentation of the adolescent 'gang' collectives, are now able to articulate that vanished sense of common purpose or belonging in any meaningful way).[5] It is in this 'ironic' collision of various forms of collective identity with the notional 'authenticity' of the subject-self, and in the forcing of these alternatives to 'speak for themselves and hang themselves by their own rope', that we will define and historicize Hinton's teen novels as a youth discourse in the terms set by Randolph Bourne.

The initial step we might take toward an accounting for Hinton's *bildungsromane* in ideological terms might lie in a sharpening of our definition of the basic group or collective as it is figured in the novels. In *The Outsiders*, the description of the two broad social strata within which Hinton sets her competing 'gangs' tells us immediately that the outer limits of this teen culture lie in the problem of class conflict itself, where the idea of the 'gang' and gang war stands in, in more or less unspoken ways, as a sublimation of antagonistic class relations. On one side we find the (upper case) 'Socs' or 'Socials', who are 'the jet set, the West-side rich kids', and on the other the (lower case) 'greasers', who are 'poorer than the Socs and the middle class', '[w]hite trash with long hair' (Hinton 1972: 8, 62)). It is this problem of 'the two different worlds we lived in' (ibid.: 48), and the occluded reasons for conflict between these 'worlds', which underlies all three novels and which haunts the thought processes of the main characters. Indeed, for a cycle of stories that seems programmed to avoid or systematically displace the broader class outlines of the 'gang' identities it discusses, the novels have a near anthropological fascination with the fine nuances and social mores of that thing which they will not permit themselves to name. 'Why did the Socs hate us so much ?' asks Ponyboy Curtis, the greaser narrator of *The Outsiders*. 'We left them alone. I nearly went to sleep over my homework trying to figure it out' (ibid.: 23). 'I thought maybe it was money that separated us': but '[i]t's not just money,' the Soc girl Cherry tells him. 'Part of it is, but not all. You greasers have a different set of values' (ibid.: 44). The intuition of Hinton's characters that a broader set of socio-economic factors are at work in the dominance of the Soc 'gang', and the fascination with which the characters dwell upon those hidden determinants, are set within a detailed inventory of the contrasting leisure niches, emotional planes and relationships with state power which differentiate the class-bound realities of capitalist life in Hinton's fictive world. So 'Socs go to The Way Out and to Rusty's, and the greasers go to The Dingo and to Jay's' (ibid.: 26). But do their girls cry, Curtis wonders to himself, 'when their boys were arrested, like Evie did when Steve got hauled in, or did they run out on them the way Sylvia did Dallas ?' (ibid.: 22). 'You know how cops are; there's a million over on the Ribbon, making sure the nice kids don't kill each other or run each other down, while we can cut each other's throats and they don't give a damn' (Hinton 1975: 29). With its 'leaders in the paper for being a public disgrace one day and an asset to society the next' (Hinton 1972: 8), 'Soc' life is defined as the universal (bourgeois) standard by which all social life should be lived, but is simultaneously imagined as a menace to society as such. Behind their notional integrity as a 'gang' united against the common 'greaser'/class enemy, the concealed essential pattern of this bourgeois class is one of entropy through internecine competition, less a gang than 'a pack', a 'snarling, distrustful, bickering pack like . . . wolves in the timber' (ibid.: 33). 'That was the truth,' Curtis tells us. 'Socs were always behind a wall of aloofness, careful not to let their real selves show through' (ibid.: 45). 'Nothing,' Cherry tells Curtis, 'is for real with us' (ibid.: 44). One could hardly hope for a more parodically faithful account of bourgeois 'values' in any of the great diagnostic novels written by Sinclair Lewis or John Updike!

This tendency to render the class relation fully present in narratives which at the same time assiduously duck the prospect of naming it as class, or as the capitalism from which the problem of class derives, provides the context within which Hinton's ironic juxtaposing of multiple models of social identity (and the relative truth or falsity of their 'values') then emerges. As *bildungsromane*, *The Outsiders*, *Rumble Fish* and *That was Then This is Now* each trace the fall out of adolescence into adulthood, and each link this falling to a single cataclysmic moment or series of events which lead to the break up of the teen collectives, and to their supersession by what looks, superficially, like a qualitatively different, more progressive kind of social relation or ethic: the 'adult' commitment to the self, or the need to account for one's actions responsibly according to the dictats of individual (rather than collective) conscience. Later in this essay we will want to broaden the context within which this defining moment arrives in the novels, and give it the historical name of 'Fordism'. For now, though, we can note that in *The Outsiders* the point of no return arrives in the death of a Soc gang member during a fight, and in the answering of the greaser killers for their actions, a course which then leads the narrator toward a rejection of the 'hatred', 'pride' and 'conformity' governing 'gang' (i.e. class) experience, and a concomitant embracing of social mobility on purely individualistic terms: the determination of the narrator 'to get somewhere', to avoid living 'in a lousy neighbourhood all my life' (ibid.: 146, 147).

Throughout the narrative, this drift toward a reinvention of social personality is accompanied by a number of statements which measure the dragging of oneself from the binding attachments of collective being against the 'natural' and 'inevitable' reincarnation in adulthood as an 'autonomous' subject or ego-self. One of the more striking instances of this comes in the narrator's recitation of Robert Frost's poem 'Nothing Gold Can Stay', where the organic cycle of growth and decay is offered as a metaphor for the slippage of youth into adulthood, and for the absolute privatizing of identity which, for Hinton, this slippage entails.

> Nature's first green is gold,
> Her hardest hue to hold.
> Her early leaf's a flower;
> But only so an hour.
> Then leaf subsides to leaf.
> So Eden sank to grief,

> So dawn goes down to day.
> Nothing gold can stay
>
> (ibid.: 85)

Spoken aloud by Ponyboy Curtis as he and the character Johnny watch the golden colours of a morning sunrise fade into daylight, the poem is included during the 'pastoral' sequence of the novel, where the pair hide out for several days in a church 'in the country', 'in the middle of nowhere' (ibid.: 72, 81), following the death of the Soc. Hiding out at the church, the characters seek to disguise their gang/class identity, cutting and bleaching the long hair which 'labelled us [as] greasers', which 'was our trademark. The one thing we were proud of' (ibid.: 78). Prefigured by the loss of this trademark, and paralleled by the elegiac decaying of the dawn in Frost's poem, these pastoral chapters culminate in the burning down of the church (the symbolic place of sanctuary), and the dramatic rebirth of the characters as they are propelled outward from the womb-like collective of the teen 'gang', and into the world of responsible (but now individualistic) adulthood. As Johnny and Ponyboy rescue a group of children from the burning building, thereby assuming a new 'parental' or adult role, this transformation is confirmed and reinforced by an equally new sense of self-scrutiny in the narrator's voice, and by the emergence of the narrator-self as a now 'unified' subject–object capable of such self-reflection. 'I should be scared, I thought with an odd detached feeling', Curtis tells us during the rescue, 'but I'm not. . . . Why aren't I scared? . . . Johnny wasn't behaving at all like his old self. . . . He wasn't scared either. That was the only time I can think of when I saw him without that defeated, suspicious look in his eyes. He looked like he was having the time of his life' (ibid.: 100–1). Sunrises and sunsets are central metaphors in *The Outsiders*. In the earlier scene at the drive-in, where Ponyboy and Cherry have tried to dissect the meaning of their antagonistic class positions, the universality of sunsets is offered as evidence for an 'authentic' subjectivity that is latent in all gang/class members, but which is stunted and held in check by the 'artifice' of collective belonging. 'It seemed funny to me that the sunset she saw from her patio and the one I saw from the back steps was the same one,' Curtis tells us. 'Maybe the two different worlds we lived in weren't so different. We saw the same sunset' (ibid.: 47–8). This moment then points the way toward the later pastoral chapters, where the elegiac passing of dawn to day heralds the arrival of that awakening 'adult' subjectivity in the burning church, and where the pastoral realm itself is offered as a site of authentic rebirth, a utopian place where the 'outside world' of collective gang/class relations appears 'unreal' or 'dreamlike' (ibid.: 87), and where all barriers to the realization of the 'liberated' self are dissolved. 'It seems like there's gotta be somewhere without greasers or Socs, with just people. Plain ordinary people,' Johnny says to Ponyboy the night of the drive-in. ' "Out of the big towns," ' I said, lying back down. "In the country . . ." ' (ibid.: 55).[6]

As Hinton herself matures in *That was Then This is Now*, the turning point of the story comes in the intrusion of a drug-taking 'hippie commune' on what remains of gang/class identity from *The Outsiders*. Here, through the story of a deepening rift between the narrator Bryon Douglas and his adopted brother Mark, the older Hinton now narrows her focus, turning initially to family and friendship as the desirable sources of embedded social belonging, before confirming again that group loyalty of whatever local or general kind is a pernicious thing ('there had to be a few sponges in a setup like that' (Hinton 1975: 21)), as the maturing narrator 'discovers' a moral imperative to inform on his drug-dealing best friend. Throughout the novel, a series of sub-narratives which detail the damaging effects of race and gang violence on individual lives repeatedly stress the notion of 'difference', and the need to privilege individual choice over and above loyalty to family, friends, gang or class. And as in *The Outsiders*, this shifting from collective to 'private' identity ('in the past I thought in terms of "we," now I was thinking in terms of "me" ' (ibid.: 79)) again appears as a more or less inevitable process, the rift between the two main protagonists arising in their contrasting responses to the fact that 'the whole thing is changin' ', that 'somethin' is coming to an end because somethin' else is beginning' (ibid.: 53). Lacking the kind of epiphanic motif which evokes this transition in *The Outsiders* (the sunset/ sunrise), *That was Then This is Now* instead develops the Salinger-esque technique of the 'rule-giving' narrator which Hinton has rehearsed in the earlier novel.[7] Here, the steady flow of axioms, principles and governing laws from the narrative voice establishes the narrator as the sovereign source of order and meaning in a story that becomes his own 'property', and from which any sense of collective authority is effectively expelled. 'A little kid like him shouldn't be reading that junk, I know, but he should at least want to' (ibid.: 10). 'If I had to be a baby-sitter day and night, I'd lose my temper and kill one of those brats' (ibid.: 11). 'Since we had surprised them, it wasn't too hard to get them pinned' (ibid.: 16). 'Parents never know what all their kids do. Not in the old days, not now, not tomorrow. It's a law' (ibid.: 60), and so on. Later, in *Rumble Fish*, where the point of view is retrospective and the collapse of the gangs is identified as the defining moment in the life of the maturing narrator, the problems which flow from this loss of collective belonging then take over as the central theme of the writing.

We will come back to *Rumble Fish* in a moment, but before we do this we should consider more fully the implications of the 'lesson' which these *bildungsromane* appear to convey. In this regard, a more comprehensive treatment of Hinton's writing would no doubt involve a closer attention to the market to which these teen novels are brought for sale, and a detailed demographic account of that readership as it has developed alongside the writer's own rite of passage into adulthood. While such an account is beyond the scope of this essay, what we can say is that these stories are packaged and marketed primarily for the adolescent reader who is preparing himself (and notwithstanding the gender of the writer these are very 'masculinist' books) for the 'adult' world. We can also note that the social education acquired by Hinton's young protagonists is reported to the reader in a stringently moral, at times quite didactic writing style. The reader is directly addressed throughout all three books. Each story turns upon a set of clearly identified mistakes or questionable choices by a main character or characters. The narrator in each case is careful to flag up the conclusions being drawn from the story of those mistakes, and so forth. If these are then *bildungsromane* where the lessons learned by the narrators tend to match up with a putative education of the reader, novels which are on some level quite authoritarian in design and execution, then the need to choose between self and class, and the inevitability of the slide into a privatized culture of strong individuals and discarded collectives, can certainly be considered within properly ideological terms. In Hinton's fictive world, where class relations are acknowledged to be the broad outer limit determining the various collective identities against which the characters set themselves, the appeal made to the reader is nonetheless to turn her back on the authenticity of those relations, and embrace instead a bourgeois ethic of private or individualistic self-fulfilment. Here it is useful to note that the origins and initial development of the *bildungsroman* form lie in eighteenth- and nineteenth-century Europe, and that the genre is thus embedded in a epoch which is itself overdetermined by the rise to power of the bourgeois class, and the supplanting of earlier political and economic formations for whom subjectivity, in the modern sense of the atomized individual self, was an unknown quantity.[8] So that when Fredric Jameson suggests that *bildungsromane* are 'machines for producing subjectivity, machines designed to construct "centred subjects" . . . The

very epitome of an ideologically charged technical apparatus or technological innovation' (Jameson 1992–3: 182–3), his description of genre is
both literary and—in a manner that literary criticism today has largely
forgotten or been taught to forget—historical in a rather broader sense.
For the new kind of subjectivity embodied in the eighteenth-century
novels of education is one that arises as both the product and the
ideological bulwark of a new kind of social and economic order: an order
whose political and economic manifestation, in the great bourgeois
revolutions of the period, is paralleled in the cultural sphere by the
adventures of the bourgeois monad, the sovereign self, the free-standing
auto/biographical subject whose discovery and moment of development
provides the raw material for those novels. In this sense, the cultural
significance of the *bildungsroman* is that it points us back out into what,
from our own moment at the beginning of the twenty-first century, can
now be recognized as a more or less universal experience in modern
history. The peculiarity of the form, as Jameson argues, being its tendency
to recur in a range of different First and Third World cultures, each of
which have experienced at different times that same moment of what
is referred to euphemistically as 'modernization': an experience whose
objective content can be read in less abstract terms as the penetration of
bourgeois social relations into pre-capitalist collectives (peasant villages
and communes, extended manors, Native American cultures and so
on), and in the displacement of identity conceived of as a collectively
embedded thing by the 'free-standing' self of the modern or bourgeois
period. As a literature which organizes itself around the construction and
fictive reproduction of the auto/biographical self, the personal, 'private',
or self-propelling subjectivity of bourgeois myth, the *bildungsroman* thus
becomes an archetypal literary form: a kind of writing whose tendency
to emerge within the culture of 'modernizing' economies appears to
reconfirm, as Jameson points out, the currently unfashionable view of 'a
universalist history, in which the most unrelated societies scattered in time
and space all dutifully come around in the end to repeating the basic
stages', to acquiring an education, and to 'working their way up out of this
or that precapitalism into their individualistic *bildungsroman* moment'
(ibid.: 174).

In the case of S.E. Hinton we might then modify this definition of
genre to take note of the writer's own historical position, and suggest
that the model of socialization proposed in these novels (where class is
imagined as a thing to be shrugged off or denounced as an illusion, but
is simultaneously retained as the ultimate standard against which all others

must be measured) is specific to a particular moment in the development of twentieth-century capitalist relations. That moment would be the period of capital accumulation sometimes called 'Fordism', which spans the years from around 1940 to 1975, and whose American hallmarks are the mechanism of collective bargaining—hailed in the Cold War liberalism of Galbraith, Hofstadter and Bell as a defusing or harmonization of the fundamental contradiction between labour and capital—and a redoubled emphasis on acts of privatized consumption in the marketplace during the 'golden age' years of deepening internal demand.[9] If this apparent harmonizing of capitalist social life under Fordism represented at best a temporary truce between irreconcilable class interests, the ideological glue which the mechanism applied to American life in the years of the long boom was certainly effective. Daniel Bell even went so far as to announce that what the post-war generation had witnessed was the very demise of class-based politics, the 'exhaustion of political ideas', and the 'end of ideology' (in the loosest sense of the word) as such. The Fordist parameters of Hinton's fiction may be glimpsed firstly in what we have seen to be the oddly class-conscious classlessness it offers as a model for the 'mature' sensibility, and secondly in the blurring of (still visible) class lines which this model implies. In *That was Then This is Now*, the catchment area of the school attended by the narrator Bryon Douglas 'included a real crummy part of town—ours—and a pretty ritzy part of town' which 'can make for problems', or 'used to anyway' (Hinton 1975: 55). Nowadays, Douglas tells us, his friends include 'what we used to call Socs', and 'it was hard . . . to tell a Soc from a greaser' (ibid.: 55), while the central dilemma confronting the narrator is the problem of political transparency itself. 'I lead with my left,' he say, 'and that's about as much as I know about Left, Right and so on. I have a vague notion that the Left is Hippie and the Right is Hick, but I really don't know much else' (ibid.: 56). If Hinton's novels are read as 'lessons' conceived and transmitted within the last years of the Fordist boom, where the problem of antagonistic class relations is both 'solved' and yet remains as a vital pressure upon the political imagination of the writer, these 'machines for producing subjectivity' then come fully alive as ideological documents. And in this regard the 'values' which emerge from Hinton's 'ironic' colliding of different models of social identity seem rather ambiguous. Written in a style where the authoritarianism of the lesson directed at the young reader is set off against the libertarian ethic of private selfhood embraced by the narrators, the further, unspoken lesson of these *bildungsromane*, is that for as long as class relations remain in place as the ultimate (but occluded) horizon within which life is lived, bourgeois selfhood is something that must be preached and inculcated rather than something which is 'naturally' lived: a doctrine or faith that requires conscious effort on the part of the individual if it is to be 'believed in', a way of looking at the world which demands a more or less active suppression of deeply rooted contradictions which remain fully alive (however blurred their outline), and which are irreducibly collective in character.

This being so it is then possible that the properly ideological education proposed by these novels is more provisional than might at first appear to be the case. For if Hinton's writing is a youth discourse in Bourne's terms, in its experimental switching between and among competing models for the socialization of identity, then the contradictions which it brings to the surface prevent it being ideological in the purely 'negative' sense alone. When it is bounced back off the novels' various statements about the intractability of class domination ('[i]t ain't fair that we have all the rough breaks,' 'you can't win against them no matter how hard you try' (Hinton 1972: 50, 17)), the appeal to classlessness which these novels make might function in a rather different way. Instead of a simple substitution of one reality for another, which serves to mask the social divisions that exist in the fictive world, the suggestion that each character possesses within themselves a common humanity which might transcend those divisions skews the 'lesson' of the novels about their own axis in unexpected ways. So that the thing which is sought, the common humanity, the autonomous subjectivity freed from external restraint, becomes a thing that is now unattainable within the kind of social relations presented to us in the fiction, and connotes instead a human potential that may only be realized within another, qualitatively different but currently absent kind of social order toward which the writing then points us. This is all the more so when we realize that the subjectivity which these novels strive to produce, the illusion of the free-standing sovereign self, seems today either hopelessly arcane, or profoundly utopian. For within our current age of unprecedented market penetration, where the circuits of capital connect up the most global of financial transactions with the tiniest details of individual lives, an age where subjectivity itself has finally become recognized as merely one 'intertext' among others, the very idea of a self-propelling 'private' self seems so out of kilter with the daily realities of 'growing up' into work and leisure, or unemployment and subsistence, as to belong to another world entirely.

This 'utopian' ideology which emerges in Hinton's 'ironic' colliding of 'group' and 'subject' identities can be traced most visibly in *Rumble Fish*, where the actually existing subjectivity of the maturing narrator, and that of his brother, is set off against a nostalgic longing for the old collectivity of the gangs. In *Rumble Fish* the concrete limitations inherent in the ideology of the free-standing bourgeois self in a world where class-relations persist, can be seen first of all in the story of the narrator's brother, the Motorcycle Boy. Identified as a prime mover in the breakup of the 'gangs' ('I thought we'd stopped this cowboys and Indians crap' (Hinton 1977: 30)), the Motorcycle Boy becomes the didactic voice in the novel, repeatedly pronouncing on or alluding to the inauthenticity of the collective 'gang' experience to which the narrator, Rusty James, remains nostalgically attached. The epitome of the fully rounded, self-authoring subject of bourgeois myth—a reformed gang leader whose everyday conversation shows his knowledge of classical Greek literature (ibid.: 57); who was expelled from school for 'perfect tests' (ibid.: 36); who 'looked like a painting' (ibid.: 84); who was 'very famous around our part of the city' (ibid.: 68); who is a mixture of 'Robin Hood, Jesse James and the Pied Piper' (ibid.: 67); who 'could get away with anything' (ibid.: 33); who is 'the coolest person in the whole world' according to his brother; 'a prince . . . royalty in exile' according to others (ibid.: 40, 85)—the Motorcycle Boy stands alone in all that he does. But this ideal type who is revered by the other characters has a tragic flaw. Born with 'the ability to do anything', but also born 'on the wrong side of the river' (ibid.: 116), the Motorcycle Boy is a character whose superhuman potential is condemned to wither and die in a class society which is unable to nurture or sustain the capabilities he possesses. Colour blind and partially deaf from early childhood, he 'would have made a perfect knight, in a different century', but 'was born in the wrong era' (ibid.: 116). Tainted by the class status of his birth, this visitor from a perfect other-world who has become part blind, part deaf, and is prone throughout the novel to near catatonic silences, is presented to us as a character alienated both from the potential that remains locked within him, and from those other 'individuals' who make up the circle of family, friends and ex-gang members around him. 'For some reason or other,' the narrator tells us, 'the Motorcycle Boy was alone, more alone than I would ever be, than I could ever imagine being. He was living in a glass bubble and watching the world from it' (ibid.: 91).

The climactic moment of the novel is framed in imagery which encapsulates the plight of the hero, and which stands in ironic counter-point to the sunset/sunrise motif of *The Outsiders*. Drawn to the Siamese fighting fish held in a local pet store, creatures which would 'kill each other' if given the chance, which would 'kill themselves fighting their own reflection', the Motorcycle Boy wonders aloud if these 'rumble fish' would 'act that way in the river'. Later that night he breaks into the store, releases the other caged animals, and is on his way to the river with the rumble fish when he is shot by the cops. In these closing scenes, the isolation of the character is depicted as something more than the accidental provenance of one individual unable to realize his potential in a class-based social system. Here, in the metaphor of the fighting fish, the typology of the bourgeois monad in general is brought under Bourne's 'white light of irony', the 'free-standing' self re-emerging in the process as a subjectivity consigned to a condition of generalized alienation, where a programming of the competitive individual toward the destruction of others connotes also (in the naturalistic drives of the rumble fish) a final absence of self-determination as such. Like Bourne's 'judge on the bench, giving men a public hearing', testing ideas 'by their social validity', Hinton's writing here sets off a series of textual aftershocks, as the breakdown of the bourgeois monad is switched rapidly between a number of implied perspectives or positions. Victimized by his class position on one hand, the Motorcycle Boy's isolation must also remind us of his own active hostility to collective or 'gang'/class categories throughout the novel, and thus of his own complicity in the forces of atomization which now seem poised to crush him. Simultaneously the reader is drawn to the fate of the narrator himself, a character who always wanted to be just like his brother and is now granted that wish, as he too becomes colour blind, with his memory (the great modernist signature of 'deep' subjectivity) all 'screwed up' (ibid.: 119, 7). Weighed against each of these positions, where the natural progression into adulthood is now marked by a breaking up of the self rather than by its triumphant emergence into a boundless world of bourgeois freedoms, we are then also forced back upon the alternatives to this process of fragmentation which are intuited by the characters: the collective 'gang' experience to which the narrator constantly harks back—'I can remember it', 'Man . . . a gang really meant somethin' back then', 'it *was* something' (ibid.: 24, 25, 93)—and which the Motorcycle Boy suspects will return 'once they get the dope off the streets' (ibid.: 94). As an 'ironic' conduit through which competing models of the 'adult' future are made to flow, Hinton's youth discourse then ultimately reinvokes precisely those contradictions which its rhetoric of private selfhood and authentic moral conscience are designed to bury or circumvent. For at the very moment when the writing is most 'authoritarian' (the concluding sequences where lessons are learned by protagonists and readers alike, and where the *bildungsroman* becomes a Fordist conduct manual), the class antagonisms which produce the gangs and which the novels have banished from view, are now returned to the surface of the writing. In this returning to view and re-evaluation of their own repressed contents, the novels then self-deconstruct, disassembling the argument which they force upon the reader. Despite the 'values' which they set out to endorse and disseminate, the final lesson given by Hinton's fiction is that meaningful social belonging cannot be articulated in the bourgeois ideologies of the society to which she and her readers belong: that the 'transparent' relation between the self and the social proposed by those values is a fiction, one that will eventually return her readers only to those problems of class and class conflict which hang over the ending to *Rumble Fish* like a shroud, and to which the *bildungsroman* itself must 'in the final instance' trace its own roots.

Notes

1 As used here, 'ideology' is defined in a specifically Marxian sense. Among other things, 'ideology' would then connote a way of looking at the world which restricts what is thinkable in any given historical period, and may refer to that network of assumptions and beliefs about the naturalness or inevitability of the extant social order, which assists in the reproduction of that order at the level of ideas or the imagination. Ultimately, the dissemination of ideology will therefore involve a glossing or outright denial of those embedded contradictions (in the final instance the antagonistic relations between competing social classes) upon which our current social life is built: contradictions which perpetually threaten to collapse that life from within and which must thus, by force or by force of ideas, be 'strategically contained' in one way or another.

2 On 'the third technological revolution', and on 'long waves' in the history of capitalism, see Mandel 1978. On the managerial disciplining of labour, see Braverman 1974.

3 On Bourne, see Lasch 1986, and May 1992.

4 On this more 'positive' or 'utopian' content of 'negative' ideology, see Jameson 1988, and Jameson 1989. On the utopian dimension of culture generally, see Bloch 1988.

5 The closest analogy would perhaps be the idea of 'seriality' as it is developed in the later Sartre. See Sartre 1976.

6 On the 'ideological multivalence' of American pastoral, see Buell 1995.

7 On the rule-giving narrator in Salinger's *Catcher in the Rye*, see Nadel 1988.

8 On European *bildungsromane*, see Moretti 1987.

9 Ostensibly a social contract between the American working class and their

employers (which arose during the militarization of the economy in the war years and was institutionalized in the Taft-Hartley Act of 1947), this system of 'de-centralized' bargains struck between business and trade unions was of course nothing of the kind. Collective bargaining undoubtedly allowed the unions to wrest significant gains from the employers (among them a guaranteeing of the wage level, and a recognition of the principle of employer top-ups for health insurance and pensions). But the terms of Taft-Hartley also signalled a widespread attack on the (relatively) progressive measures of the Wagner Act of 1935, severely limiting the legality of working-class activism in a range of very specific scenarios (including action taken against the unilateral restructuring of working conditions by employers), whilst extending to the state, in the name of de-centralization, the power to intervene directly in conflicts which might 'endanger the national economy'. Notwithstanding the recessions of 1953–4 and 1957–8, and the widespread adoption of more openly aggressive 'Boulwarist' management strategies during the final years of the Eisenhower administration, the assumption that Fordism represented a practicable and very American solution to the 'problem' of social class remained more or less intact until the sharp recession of 1974–5, when the integrated coherence of the 'golden age' would finally unravel and pave the way for the structural readjustments of the Reagan era. See Aglietta 1979, Davis 1986. On American collective bargaining, see Bok and Dunlop 1970, and Litwack 1962.

Bibliography

Aglietta, M. (1979) *A Theory of Capitalist Regulation*, London: New Left Books.

Appleby, J. (1984) *Capitalism and a New Social Order*, New York: New York University Press.

Bloch, E. (1988) *The Utopian Function of Art and Literature*, Cambridge: MIT.

Bok, D.C. and Dunlop, J.T. (1970) *Labor and the American Community*, New York: Simon and Schuster.

Bourne, R. (1977a) 'Youth' in *The Radical Will: Selected Writings 1911–1918*, Berkeley: University of California Press, pp. 93–105.

——(1977b) 'The life of irony', in *The Radical Will: Selected Writings 1911–1918*, Berkeley: University of California Press, pp. 134–48.

Braverman, H. (1974) *Labor and Monopoly Capital: The Degradation of Work in the Twentieth Century*, New York: Monthly Review Press.

Buell, L. (1995) *The Environmental Imagination: Thoreau, Nature Writing and the Formation of American Culture*, Cambridge: Harvard University Press.

Davis, M. (1986) *Prisoners of the American Dream: Politics and Economy in the History of the US Working Class*, London: Verso.

Hinton, S.E. (1972) *The Outsiders*, London: HarperCollins.

——(1975) *That was Then This is Now*, London: HarperCollins.

——(1977) *Rumble Fish*, London: HarperCollins.

Jameson, F. (1992–3) 'On literary and cultural import-substitution in the Third World: the case of the testimonio', in Gugelberger G.M. (1996) *The Real Thing: Testimonial Discourse and Latin America*, Durham: Duke University Press, pp. 172–91.

——(1989) *The Political Unconscious: Narrative as a Socially Symbolic Act*, London: Routledge.

——(1988) 'Of islands and trenches: neutralization and the production of utopian discourse', in *The Ideologies of Theory, Essays 1971–1986: Volume 2, The Syntax of History*, Minneapolis: University of Minnesota Press.

Lasch, C. (1986) *The New Radicalism in America 1889–1963: The Intellectual as a Social Type*, New York: Norton.

Litwack, L. (ed.) (1962) *The American Labor Movement*, Englewood Cliffs: Prentice Hall.

Maidment, R. and Dawson, M. (1994) *The United States in the Twentieth Century: Key Documents*, London: Hodder and Stoughton.

Mandel, E. (1978) *Late Capitalism*, Verso: London.

May, H.F. (1992) *The End of American Innocence: A Study of the First Years of Our Own Time, 1912–1917*, New York: Columbia University Press.

Moretti, F. (1987) *The Way of the World: The Bildungsroman in European Culture*, London: Verso.

Nadel, A. (1988) 'Rhetoric, sanity, and the Cold War: the significance of Holden Caulfield's testimony', *The Centennial Review*, 4(32), pp. 351–71.

Rees, D. (1984) *Painted Desert, Green Shade: Essays on Contemporary Writers of Fiction for Children and Young Adults*, Boston: Horn Books.

Sartre, J.-P. (1976) *Critique of Dialectical Reason*, London: New Left Books.

Toffler, A. (1970) *Future Shock*, New York: Random House.

Whitman, W. (1977a) 'Song of Myself', in *The Complete Poems*, London: Penguin.

——(1977b) 'Pioneers! O Pioneers!', in *The Complete Poems*, London: Penguin.

SIX

'Something you can't unhear': Masculinity, Youth and History in Larry Watson's Montana 1948

Neil Campbell

What you have to understand, about Westerns and the people who were part of them is that it was a great way not to grow up[1]

(Gene Autry)

The chain lightning of memory and family never quits in us[2]

(Ivan Doig)

The burden of the past that weighs like a nightmare on the brain of the West is an imperial burden, the anxiety that it might not all be of one piece, that secret histories, forgotten facts, other imaginations operate in all that we do and make, and our massive ignorances of these Othernesses is working to undermine what we do[3]

(Jerome McGann)

Secrets. Jack knew his town had secrets; every town did . . .[4]

(Larry Watson)

Youth and Nation

America has often drawn special connections between itself as nation and the concept of newness and youthfulness:

> We are young, vigorous, unique; 'on the cutting edge of history'. Since we
> are new, what is young, or vigorous, or unique is good to use *prima facie*
> . . . All people, everywhere, value youth . . . but America is the 'fountain of
> youth' . . .
>
> (Robertson 1980: 348)

Here, the nation is envisioned as a masculinist place of renewal, a re-birth
in which the energy of youthfulness represents beginning again and
undoing the corruption of the Old World. This investment and vision
became inscribed as the American Adam found in Emerson, Thoreau and
Whitman, and summed up in D.H. Lawrence's statement, 'She starts old,
old, wrinkled and writhing in an old skin. And there is a gradual sloughing
of the old skin, towards a new youth. It is the myth of America' (Lawrence
1977: 60). The Old World was a persecuting and alienating 'parent
culture' grown authoritarian in its power, and the rebellious 'children'
who opposed it would provide the vital, new future.

However, Robertson's 'cutting edge of history' further signifies
youth's capacity to question and reject accepted realities. The child, seen
as innocent and regenerative, could also be seen as on the border of the
new, challenging, demanding and even radical. These dual images of
youth persist in American culture, embedded in a variety of discourses
explored throughout this collection of essays. It is as if the child could
never be 'childish' for long in American cultural myths, for they had a
more significant, symbolic presence: 'To follow blindly the footsteps of
past masters was to remain forever a child; one should aim to rival and
finally to displace them. Inherited wisdom should be assimilated
and transformed, not simply revered and repeated . . .' (Lowenthal 1985:
72). Encoded here are mythic ideas about the inevitability of American
progress, as though the growth of the child was emblematic of the natural
growth of the nation toward a brighter, purer future. Thus, childhood
became the site for conflicting discourses: representing the child as the
natural rebellious inheritor of virtue born out of the struggle against
the parent culture, and simultaneously as the vision of naive innocence,
untarnished by the grubby adult world of materialism and moral decay.

Hence, writers have used the child as a source for their examinations
of cultural formations, linking the individuation of the child to that of
the unfolding nation. This has been a particular theme in narratives
of the American West, with the region seen as a microcosm of the
nation: 'the West is America only more so'. A male child learning the
supposed lessons of frontier life—hard work, determination and rugged

individualism—became emblematic of an American ideological vision of national identity. Inscribed here is both the myth and its critique, since the honest child growing up with the nation provides an opportunity to interrogate the underlying assumptions and values taken for granted in these stories. Elliot West writes that the child's 'values, visions of the future, and perceptions of themselves emerged' with westward expansion to the extent that 'the growth of the two cannot be separated' (West 1989: 245). This chapter shows how the child can be used to pose fundamental questions about America, the West and the very ways we record history itself.

Autobiography and Memoir: 'a new western emotional history'?

The 'new western history' set out to rewrite the histories of the West as a conquered land whose many voices had been reduced to those of the dominant and whose multiple stories had been compressed into myths and fables. Elliot West argues that 'until its children are heard, the frontier's history cannot be truly written' and it will remain 'incomplete, and thus distorted' (West 1989: 245). Indeed, a characteristic of this revisionist history was its willingness to connect personal experience with a wider, regional and national story. The pretence of historical objectivity, of neutral history, was rejected in favour of the inclusion of previously excluded stories, from wherever they might be found. In the words of Donald Worster, there was 'an inner cultural history' to be told as well as the 'outer ecological one', consisting of 'how people in the West have thought and felt in distinctive ways', what their dreams and disappoint-ments were, what they believed, how they acted and how they lived (Worster 1992: 231). Historians' own stories are part of this inner cultural history and often surface in their work. Worster wrote 'I know in my bones, if not always through my education . . .' (ibid.: 24), while Patricia Nelson Limerick's work is infused by her life and childhood:

> There has been a great tradition in western American history, a tradition in which I am proud to play a small part: taking one's home seriously . . . and after a spell of wondering why I had grown up in a town that seemed so far from the main course of American history, I ended up taking Banning seriously.
>
> (Limerick 1991: 81–2)

The process of growing up, its memories and imaginings are a part of the wider, more inclusive canvas of a new western history that revised the region 'as many complicated environments' (Limerick 1987: 20) which had so often been simplified or hidden behind the screen of mythology. Pre-dating 'new western history', Wallace Stegner contrasted his child-knowledge and the version of the world he was handed: 'I am the product of the American earth and in nothing quite so much as in the contrast between what I knew through the pores and what I was officially taught' (quoted in West 1989: 260).

In 1996, Richard Maxwell Brown described such autobiographical works as a 'new emotional history of the West' that 'engrave a lesson of courage without illusions . . . [demonstrating] the grassroots western heritage of courage without the disabling illusions that have misled so many into failed and fruitless lives across the western dreamscape' (in Milner 1996: 56, 60). The works he discusses are primarily white American autobiographies, although what he identifies is a trend more established in ethnic writing where official history has ignored or erased groups from its records. Life stories became the space to articulate a counter-history to the legitimized version and present a text 'talking back' to dominant cultural voices. As Maxwell Brown argues, these works, expose illusions through the hidden histories of the West silenced in conventional accounts in a similar way to 'new western history'.

Autobiographies by Anglo-Americans reconstruct the past because the official history has been incomplete and has excluded diverse, personal stories and perpetuated instead myths of power and dominance in need of critique. Toni Morrison explains this from an African-American point of view, arguing that in the slave narratives, written with a specific readership in mind, much was omitted. There was 'no mention of their interior life' and consequently her fiction is concerned with 'memories and recollections', 'the act of the imagination', 'a kind of literary archaeology . . . to reconstruct the world that these remains imply' (1987: 111, 112). Morrison's version of 'inner cultural history' is echoed in Native American Leslie Marmon Silko who believes 'through the stories we hear who we are' with 'remembering and retelling . . . a communal . . . self-correcting process in which listeners were encouraged to speak up . . . [in order to create] a communal . . . not an absolute truth. For them this lived somewhere within the web of differing versions' (Silko 1996: 30–31, 32). Recent white personal histories of the West by writers like Ivan Doig, William Kittredge, Teresa Jordan, Gary Holthaus, Terry Tempest Williams, Kim Barnes, Cyra McFadden, Roxanne Dunbar-Ortiz and others, serve a similar corrective, 'archaeological' purpose. Reviewing experiences of family life in the West becomes a means of reviewing the public histories of America and reflecting upon how those histories have been constructed, perpetuated and embellished. Through the eyes of youth, in particular, such memoirs chart the slippage from the dream-world of the western myth toward a more complex, multiple and often painful recognition of both their own history and the wider history of the nation. In the youthful territory between dream and memory, these texts explore the secret histories of the West as they simultaneously uncover the unspoken histories of family and land. At the intersection of personal and public, these writings of fiction and autobiography and the grey generic area in-between, form a new body of white western representation whose effect is to rememory the West. The child or youth becomes a way of seeing, of looking back, that allows adult writers to step outside the representational norms to explore and rethink their lives in the West and their relationships to a wider America. Ivan Doig describes being a child as like having 'honorary membership with the grown ups' whilst 'standing back and prowling with your ears' (1993: 29) and therefore gaining a view of the world which is a 'pattern of remembered instants so uneven, so gapped and rutted and plunging and soaring' (1978: 10). Doig recognizes the parental controlling vision, like any meta-narrative, is 'uneven . . . gapped and rutted' when looked at anew from another angle of vision. Teresa Jordan terms these gaps 'unconformities' because they force one to see the 'conformities' that construct the established norms and visions of history and family. Through the child's eyes the gaps in 'adult', normalized stories and histories are scrutinized, engaging the reader in counter-memory and alternative voices within and behind the official, dominant history. Doig's own story begins significantly with 'new silence' following the death of his mother, and from this break with dependency he begins his 'remembering' back 'into these oldest shadows for the first sudden edge of it all' (ibid.: 3) Again and again, the child/adolescent stands on the edge, in the border territory of youth, present yet invisible, aware but silenced, attentive but unacknowledged, and from here they observe, report and comment in ways which allow the adult writer to reassess and re-evaluate the voices that have for so long controlled the centre's official history.

   William Kittredge's memoir *Hole in the Sky* (1992) begins with the sixty-year-old author remembering his child 'self', confessing a desire to 'reinhabit . . . himself, to know as that child knew', and 'to be like the child for whom it was so simple to let himself go into affection for what we are'. Voicing a desire for the dream-like patterns of childhood, Kittredge longs to be 'seamlessly wedded to everything', and for 'things to be radiant and permeable' (1992: 3, 8). Yet childhood's radiance is intruded upon by the revelations and knowledges of a world beyond this dream—in his case a world of secrets and lies, of myths and deceptions about his family and the West. Thus, for Kittredge, the dream-world of childhood is like the myths of the West and America itself, in need of revision.

The sub-title of Kim Barnes' memoir *In the Wilderness* (1996) is 'coming of age in unknown country', indicating that, like many similar works, she is concerned with the dual process of growing up personally and in relation to the 'country' itself. However, the easy connection between self and society is problematized, almost as if it rebuts Horace Greeley's 1850 statement, 'Go West, young man, and grow up with the country'. Now the country is as 'unknown' as her own identity and its relation to the world beyond her. The child, once again, is a channel through which myths are encountered and secret histories revealed. Teresa Jordan's *Riding the White Horse Home* (1993), like Kittredge's book, looks back over personal history to understand the forces that constructed her identity and to discover the 'unconformities', that is, those things that don't conform to the usual pattern or expected mythology:

> I think of unconformity as something similar to the white space or break on the page writers sometimes use to leap from one idea to another. Or perhaps an unconformity is like all that hazy history that lies between the legends we have of our ancestors and the realities of our own particular lives.
>
> (Jordan 1994: 9–10)

The 'break' between 'legends' and 'realities' is a liminal territory best charted by youthful protagonists and narrators able, as Jordan puts it, 'to excavate the unconformities that connect my heritage with who I am now', not just to understand herself, but to see how those same forces 'shaped the rural West' too (ibid.: 15–16). This quest for 'knowing' all the 'hazy history' (ibid.), is another call for a 'literary archaeology' to retrieve lost histories and voices to put alongside the dominant mythic ones. Of course, such an excavation is not easy since childhood memories are problematic, as Ivan Doig has explained, it 'is a most queer flame-lit and shadow-chilled time' with parents like 'tribal gods, as old and unarguable and almighty as thunder' (Doig 1978: 10). However, even if unreliable and half-formed, these recollections and histories intervene in dominant discourses, uncover unpleasant truths and hidden histories, and as Morrison has commented about her writing, 'rip that veil drawn over "proceedings too terrible to relate" . . .' which is 'critical for any person who is black, or who belongs to any *marginalized category*, for, historically, we were seldom invited to participate in the discourse even when we were its topic' (Morrison 1987: 110–11; my emphasis). The 'marginalized category' is both the child-as-observer/participant and the untold voices of history they manifest.

Increasingly, white writers have argued, like Kittredge, they 'were enclosed in stories and often couldn't see out . . . driven to repetitively act out certain stories in hopes the enactments might defend us, save us, protect us' (Kittredge 1996: 45, 47). The challenge is new writing that counters the older, privileged stories so westerners can remix and reinvent themselves (ibid.: 5). Childhood memories can tell a 'new story' to counter the archetypal western youth as a symbol of innocence, a 'radically new personality . . . happily bereft of ancestry, untouched and undefiled by the usual inheritances of family and race; an individual standing alone, self-reliant and self-propelling . . .' (Lewis 1955: 5). Ancestry now becomes the focus for memoir, tracing in the family and the community the particular roots of the illusions and the cultural contradictions they perpetuate.

Reviewing the mistreatment of the Native Americans, for example, Kittredge comments 'In Warner Valley we lived surrounded by ghosts, but we forgot' and 'We knew a history filled with omissions, which can be thought of as lies' (1992: 19, 23). Kittredge—echoing 'new western history' —invokes the 'ghosts' of his own forgotten past, and uses them to counter the omissions of public history. In a crucial passage he writes, 'I find myself searching for history out of books and dim rememberances, trying to fit it together in strings which reach from generation to generation, trying to loop myself into lines of significance' (ibid.: 27). The childhood memoir begins this 'loop' by giving voice to and re-examining the 'rememberances' not as nostalgia or triumphalism, but as analysis and critique. From child to adult, Kittredge is witness to the process of westward expansion and destruction, literally growing up and into the land itself:

My people drained the swamps and farmed them, and built roads and fences across the enormous sweep of that country as if they were inscribing their names onto the land. This is ours, they said, we own it. But they didn't, not in any significant way.

(ibid.: 232)

This possessive inscription marked the land with his presence and his memoir becomes a rewriting, reinscribing a different version, a new responsibility for identity and place aimed at the future. Developing alongside new western history's desire for revision and western memoirs' relentless recovery of forgotten stories, many other writers have employed the child as a starting point for reinscription in autobiography, or the symbolic device through which the hidden is revealed to us in fiction.

Montana 1948: 'That sure was the Wild West, wasn't it?'

Larry Watson's *Montana 1948* (1993) dramatizes ideas about the West and history itself, through the eyes of a male child discovering his family's past. Watson's novel has parallels with new western autobiography, but like Morrison, it is fiction that provides 'total access to the unwritten interior life of these people . . . —to fill in the blanks . . . to part the veil that was so frequently drawn' (Morrison 1987: 111, 113). Don DeLillo has written in a similar vein about his novel *Underworld* (1998): 'It is fiction's role to imagine deeply, to follow obscure urges into unreliable regions of experience—child-memoried, existential and outside time . . . Language can be a form of counterhistory' (DeLillo 1998: 4). DeLillo is interested, like Watson, in 'a version of the past that escapes the coils of established history and biography' and which he recovers in 'the small gathered fragments of overheard voices . . . the voices of friends and the barely seen gestures of total strangers—retrieved, remarkably, in the sensuous drenching play of memory' (ibid.). The marginalized child gathers up 'the layerings of memory' normally excluded from mainstream history, into what Michael Fischer has called 'Mosaic Memory' (in Ashley, Gilmore and Peters 1994: 122).

The Prologue to *Montana 1948* is a powerful rumination on history and how it is told and received. It begins with the heady mosaic of childhood memories, 'a series of images . . . vivid lasting' (1996: 11), sounds, smells and other senses analysed as an alternative method of constructing history. The images are 'rapid and tumbled together' in such a way that 'chronological sequence seems wrong' (ibid.: 12) and inadequate:

> Imagine instead a movie screen divided into boxes and panels, each with its own scene, so that one moment can occur simultaneously with another, so no action has to fly off in time, so nothing happens before or after, only

during. That's the way these images coexist in my memory, like the Sioux picture calendars in which the whole year's events are painted on the same buffalo hide, or like a tapestry with every scene woven into the same cloth, every moment on the same flat plane, the summer of 1948.

(ibid.: 12)

The narrator, David Hayden, has lived through an experience for which traditional linear history is an inadequate mode of expression. His must be an alternative history inflected with memory and imagination, not rooted in empiricism, evidence and fact, but full of 'indelible' memories, love and the sense of place. Michel Foucault's genealogy is a more appropriate way of defining David's alternative history, for it means in one sense the examination of ancestral history, but also, 'a field of entangled and confused parchments . . . documents that have been scratched over and recopied many times' (Foucault 1993: 139). Genealogy 'retrieves' histories from 'the most unpromising places' and 'lost events' (ibid.: 155) via 'subjugated knowledges' given no importance in the hierarchies of historical meaning (Foucault 1980: 82). These 'disqualified knowledges' emerge through marginalized, 'lowranking' voices or 'naive knowledges', like those of children, in order to unsettle 'the tyranny of globalising discourses' and introduce critical interventions into the process (ibid.). The child's vision introduces alternatives to the official, 'centralising powers' of an 'adult' dominant discourse. Larry Watson's parallels between the movie screen, the Sioux calendar and the tapestry reject traditional history and show that different sources and ways of telling exist in different cultures, classes and genders, many of which have been disregarded in the obsession for a linear, meta-narratival 'history' that appears to speak for all. For Watson, as for many contemporary writers, historians and artists in the American West, there is no single story to be told, no dominant voice that should command the telling, and no authoritative group that holds sway over all others. Hence, Watson's novel employs the child's consciousness to question many established patterns of behaviour and belief, including history itself.

The child overhears from the edges, collects the fragments thrown away in adult language, which when reconstructed, create an alternative history of family, community and nation. It is the child that is awakened into the complex layers of the adult world and who, in turn, awakens the reader from the dream-world of myth and complacency. The child is no romantic vision of innocence, but rather an outsider constantly at the threshold, always about to become something else, curiously peering over life's borders and bringing into 'consciousness' that which had been repressed to problematize the adult's habitual, forgetful vision. However, this is no reduction of larger issues down to the 'pre-limited terms of the family narrative' (Jameson 1986: 22), but rather a means to connect the secret histories of the family to the wider, ideological movements of history itself.

Watson's novel is poised literally and metaphorically on the borders, with all the sense of possibility and change that the state suggests. It is set alongside an Indian reservation, on 'the western edge of the county', 'barely inside the state's borders', at a time on the edge of the war and on the borders of the 1950s' significant social and cultural change, at the heart of which is a boy, aged 12, 'on the cusp of adolescence' (Watson 1996: 15, 22). Amidst these borders exists David Hayden whose inter-action with Bentrock, Montana and the events of 1948, form the spatial centre of the novel. From here a buried, forbidden knowledge emerges (his uncle's abuse of Indian girls) as a new form of historical fiction, like that written by other marginal groups such as women and African-Americans—creating a new history which includes the personal. The reinvention of autobiographical/historical writing in the American West is a further assault on dominant histories to voice the 'silences' from the margin. Children, like women, are often 'kept away from the scene of action . . . not to be seen or heard . . . [unable to] stray very far from the bounds of home' (Paul in Hunt 1990: 150–1) and so any process of revision must include children's voices as well as women's and other subordinated groups.

Like those autobiographical works with which I began, Watson's fiction is concerned with personal history, memory and 'counter-memory', alongside the conventional, normalized and mythic history of the West. Counter-memory is defined by George Lipsitz as

> a way of remembering and forgetting that starts with the local, the immediate, and the personal . . . with the particular and the specific and then builds outward . . . [It] looks to the past for *the hidden histories excluded from dominant narratives . . . forces revision of existing histories by supplying new perspectives about the past to reframe and refocus dominant narratives purporting to represent universal experience.*
>
> (Lipsitz 1990: 213; my emphases)

Fiction is a source of counter-memory because it exists between history and myth and 'draw[s] upon oral traditions, vernacular speech' as well as showing an interest in 'the concerns of everyday life' (ibid.: 230). The child in fiction can provide just such a counter-memory, naively revealing the unspoken and hidden from within the sealed world of adulthood. Mikhail Bakhtin, writing about forms of the *bildungsroman* (the novel of education) claimed that in one of its most interesting guises it is about 'the process of becoming' within a social context:

> It is no longer man's own private affair. He emerges along with the world and he reflects the historical emergence of the world itself . . . on the border between epochs, at the transition point from one to another. This transition is accomplished in him and through him . . . [It is] the emergence of a new man.
>
> (Bakhtin 1990b: 23)

Hence, the emerging child confronts society as revelation and burden, forcing him/her into a new realm which is always more than personal, containing as it does the secrets of a wider world. The child provides 'new perspectives about the past', a living counter-memory to the privileged and accepted history of the adult world fixed as myth.

Bearing this in mind, it is no surprise that Larry Watson launches *Montana 1948* with his direct assault on historicism and the tenets of conventional history-writing. His novel writes history but in a different way; what Edward Soja, glossing Hayden White, might term 'real-and-imagined'. Soja argues for a new inclusive history 'filled with multiplicities, [on] many different planes of social time, as well as with hidden experiences, undecipherable coding, unexplainable events' (Soja 1996: 175). For Watson, place or location provides the arena for this new exploration of 'telling', hence the novel's specific and precise title. From and through this particular moment the 'movie screen/tapestry/Sioux calendar' opens up to reveal layered history of one small town family as it inter-links with the social-historical patterns of its age and its region—the West. The narrator tells of the events' simultaneous occurrence, not linear, or systematized, but coexisting on the 'same flat plane' where things happen together outside of any obvious privileging or hierarchizing. Soja writes that 'there is a growing awareness of the simultaneity and interwoven complexity of the social, the historical, and the spatial, their inseparability and interdependence' (Soja 1996: 3) influencing how we think about space, history and society. Bakhtin saw this in Dostoevsky's fiction which sought 'to juxtapose and counterpose . . . to see everything as coexisting, to perceive and show all things side by

side and simultaneous, as if they existed in space and not in time . . .'
(Bakhtin 1997: 28). This approach rejects the linear in favour of the
complex, ambiguous and multi-structured, where many things go on
together, as in the emerging perceptions of a child.

Similarly, simultaneity and spatial history enables one to see the
American West as a coexistence of tensions where there are negotiations
and struggles over power and meaning rather than a single, fixed outcome.
As David Hayden simultaneously reaches a personal border and faces the
truth of the shady reality of his own family in *Montana 1948*, Watson
examines the construction of identity and history as intertwined. As we
witness David's subject formation, he *becomes* that history, constructed
around him by what is approved and authorized and what is not. The boy
is, as Bakhtin put it earlier, emerging with the world, but in so doing,
recognizing the disjunctions between what he is supposed to know and
what he actually does. The 'unconformities' in his own family draw
attention to the wider instabilities in history itself, reminding the reader
that history is a series of constructions and representations rather than
some sacred and absolute truth.

Just as David's father rejects 'a nickel-plated Western Colt .45,
something with history and heft' in favour of 'a small .32 automatic,
Italian-made and no bigger than your palm' (Watson 1996: 17), so the
novel resists the traditional, mythic 'history and heft' of the West for
something smaller and more complex. Through the micro-narratives of
the New West, Watson builds a counter-history to the totalizing norms—
as Frederick Jackson Turner's Frontier, as Gunfighter Nation or Virgin
Land. These are dominant, masculinist narratives retold in various media,
gaining immense authority and power against which have emerged smaller
(micro-) stories which 'rather than confirming a monological [one voiced]
conception of truth . . . offer an alternative model of knowledge' (Clayton
1993: 100), akin to Foucault's genealogy. This process is about giving
voice to the 'buried and disguised' (Foucault 1980: 82) which though
present, has been 'disqualified as inadequate or insufficiently elaborated'
(ibid.). These might be seen as 'naive knowledges', like the voices
of children, and therefore unworthy of cultural space, but Foucault argues
that these 'buried, subjugated knowledges' give rise, through 'rude
memory', to a broader history consisting of 'multiplicity . . . struggles . . .
conflicts' (ibid.: 83) which may have remained hidden by the 'unitary body
of theory which would filter, hierarchize and order them in the name of
some true knowledge' (ibid.).

In Watson's novel, as in his later books, *Justice* (1995) and *White*

Crosses (1997), a prominent motif is that of hiddenness and secrets. We are told that David's mother, who 'always held something back' and was a 'little reserved', is suspicious of charm, seeing it as existing 'to conceal some personal defect or lack of substance' (Watson 1996: 44). Similarly, David's father is the local sheriff who kept his gun in a 'locked case', 'never wore his badge' and 'didn't fit [his son's] ideal' of the mythic western man (ibid.: 18, 19). He cannot 'be fully himself' and was 'a man who tried to turn two ways at once' (ibid.: 19, 21)—to his own father's expectations of the old masculinist ideals and those of his wife for a different, 'civilized' life. This is a world of withheld feelings and un-spoken desires, mirroring the wider tensions obfuscated by the dominant (hi)stories of the West itself. Watson's fiction explores the territory opened in Kittredge's work, who wrote: 'Like anybody, we were enclosed in stories and often couldn't see out. We wanted various coherencies to stand as valuable in ultimate ways, worth any defense necessary' (Kittredge 1996: 45).

The Haydens are enclosed in their own 'usual pattern', just as the mythic stories of the Old West, of gunfighters and lawmen, of rugged individuals and stoic determination, enclose them in 'coherencies' that structure and order existence. Yet all that is hidden in this vision— both personal and public—can intrude into the picture and disturb its complacency. These stories are epitomized by Julian Hayden, David's grandfather:

> a dominating man who drew sustenance and strength from controlling others. To him, being the law's agent probably seemed part of a natural progression—first you master the land and its beasts, then you regulate the behavior of men and women.
>
> (Watson 1996: 20)

The Old West is part of a mythic frame that appears 'natural' and eternal to the likes of Julian Hayden, for it has taken on the characteristics of myth, of the Manifest Destiny of white, male dominance and divine right in the West. Stripping these old stories away, Watson brings back the hidden and the repressed through the figure of the child, forcing the Haydens to make choices outside their own psychic jurisdiction and risk the disruption of both family and community. Watson emphasizes ways in which the personal, familial, communal and national histories are all bound up together, and to learn about one is, ultimately, to learn about another.

In a very literal sense, in *Montana 1948*, the law is put under question because the law of the Father is the law— hence the history of self and community are both represented as the Father prefigures the son, and the father as sheriff upholds the community's sense of order and justice. In *Justice* (1995), Watson describes how the younger Frank and Wes (David's uncle and father) felt in relation to their father as sheriff: 'Only when they got out of town, out of the county, out of the jurisdiction, did they feel as though they could be other than the sons of Julian Hayden' (1995: 16). The law of their father, or patriarchy, is inscribed in them and determines their actions within the boundaries of his jurisdiction, but the desire to step outside those boundaries is clear for it suggests 'they could be other'.

Similarly, David Hayden's world is inscribed by his father, grandfather (Julian), and by the inheritance of a mythic, masculinist West, but the lure of the 'other' is central to the action of *Montana 1948*. The child David— who 'was never sure how to behave'—is caught between the small town respectability of Bentrock, 'social order, good manners, the chimed schedules of school and church . . . the rule-makers, the order-givers, the law-enforcers', and his desire for 'wildness' (ibid.: 22). Wildness here means to be beyond 'jurisdiction' and 'unmalleable' (ibid.: 24) within the controlled social order he resents. Typically, this is a familiar desire in youth literature; to exist beyond parental and communal discourse as it constructs and shapes the subject-child. Ironically, David's journey is toward some new 'law' or jurisdiction, prompted by the 'secret knowledge' (ibid.: 22) of his community and family—revealed as fragments, half-hidden rumours and overheard conversations which unsettle the cosy, small townism of Bentrock. David is destined to be constructed by dark knowledges that he cannot escape for they will determine so much of his life to come.

David is a child, like Ivan Doig, 'prowling with [his] ears' (Doig 1993: 29), over-hearing the muffled conversations of the adult community revealing its 'unconformities'. Watson invents a focalizer-child-detective-historian who gathers up these snippets and remnants—'I explored; I scavenged . . .' (ibid.: 23)—in order to construct the secret knowledge he senses is all around him. This is exactly the role of the radical historian as described by De Certeau:

> He or she works in the margins . . . becomes a prowler. In a society
> gifted at generalization, endowed with powerful centralizing strategies, the

historian moves in the direction of the frontiers . . . going back to . . . all
these zones of silence.

(De Certeau 1988: 79)

The child becomes the quasi-historian 'situated in places of transit, where
"borderline", "borrowed", or "rejected" phenomena can be perceived',
acting against the 'powerful centralizing strategies' that would define a
particular story as the true and only version of events (ibid.). In 'going
back to the zones of silence', David, as adult narrator, enters the realm of
childhood in order to retrieve the memories that haunt and shape his life.
Ironically, the adult-historian-narrator who we are told has succumbed to
the social norms of what history is, recalls an earlier lesson, as a child, of
what history might be in a fuller, more complex sense.

The literal and metaphorical basements of Bentrock produce untold
knowledge for David: Frenchy's 'fat, toothless old Indian woman whom
anyone could have sex with for two dollars' (ibid.: 24–5), Marie's naked-
ness, his Uncle's crimes, imprisonment and suicide. Below the town's
surface percolates racism, sexism and class hatreds that Watson's micro-
narratives raise up through the child David; such as when he first
overhears the dark truth of his uncle's abuse of Indian girls: 'I flinched and
a part of me said leave, get away, run, now before it's too late, before you
hear something you cant unhear. Before everything changes' (ibid.: 47).

David's 'coherent' life is unsettled by the intrusion of secret knowledge
into his safe, lighted chamber of dreams, myths and expectations.
Suddenly, the shattering entry of an overheard fragment contradicts and
challenges the foundations of security and order, and 'charming, affable
Uncle Frank was gone for good' (ibid.: 49). The family, who 'were as close
as Mercer County came to aristocracy' are about to be undone by
'perversion, scandal, family division, and decay' (ibid.: 126–7). Watson's
use of personal history, of history from below, punctures the 'official'
family history with its public face and gloss just as alternative histories can
be seen as intruding into the neat flow of accepted public, authorized
history. David is positioned as an outsider by the words 'Not in front of
the boy' (ibid.: 39–40); sheltered by his parents from a hidden language
that gradually emerges bringing with it new knowledge; 'Rape. Breasts.
Penis. These were words I never heard my mother use—never' (ibid.: 48).
Suddenly, his mother, a beacon of civilization, 'who hated talk about
bodily functions even more than she hated swearing' (ibid.: 70), is using
language that ushers in transgressive family history, making David aware
of a fuller picture that he 'didn't want to see' (ibid.:53), and making him a

secret historian reading the signs for the reader. Once the boundary is crossed, the apparently stable world-view is unsettled by other histories long repressed: 'You know Frank's always been partial to red meat. He couldn't have been any older than Davy when Bud caught him down in the stable with that little Indian girl' (ibid.: 72). Once punctured, the authorized version of history is destabilized and the ultimate result is a world turned upside down: 'This county is going to get torn up over this . . . We'll be a long time coming back from this' (ibid.: 145). The border-child, always on the outside of official history, at the edge of things, seen but not heard, becomes the ironic harbinger of this shattering otherness. However, David's subjugated knowledge crashes into the enclosed, hermetic realm of familial and communal history to remind us of all that is excluded and to question the authority of masculine subjectivity.

David's emergence, his education, involves a series of lessons about family and community, race, sex, gender and death. For example, Native Americans are patronized by whites, prejudiced against and ultimately seen as dispensable in the attitudes and institutionalized racism deeply embedded in Bentrock. His own father, a decent man, 'simply held them in low regard . . . [as] lazy, superstitious, and irresponsible' (ibid.: 34). Sexuality is a significant part of the border territory David exists within; attracted by the sight of the naked Marie Little Soldier stepping from the shower, suppressing thoughts about his Aunt Gloria (ibid.: 77), over-hearing sex between Gloria and Frank and even finding himself 'stirred . . . sexually' by the thought of his uncle abusing one of his class-mates (ibid.: 129). All of these intense moments are signs of the disintegration of David's safe, domestic, childhood world and mark the passage to the darker adult realm beyond. As he feels himself stirred he 'didn't want to feel any of what [he] was feeling . . . [he] hugged [his] sack of groceries and ran home' (ibid.). The child retreats from sexuality and forbidden desire to the familiar world of groceries and home, and yet there can no longer be comfort there since it is within the home itself, in its basement, that Frank is imprisoned. For David, personal and public history are turned upside down, an idea Watson articulates in a stereotypically western moment of violent revelation for the boy as he rides out to kill birds on the range. The confused desires, revelations and anger at the 'events, the discoveries, the secret of the past few days' (ibid.: 81) are vented as David kills a magpie, traditionally signifying sorrow, and feels 'something new' as he ponders over his kill:

Looking in the dead bird's eye, I realized that these strange, unthought-
of connections—sex and death, lust and violence, desire and degradation
—are there, there, deep in even a good heart's chambers.

(ibid.: 82)

A conventional act of masculine, western action is transformed here. In a
gesture of repression, shocked by this revelation, David buries the dead
bird with its Poe-like eye 'just enough to dull the sheen of its feathers'
(ibid.). For he has seen in his 'good heart's chambers' and in the heart of
his community's history, a dark, unconscious 'uncanniness', where the
uncanny is 'something repressed that recurs' (Freud 1990: 363). However,
as Freud argues, 'this uncanny is in reality nothing new or alien, but
something which is familiar and old established in the mind and which has
become alienated from it only through the process of repression' (ibid.:
364). Within David's family, within his house, both his uncle's corruption
and the willingness of others to collude in that corruption has been
revealed. The scene that began with David's desires and his violent killing
of the bird, ends with him lining up his unloaded gun to shoot Uncle
Frank talking with his father—'brothers in posture and attitude' (ibid.:
83). For a moment, David speculates on whether killing Frank would solve
'everyone's problems', as if in his mind he would be making the ultimate
act of repression, like burying the magpie's eye in the earth, but perhaps
because of his father's closeness he holds back and carries his feelings back
to the house.

Yet David's knowledge and feelings cannot be suppressed; it is the
uncanny of history, the return of the repressed, like 'death in our house' as
he calls it (ibid.: 95). The home was important to westerners: 'A house
[was where] pioneers expressed themselves most clearly . . . [it] epitomized
the intentions of adults, including what they hoped to pass on to their
young' (West 1989: 69). Yet, for David, the home is made unhomely, as if
'There always seemed to be a sound—a whisper—on the edge of your
hearing, something you couldn't quite make out' (Watson 1996: 95). As
De Certeau puts it,

what was excluded re-infiltrates the place of its origins—now the present's
'clean' . . . place. It resurfaces, it troubles, it turns the present's feeling of
being 'at home' into an illusion, it lurks . . . within the walls of the
residence . . . it inscribes the law of the other.

(De Certeau 1997: 4)

The house's familial space becomes the focus of David's collision with hidden history, as the boy moves from the margins of the story to its centre with the revelation that he had seen Frank leaving the house after Marie's death. Suddenly, from passive over-hearer, David is centre stage being listened to by his parents: 'Shh, Gail. Let David tell it', says his father (ibid.: 97). No longer repressed, David lets out 'the secret . . . held, the fearful knowledge' (ibid.: 88) and becomes bound in to his uncle's fate. Curiously, in finding his own voice and articulating the hidden history, David unsettles the order of his own family and disturbs long-held notions of law and stability.

With his uncle literally imprisoned in the basement laundry room, clean, domestic space is contaminated by crime and the symbolic division is a stark reminder for David:

> that the floor beneath my feet suddenly seemed less solid, like those sewer grates you daringly walked over that gave a momentary glimpse of the dark, flowing depths always waiting below.
>
> (ibid.: 144–5)

All 'usual pattern' (ibid.: 33, 106) and order is broken and the righteous, wholesome, family image of the West is shattered by the intrusion of the 'dark, flowing depths' associated with the sewer in David's mind. The social law of the family and the judicial law of the community have been broken and, increasingly, order becomes chaotic, with relationships strained or in tatters and old tensions bubbling to the surface. Julian Hayden's disapproval of Wesley's arrest of Frank culminates in a verbal battle in which Julian's disrespect for Wesley is apparent, followed by a physical battle between Julian's men and the Hayden household. Using a mock western showdown, Watson reverses roles and has David's timid, civilized mother arm herself to fend off the men coming to free the outlaw Frank. Truly, this is a changing world turned upside down to the extent that David momentarily imagines himself as part of a 'new family' without his father (ibid.: 140). Facing the familial unconscious, the dark unspoken past, David's house takes on a strange silence: 'stunned, still vibrating, the way the air feels in the silence immediately following a gunshot' (ibid.: 148). However, all the community are involved: 'in the houses up and down the block—human ears were tuned to our frequency, listening to our silence and wondering . . .' (ibid.). The once aristocratic family are exposed and vulnerable, divided by the reality of the past risen up and confronting their complacency.

Watson uses the family narrative as a microcosm of the western story itself; the complacent, enclosed white family history locks out all that it cannot or will not deal with from its past—Native American removal, ethnic and gender bigotry, environmental destruction and land possession —and here we see it all breaking apart:

> I suddenly felt a great distance between us, as if, at that moment, each of us stood on our own little square of flooring with open space surrounding us. Too far apart to jump to anyone else's island, we could only stare at each other the way my mother stared at my father.
>
> (ibid.: 151)

The effects upon the family are continually expressed in spatial images, reminding the reader of the dissipation of family space and the explosion of its enclosing narratives: it 'signalled such a breach in our lives, a chasm permanently dividing what we were from what we could never be again' (ibid.: 159). Watson's story blows apart the 'homeliness' of the (bourgeois) family and forever questions in David's mind (and the reader's) the ideologies embedded in America's traditional defining notion of itself. The core of 'family values' that have scripted American national identity are destabilized and within that, the idea of individual subjectivity and centredness brought under question.

Ironically, with the suicide of Frank, the novel shows how history continues to create secrets, for nothing is, finally, revealed about his crimes or his suicide. These 'postmortem cover-ups' (ibid.: 166) save the public dignity of the Haydens but cannot heal the family's inner strife, the 'unbridgeable gulf between us' (ibid.: 167), and they are forced to leave their home and cross the border out of Montana to North Dakota feeling 'dispossessed' (ibid.: 169). In the epilogue to the novel, David tells how he became a history teacher whose personal experience has taught him much. In bringing together the public and the personal he finds

> history endlessly amusing, knowing, as I do, that the record of any human community might omit stories of sexual abuse, murder, suicide . . . Who knows—perhaps any region's most dramatic, most sensational stories were not played out in the public view but were confined to small, private places.
>
> (ibid.: 170)

Through uncovering his family secrets, David has learned not to believe in 'the purity and certainty of the study of history' and that no 'historical documents' can tell the whole story (ibid.: 170). For the West is a space made of many different histories, personal and public, and those beyond both—'whatever lurid and comical fantasy my imagination might concoct' (ibid.). However, Watson's final twist is to have David admit that this revelation about history is itself a secret hidden from his students to whom he pretends 'that the text tells the truth, whole and unembellished' (ibid.). Finally, there is no emancipation from the norms of historical processes, for the cycle of closure and silence appears maintained. For the novel that begins on the borders of possibility ends with silence, refuting the hopes of radical educators like Henry Giroux, that teachers themselves might become 'border-crossers' who make 'available for their students those narratives, local histories, and subjugated memories that have been excluded and marginalized in dominant renditions of history' (in Giroux, Lankshear *et al.* 1996: 51).

Fortunately, for the readers of Watson's novel, as opposed to David Hayden's students, we have seen and been shown the different levels that constitute history and have been educated, like the narrator, into knowing that there can be no universal or absolutist version, only plural and contesting histories, only different stories. At one point in the middle of the novel, David's father comments about his brother's history, 'It can't be undone. That's passed. That's over and done' (Watson 1996: 85), and this could stand as a comment on history itself. The novel suggests, through the figure of David Hayden, a strange duality in its treatment of history. On one hand, history has to be revised, allowed to speak through its many forgotten voices, and yet, simultaneously, it seeks to withhold and smother those stories with established official versions. Perhaps this is what the novel's opening comments about recording history on a split screen means; that the reality is of a perpetual struggle between knowledge and suppression, between silence and speech, between myths and realities. After all, a screen both shows and hides at the same time.

The final visions of the novel are a series of contrasting, remembered moments; his family wracked by the secret it has kept and their suppressed anger at the consequences, and a dream-like memory of David at play with two Indians, Marie and Ronnie. In the latter moment, David, 'unhappy with [his] general lack of success at team sports', decides to improve his game with practice. The nature of team sports in the West was significant for it was 'a ritual . . . crucial to the children's search for their community . . . it rewarded players who knew each other well, worked together smoothly . . . It embodied a cooperative individualism . . . an achievement culture writ large' (West 1989: 110, 111). It is also a ritual of masculine identity formation. However, David doesn't feel comfortable in such a 'community' or with such an 'identity', and instead recalls an alternative game played with Marie and Ronnie: 'It was a game, yet it had no object and no borders of space or time or regulation. It was totally free-form . . . I felt, for that brief span, as though I was part of a family, a family that accepted me for myself and not my blood or birthright' (ibid.: 173). In this fantasy play, David moves temporarily outside the dual constructions of history and identity, beyond the rituals of an ideal masculinity, an American co-operative individualism, outside 'real' family and the burdens that all carry, into an undivided space with 'no borders of space or time or regulation'. The typical *bildungsroman* asserts the formation of the adult through the child by a process of subject construction with David socialized through family and community into his maculine role. However, in David's last dream-memory, he rejects the tenets of bourgeois subjectivity and finds a space with Marie and Ronnie that exists beyond the confines of his parents' world. The game and 'how we played, had its origin in Ronnie and Marie's Indian heritage' (Watson 1996: 173) and a stronger feeling of tribal connectedness, not within a bourgeois family structure, but something broader and more integrated with the place itself. As David comments, he was 'accepted' for being himself and not because he was part of the pattern of the Hayden family, with its 'blood or birthright' (ibid.). This is similar to Jameson's idea of 'anonymity', by which he means 'not the loss of personal identity . . . but the association of one individual with a host of other names and other concrete individuals . . . a new conception of collectivity' (in Gugelberger 1996: 186). Jameson connects this anonymity with 'the passing of the older psychic subject, in the return to storytelling and a literature of wishes and of daily life, and in the experience of History "anonymously" rather than under the aegis of great men' (ibid.: 189–90). On one level, this is very close to the novel's prologue and the alternative visions of history and storytelling, but, of course, David Hayden cannot remain in a world with 'no borders' and has to live his life in the knowledge of two worlds—the world he has and the world he desires. As the narrator, he remains caught between the two worlds, on a border as ever, constructed by the events of his own life, aware of the hidden history, but unable to teach it to his new bourgeois subjects being prepared for life as part of a familiar pattern, a cultural master-narrative.

Don DeLillo has written that it is 'lost history that becomes the detailed weave of novels. Fiction is all about reliving things. It is our second chance' (DeLillo 1998: 4). However, although Watson's novel reminds us of the complexities of history, its 'genealogy', and its existence in the secret heart of the present, the 'second chance' and its implication of emancipation, appears not to be the lived reality for David Hayden, a man who, although 'awakened' by his youthful knowledge, seems trapped on the borders, within the endless deceits of history and subjectivity, unable and unwilling to break the spell of the past or the powerful discourses that surround him. As Kittredge put it, 'For a time I wondered if there were secrets nobody told me, thinking I was a child and wouldn't understand. Now I know there were many secrets they didn't even tell each other' (Kittredge 1992: 61). In arriving at this recognition in a 'coming of age' novel, Watson weaves a painful story about the loss of personal and cultural innocence revealing much *en route* about how history is constructed and recorded. There is no simple division between history and myth for both are real and imagined, and revisionism does not lead to a neat, new vision to replace the old one. Finally, the novel leaves David on the border able to see the significance of both sides and all the places in between, and dramatizes, through the child, what Fredric Jameson has argued, 'History is what hurts' (Jameson 1986: 102).

Notes

1   Gene Autry quoted in Patricia Nelson Limerick, 'The Shadows of Heaven Itself' in *The Atlas of the New West*, New York: W. W. Norton, 1997, p. 161.
2   Ivan Doig, *Heart Earth* (1993).
3   Jerome McGann, 'The Third World of Criticism' in K. Ryan (ed.) *New Historicism and Cultural Materialism: A Reader*, London: Edward Arnold, 1996, p. 168.
4   Watson 1997: 63.

Bibliography

Aram Veeser, H. (ed.) (1989) *The New Historicism*, London: Routledge.
Bakhtin, Mikhail (1990a) *The Dialogic Imagination*, Austin: University of Texas Press.
——(1990b) *Speech Genres and other late essays*, Austin: University of Texas Press.
——(1997) *Problems of Dostoevsky's Poetics*, Minneapolis: University of Minnesota Press.

Campbell, N. and Kean, A. (1997) *American Cultural Studies*, London: Routledge.
Clayton, Jay (1993) *The Pleasures of Babel*, New York: Oxford University Press.
Cronon, W., Miles, G. and Gitlin, J. (eds) (1992) *Under an Open Sky: Rethinking America's Western Past*, New York: W. W. Norton.
De Certeau, Michel ([1975], 1988) *The Writing of History*, New York: Columbia University Press.
——([1986] 1997) *Heterologies: Discourse on the Other*, Minneapolis: University of Minnesota.
DeLillo, Don (1998) 'The moment the Cold War began', in *The Observer Review*, 4 January, pp. 3–4.
Doig, Ivan (1978) *This House of Sky: Landscapes of the Western Mind*, San Diego: Harcourt Brace Jovanovich.
——(1993) *Heart Earth: A Memoir*, New York: Atheneum.
Fischer, M.M.J. (1994) 'Autobiographical voices (1,2,3) and mosaic memory: experimental sondages in the (post)modern world', in K. Ashley, L. Gilmore and G. Peters (eds) *Autobiography and Postmodernism*, Amherst: University of Massachusetts Press.
Foucault, Michel (1980) *Power/Knowledge: Selected Interviews and other Writings 1972–77*, London: Harvester Wheatsheaf.
——([1977] 1993) *Language, Counter-memory, Practice: Selected Essays and interviews*, Ithaca: Cornell University Press.
Freud, Sigmund (1990) 'The Uncanny', in *Art and Literature*, Harmondsworth: Penguin.
Giroux, H., Lankshear, C., McLaren, E. and Peters, M. (1996) *Counternarratives: Cultural Studies and Critical Pedagogies in Postmodern Spaces*, London: Routledge.
Gugelberger, G. (ed.) (1996) The Real Thing: Testimonial Discourse and Latin America, Durham: Duke University Press.
Jameson, Fredric ([1981] 1986) *The Political Unconscious: Narrative as Socially Symbolic Act*, London: Routledge.
——(1992/3) 'On literary and cultural import-substitution in the Third World: the case of the testimonio', in G. Gugelberger, (1996) op. cit.
Jordan, Teresa ([1993] 1994) *Riding the White Horse Home*, New York: Vintage.
Kittredge, William (1987) *Owning It All*, St Paul: Graywolf Press.
——([1992] 1993) *Hole in the Sky: A Memoir*, New York: Vintage.
——(1996) *Who Owns the West?* San Francisco: Mercury House.
Lawrence, D.H. (1977) *Studies in Classic American Literature*, Harmondsworth: Penguin.
Lewis, R.W.B. (1955) *The American Adam*, Chicago: University of Chicago Press.
Limerick, Patricia Nelson ([1987] 1988) *The Legacy of Conquest: The Unbroken Past of the American West*, New York: W. W. Norton.
——(1995) 'Common cause? Asian American history and Western American history, in Gary Y. Okihiro, *et al. Privileging Positions: The Sites of Asian American Studies*, Pullman: Washington State University Press.

Lipsitz, George (1990) *Time Passages*, Minneapolis: University of Minnesota Press.

Lowenthal, D. (1985) *The Past Is A Foreign Country*, Cambridge: Cambridge University Press.

Maxwell Brown, R. (1996) 'Courage without illusions' in C. Milner, *A New Significance: Re-envisioning the History of the American West*, New York: Oxford University Press.

Milner, C. (ed.) (1996) *A New Significance: Re-envisioning the History of the American West*, New York: Oxford University Press.

Morrison, Toni (1987) 'The site of memory', in W. Zinsser (ed.), *Inventing the Truth: The Art and Craft of Memoir*, Boston: Houghton Mifflin.

Paul, Lissa (1990) 'Enigma variations: what feminist theory knows about children's literature', in Peter Hunt (1990) *Children's Literature: The Development of Criticism*, London: Routledge.

Rich, Adrienne (1987) *Blood, Bread and Poetry: Selected Prose 1979–85*, London: Virago.

Robertson, James Oliver (1980) *American Myth American Reality*, New York: Hill and Wang.

Robinson, Forrest (ed.) (1997) *The New Western History: The Territory Ahead*, Tucson: University of Arizona Press.

Silko, Leslie Marmon (1996) *Yellow Woman and the Beauty of the Spirit*, New York: Simon and Schuster.

Slotkin, Richard (1973) *Regeneration Through Violence*, Middletown: Wesleyan University Press.

Soja, Edward (1996) *Thirdspace*, Oxford: Blackwell.

Watson, Larry ([1993] 1996) *Montana 1948*, London: Pan Books.

——(1995) *Justice*, New York: Washington Square Press.

——(1997) *White Crosses*, London: Michael Joseph.

West, Elliot (1989) *Growing Up With The Country*, Albuquerque: University of New Mexico Press.

Worster, Donald (1992) *Under Western Skies: Nature and History in the American West*, New York: Oxford University Press.

SEVEN

'Teensomething': American Youth Programming in the 1990s

Simon Philo

In her book *Defining Visions: Television and the American Experience since 1945*, Mary Ann Watson writes:

> Television's most transforming power has been to provide social scripts for post-war America. Television has been the primary means of socialisation for Baby Boomers and their progeny. From the home screen they've derived lessons about what society expects from them and notions about and of what they expect from society. [. . .] The national psyche has been permeated—in both obvious and discreet ways—by television's defining visions.
>
> (Watson 1998: 266)

As David Marc concurs, 'the lives of the vast majority of Americans born since the defeat of the Axis forces have been accompanied by a continuing electronic paratext of experience' (Marc 1996: 135), with television functioning as a 'primary delivery system offering broad ranges of representational and presentational programming' (ibid.: 135–6). For many commentators, acknowledging television's key role in socializing viewers brings with it inevitable concerns over the content of its 'scripts'. Predictably, concern has been registered most forcibly in relation to television's perceived impact upon the hearts and minds of the nation's youth. There has not been a great deal of academic work devoted to the study of television specifically tailored for adolescent viewers. In fact, what little there has been has mined that 'well-worn area of young people and moral panics' (Oswell 1998: 36). Watson's fears, for example, concerning the malign effects of contemporary TV's 'scripts' on impressionable young minds recall the hysteria witnessed in the 1950s, when television first entered the majority of American homes and it became clear that the westerns and crime series that clogged those nascent prime-time schedules were attracting a sizeable young audience. As public concern over juvenile delinquency peaked in the mid-1950s, a Congressional committee headed by Senator Estes Kefauver was convened to investigate its possible causes. The investigation centred on three likely areas of influence within the mass media—film, comic books and television. In the case of the latter, shows were monitored, expert witnesses were called and numerous academic reports read. Despite the fact that no hard, causal evidence could be found to prove that television led directly to delinquency—most experts identifying the quality of home life as the main cause—the findings published in August 1955 argued that television was potentially more injurious to impressionable young minds than either movies or comics. Since it was readily available to the nation's teenagers, who already watched an average of four hours every day, Senator Robert Hendrickson spoke for his fellow committee members when he concluded that: 'television is perhaps the most powerful force man has yet devised for planting and spreading ideas' (in Spring 1992: 185).

Forty years on, Mary Ann Watson writes with some horror that 'more than two thirds' of American teens surveyed in 1995 'agreed that television shaped their values' (Watson 1998: 125). Yet, whilst Watson finds this a 'shocking statistic' in the context of what she identifies as a decline in 'responsible television', she clearly ignores the potentially constructive and instructive function many of today's teen shows perform (ibid.: 125). Far from witnessing television's major contribution to the so-called 'dumbing down' of American youth, might we be seeing—in the case of the teen dramas discussed in this chapter at least—something akin to the opposite effect? One criticism frequently levelled at *Dawson's Creek*, for example, is that its characters employ the kind of sophisticated vocabulary that in reality high school teenagers simply do not possess or employ. Notwithstanding debates over the accuracy of such criticism, surely there is—at the very least—a case to be made for the potentially instructive value of weekly exposure to long words and difficult concepts? To further reassure the likes of Watson, closer inspection might appear to reveal that youth TV in the 1990s is rather safe. For although self-definition remains a vital concern in dramas which position teens at the very heart of their constructed world, American screen-teens are almost exclusively voiced by adult writers. Therefore, it is not surprising to discover that many of these TV texts exhibit a tendency towards 'responsible' discourses that many critics overlook in their rather selective analyses. Despite the poses that many TV teens strike and the rhetoric they might occasionally spout, one often finds that a touching—though not necessarily Victorian—moralism, faith in the future, and teen-typical fusion of idealism and pragmatism prevail over nihilism, cynicism and despair. Echoing Mark Twain's description of Tom Sawyer, youth TV is by and large then crammed full of non-threatening, 'rightly constructed' boys and girls. It is replete with 'sanctioned rebels' for the TV age. Like Jim Stark in *Rebel Without A Cause*, many are redeemer-conformists on a mission to 'clean up' the adult world before they can fully enter it.

Ostensibly wise beyond their years, typically self-obsessed, and frequently prone to spouting psycho-babble at the slightest provocation, these are some of the most [pseudo-]sophisticated teenagers in American TV history. Of course, it is perhaps not altogether surprising to find that small screen representations of teens should be so sensible. If one looks at the set of imperatives which determine the shape and scope of television output and the centrifugal force this exerts on material and meanings, then it is surprising that shows are able to find the time and space to offend. The hotchpotch of commercial, artistic and moral pressures which impact upon the programme-making process work to make television the most risk-conscious of all cultural media. As a result, contemporary teendramas like *My So-Called Life*, *Dawson's Creek* and *Party of Five* are distinguished by witty, literate scripts that breathe life into bright, communicative teenagers, who are the antithesis of the rarely seen sullen, uncommunicative outcasts so feared by parents and educators. Responding to criticism which objected to the fact the characters in *Dawson's Creek* were too good-looking and well-spoken to be believed, one reviewer urged anyone who had 'a problem' with this and who would 'rather watch unattractive, inarticulate youngsters' to 'go rent *Kids*' (Fretts 1998b: web). Ever willing to analyse, dissect and explain their thoughts and deeds, the most irritating thing about today's small-screen-teens could well be that they do not shut up. Whilst *Dawson's Creek*'s Joey Potter claims that she is 'so sick and tired of talking all the time', this realization does nothing to stem the flow of words which tends to characterize these dialogue-engorged dramas.

Youth Must Be Served

The practice of tailoring shows to specific audiences had arguably begun in the 1970s, but it was not until the late 1980s that the networks began focusing their energies and attention on capturing 'the hearts and minds (and brand loyalties) of those most elusive of all TV viewers: teenagers' (Mahler 1989: 10). The arrival on the scene of Rupert Murdoch's Fox network, with its deliberate targeting of a much younger core audience, undoubtedly contributed to the increasing ghetto-ization of US TV precipitated in the late 1970s by the arrival of VCRs and greater viewer choice available via the proliferation of cable TV channels. The combined effect of these had resulted in a dramatic drop in audience share for the three major networks (ABC, NBC, CBS), and forced them into examining the nature of programming which had until this point been driven by a desire to capture the broadest possible audience. As their combined audience share dipped from 90 per cent to a figure nearer to 50 per cent, the so-called Big Three networks looked to follow Fox's example and target more sharply defined, but potentially lucrative demographic bands.[1] With the emergence of 'satellite and cable television [programmers] no longer define[d] youth as a point in the schedule, but as niche markets with their own particular channels' (Oswell 1998: 45). In the 1990s, Rob Owen has observed that 'TV's demographic dial is set for youth and that is unlikely to change' (Owen 1997: 204).

Fox declared its intention to go after the youth market from the moment it began broadcasting in 1986. Andy Fessell, Fox Vice President for Research and Marketing in the late 1980s, stated that the network would work assiduously to appeal to the 18–34 demographic, and this policy had been so successful that by 1993 the average age of the Fox viewer was just 29 years old.[2] In its first full season, Fox scheduled the teen police drama *21 Jump Street* (starring a pre-movie stardom Johnny Depp) in a clearly signalled, and ultimately successful, attempt to draw younger viewers to the channel. Up until this point, American television had all but ignored the dramatic needs of adolescents. Even Mary Ann Watson is forced to admit that pre-Fox youth programming could be best described as 'goofy' (Watson 1998: 44), with teens 'only seen on TV as part of a family sitcom unit' (ibid.: 49).

Historically, teen audiences have always proved difficult to reach, capture and retain. This is a group that has traditionally spent less time watching TV than any other section of the population.[3] Searching for an explanation, programmers and media analysts concluded that the principal reason for this was that adolescent viewers simply could not identify with the on-screen teens mainstream shows set before them. As David Oswell points out:

> The relationship between youth and television is [. . .] an unhappy one. Teenagers have been caught in a double-bind. On the one hand the construction of television as domestic and familial has meant that young people have had little desire to stay at home and watch. Attempts by television producers to escape this problem have always fallen short of the 'real thing'. And on the other hand, those teenagers who have stayed at home watching television have been constructed as addicts and pathological.
>
> (Oswell 1998: 45)

TV's traditional lack of appeal to teenagers, then, is largely attributable to the fact that it both represents and symbolizes family authority which many adolescents instinctively rebel against—'an implicit rejection of family order accompanies the search for sexual identity, and television, as a centre of family life, must bear a share of adolescent resentment' (Marc 1996: 137).

However, Fox's highest-rated pre-*Simpsons* show proved very popular with this previously ill-served audience, who connected with the somewhat implausible but apparently fact-based premise of four young police officers going undercover in high schools to root out teen crime. Described by *TV World* as 'fearless and uncondescending in portraying contemporary issues that face teens [such as] arson, teen prostitution, gang vandalism, child abuse, teen runaways and cocaine' (in Paterson and Thompson 1996: 20), *21 Jump Street* apparently took its responsibilities seriously enough to follow up these issue-led episodes with information on relevant toll-free helplines—an innovative feature replicated by Fox's next and, to date, biggest teen drama success, *Beverley Hills 90210*.

David Marc argues that one positive side-effect of the 'decline of the three-network hegemony' has been an increased 'literacy' in programming. This has come about because catering for smaller, more homogeneous audiences 'inspires frankness [and] a form of truth [. . .] which usually makes for better drama'. Thus, in contrast to the days before narrow-casting, when '[a]t the peak of network dominance the problem was always the same: get more viewers', the late 1980s and 1990s have seen the 'compromises of least objectionability yield to the strong metaphors that are possible when a preacher speaks to the converted'

(Marc 1997: 136). Good news, then, for America's adolescent viewers. However, whilst media critic and Gen-X champion Rob Owen has sought to credit the fact that 'television today is better than it has ever been' to the 'discerning tastes of [younger viewers] who will not settle for the same old shows' (Owen 1997: xi), youth programming in particular has undoubtedly benefited from a combination of institutional, technological and economic shifts that have shaken up US television in the past fifteen to twenty years.[4]

One of the biggest hits with American teen audiences in the 1990s has been Fox's drama *Beverley Hills 90210*. First aired in October 1990 and produced by Aaron Spelling—the man responsible for adult shows like *Dallas* and the *Love Boat*—*90210* arguably 'jump-started the whole youth ensemble drama trend' (Owen 1997: 76). Whilst its glamorous setting and glossy production values might have put off many, closer inspection revealed that here was a show which extended the limited thematic range of teen-centric dramas. In the face of almost inevitable critical opprobrium, *90210* proved itself to be 'more than just a show about the wealthy and winsome' (Wax 1991: 37). By-passing the soapy sheen cast by perfect smiles, faultless skin and a Californian sun that never set, many young viewers discovered that—much like *21 Jump Street* before it—unlikely settings did not necessarily preclude an engagement with relevant teen issues and concerns. Executive producer Charles Rosin had intended the show to stress the sheer 'complexity of teenage life' (ibid.: 37); and, as Douglas Durden agreed, it appeared to have largely achieved what its creators set out to do: 'Despite its exclusive zip code, *90210* began its career as a realistic look at teenagers from the perspective of teenagers' (in Owen 1997: 73).

In a 1993 piece in the e-journal *Bad Subjects*, academic Crystal Kile reported with a mixture of exasperation and barely disguised disdain that:

> well over 80% of [her] students' essays about the series could be condensed into three sentences: 'I can totally identify with *Beverley Hills 90210*. It is the only show on television that really addresses the issues facing young people in America today. It is not like *Saved By the Bell*, it is an important show because it is so realistic.
>
> (Kile 1993: web)

Kile was dismayed that classroom debates about the show invariably revolved around its realism. This in spite of her frequent attempts to stress the fact that 'the metaphoric real world displayed on TV does not display the real world, but displaces it' (ibid.). Her students, she lamented, simply did not 'get' that *90210* reflects symbolically the structure of values and relationships beneath the surface' (ibid.), and that ultimately such values are those of a conservative and presumably adult mainstream. Whilst she is probably correct in arguing that the show engages in such ideological work, in her rush to condemn she fails to 'read' as a teen viewer might. For example, the very utopian drive that lies at the heart of *90210*—what Kile calls its 'deep yet blank nostalgia for the kinder, gentler Californian youth cult mythos of the late 1950s and early 1960s' (ibid.)—is arguably a variant strain of that desire for the comfort and securities of the past found in so many youth texts, and clearly resonates here for precisely this reason.

For some members of its non-teen audience, the show served as a useful teaching prop, becoming popular with both parents and educators who employed episodes 'to jump-start talks about sex, drug and alcohol abuse, AIDS and teen pregnancy' (Wax 1991: 37). Such admittedly anecdotal evidence suggests that it functioned as instructive text—a role at odds with Mary Ann Watson's assessment of the series as symptomatic of 'the tempestuous bed-hopping and dirty talk' that was the 'hall mark of the Fox network in the 90s' (Watson 1998: 123). Watson argues that the show actively endorsed teen promiscuity in giving 'the clear impression that the cool kids in big school were having sex' (ibid.: 121), in the process exerting harmful pressure on young viewers by highlighting the embarrassment felt by characters in the programme who were not yet sexually active. Yet, whilst she might well have a point in arguing that *90210* has packaged a made-for-TV morality by 'essentially [glamorizing] what it professed to caution against' (ibid.: 121), it should be noted that the character Brenda Walsh (Shannen Doherty) does not take the decision to lose her virginity lightly, and that she learns that every action has consequences if not a price.[5] Darren Star, the show's creator and producer, claimed that *90210* was not in the business of moralizing and that it simply wanted to air issues vital to young Americans. However, Watson found an ally in conservative media critic Michael Medved, who lamented that at the very moment *90210* was heading for the number one teen ratings slot:

> any American youngster who watched television with even moderate regularity would have received the unequivocal impression that the popular culture expected that he or she should become erotically experienced and cheerfully enter the brave new world of adolescent intercourse.
>
> (Medved 1993: 114)

In his book *Hollywood vs. America*, Medved has argued that the Fox network in particular must be held responsible for 'regularly and powerfully encourag[ing] casual sex' (ibid.: 108) on its youth-targeted programming. Much like Watson, he believes that shows like *90210* justified their prurient focus on teenage sex on the grounds of public service—that they were tackling important issues as part of a noble campaign to raise viewer awareness about sexual diseases and birth control. Yet, Medved also notes that, despite the consultative, on-set presence of a birth control expert, when Brenda loses her virginity to Dylan McKay (Luke Perry), little attempt is made to teach or educate as the couple never openly discuss the matter. More importantly, he points out that Brenda's subsequent pregnancy scare suggests that precautions were not taken. In defence of the show, it might be argued, however, that such a scare can function very effectively as a cautionary tale to its millions of teen viewers.

Stylistically the show undoubtedly took its cue from MTV, with its emphasis on rapid cuts and slick editing of brief scenes that might have been drawn directly from rock videos. The use of a rock sound-track featuring new and established bands worked to comment upon the plotlines, articulating characters' feelings by providing 'a modern musical accompaniment that fits the emotions flitting across the screen like a tailored glove' (Crosdale 1999: 8). Although heavily reliant on dialogue, teen dramas are also characterized by their use of rock music, which—as Simon Frith suggests—'amplifies the mood or atmosphere and also tries to convey the "emotional significance" of a scene: the true *real* feelings of the characters involved in it' (in Turner 1993: 59). The 'emotional reality' of the music can, then, help deepen the sense of realism depicted, supplying added emotional texture.

Formally and thematically, *90210* has arguably influenced those more critically-acclaimed teen dramas which followed in its wake, convincing network executives of the commercial viability of the teen drama and demonstrating to programme-makers the key ingredients for a hit show with a notoriously elusive, but potentially lucrative demographic.

The Rise and Rise of Teen Dramas—My So-Called Life and Party of Five

By the 1994/5 season, despite the exodus of several of its original and popular stars, *Beverley Hills 90210* continued to hold onto its number one position in the Nielsen ratings for 18–24-year-olds. Predictably, in response to the success of *90210*, the major networks were alerted to the commercial potential of the hit teen show and ABC showed first in premiering *My So-Called Life* in August 1994. Focusing on the life, loves and crises of high school teenager Angela Chase (Claire Daines) and her close circle of friends, this show—unlike *90210*—prompted immediate critical favour. Notwithstanding the undoubted quality of both scripting and acting, *My So-Called Life*'s positive reception with the critics must be attributable at least in part to a discernible snob factor. For here was a show aired on an established network and, more importantly, created and written by the team responsible for one of the most critically lauded drama series of the late 1980s—*thirtysomething*. Aired from 1987 to 1991, *thirtysomething* has much in common with the teen dramas discussed in this chapter. For whilst—as its title suggests—it focused on the lives of adult characters, the show's 'coming-to-terms-with-our-parents, coming-of-age narratives' (Feuer 1995: 71) made it something of a template for nineties teen-based dramas playing out surprisingly similar dilemmas.[6] *thirtysomething* was also characterized by a high level of soul-searching and -bearing, which some unkind critics labelled 'whining' (ibid.: 61). This propensity for heavy bouts of on-screen self-analysis is arguably one of the features of the show that links it explicitly to teen dramas like *My So-Called Life*, *Party of Five* and *Dawson's Creek*, in which a 'spiritual crisis' precipitated by eighties 'yuppie envy and guilt' (ibid.: 60) is replaced by one brought about by travails of the journey through adolescence. All of these shows, then, are characterized by the sheer amount of self-examination that goes on within them, and, as such, might well be bracketed together as 'teensomethings' in recognition of the show that arguably helped spawn them.[7]

Sometimes referred to as the 'anti-*90210*' (Owen 1997: 139), *My So-Called Life* was praised for the realism and honesty of its portrayal of teens and teen life, winning the TV Critics' Association award for Best Drama in 1995. In contrast to the somewhat air-brushed, one-dimensional characterizations found on *90210*, Angela Chase was presented as a more complex fictional teen— the depth of her character most effectively revealed in the accompanying monologues she delivered. Unlike the popular high school kids portrayed in *90210*—'class presidents and homecoming queens'—*My So-Called Life* featured 'outsiders who didn't seem to fit in' and consequently struck a more realistic chord with many viewers (ibid.: 139). The show gave at least some expression to that brand of youthful nihilism rarely found on the tightly-policed cultural medium of mainstream television; and whilst we did not quite witness TV's equiva-lent of the 'dark cinema of youth' epitomised by movies like Larry Clark's *Kids*, we came as close as we might expect—or hope—to get (Campbell and Kean 1997: 233). In line with those classic youth narratives identified by Paula Fass which situate adolescents at a 'splendid cross-road where the past meets the future in a jumble of personal anxieties and an urgent need for social self-definition (ibid.: 215), Angela and her intimate circle of peers are shown facing up to the emotional turmoil of grow-ing up. Writer/creator Winnie Holzman was at pains to emphasize the universality of problems faced by teenagers down the years—problems which she presumably hoped would prompt a not altogether unpleasant mixture of the shock of recognition and nostalgia in non-teen viewers:

> Who am I? What does it mean to find yourself? These are the basic struggles, and they don't change with generations. That to me is the meaning of my show.
>
> (in Owen 1997: 141–2)

Issues surrounding sex and sexuality typically dominated proceedings, but the breakdown of her parents' marriage, which culminates in her discovery of her father's clandestine affair, provided an additional source of confu-sion and pain for the already angst-ridden Angela. As previously noted, *My So-Called Life* quickly found favour with both adults and adolescents. 'I identified with Angela', Joyce Millman has written in a retrospective piece seeking to make *Dawson's Creek* look poor in comparison:

> I'm not saying that everything that happened to her happened to me when I was fifteen; what I mean is, there's a little Angela in every woman [. . .] *My So-Called Life* was the most soulful, realistic, wise and empathetic show about high school ever. [. . .] Watching it was like being ambushed by your secret self, the person you were before you became you.
>
> (Millman 1998: web)

The fortysomething Winnie Holzman suggested that this pan-genera-tional appeal could be put down to the fact that the show was not aimed at an exclusively teen audience:

> I didn't think in terms of teenagers [. . .]; that's not my approach. I was thinking in terms of having characters that would be interesting. I was attempting to be honest [. . .] and I did not want the teen characters to be

clichés, but at the same time it was important to me that the parents not be cliché, and in many ways it was harder.

(in Owen 1997: 140)

Whilst the problems of Angela Chase inevitably took centre-stage in a drama which by and large offered a world through her eyes, Mr and Mrs Chase were rarely represented as mere ciphers or stereotypical authority figures. Certainly, Angela has predictable run-ins with her mother— commenting memorably in one episode that 'lately [she] can't even look at [her] without wanting to stab her repeatedly'—but the complex, and hence arguably more realistic, dynamics of her relationship with Patty Chase are best highlighted by the uneasy cease-fire that closes this same episode which sees Angela curled up in her mother's bed apologizing for her bad behaviour of late. However, whilst such an apology might suggest that a reassertion of some kind of righteous adult order has occurred, what sets this and a number of other nineties teen shows apart from earlier shows featuring parent–child battles are serialized storylines which lend realism by resisting easy closure and moral lessons learned. These, then, are shows invariably scripted by adults, but crucially they do not always valorize or work to (re)establish the adult order.

In the early 1980s, a colloquium investigating screen images of adolescence questioned whether the full range of teenage experience was being dealt with on screen and what, if anything, might be missing from film and television portrayals. Concluding that screen-teens were often stereotyped, several members of the discussion group called for more realistic representations built around the predominant emotion of life during adolescence that they identified as *ambiguity*. Television, in particular, it was noted, seemed 'scared to death of ambivalence', pre- ferring wherever possible to 'answer all the questions' (Roth 1982: 33). Teenagers surveyed at the time—it was also noted—were desperate to see on-screen adolescents dealing with their own problems, not necessarily having adult authority figures asserting their dominance and control by solving problems and defusing crises for them. Yet, as *TV Guide* writer Sally Bedell pointed out, she had 'seldom seen an adolescent [on television] who goes through some kind of *sturm und drang* come up with his own solution' (ibid.: 33). By the 1990s, shows like *My So-Called Life* had taken considerable steps to address this shortcoming, with teen characters shown tackling their problems with varying levels of success and competence. Indeed, one of the defining features of youth shows in the 1990s has been their focus on a supportive circle of friends as a replacement for ineffectual or possibly non-existent family units. Allied to this, parental figures like the Chases or the Leerys (*Dawson's Creek*) are pictured as fallible individuals with problems often far out-weighing those of their offspring, making it near impossible for them to demonstrate 'the necessity for renewed, coherent social order' identified as pivotal to the praxis of so many youth texts in the past (Campbell and Kean 1997: 217).

Despite the critical praise heaped upon it, *My So-Called Life* was cancelled after a run of just nineteen shows. Somewhat ironically, given American TV's slide towards narrowcasting in the 1990s, ABC decided that the show's ratings were simply not healthy enough to warrant its re-commissioning.[8] At Fox, however, the ratings success of *90210* led to the appearance of *Party of Five*. Just as Fox had stood by *90210* while it struggled to find an audience in its first season, so the network indulged *Party of Five* as it finished its first run ranked a less-than-impressive 99th out of 103 shows. Positive reviews for the new teen drama and—perhaps more importantly—evidence that it was a ratings success with teenage girls and young women in particular convinced Fox executives that it was worth persevering with.[9] In contrast to its much-maligned stablemate, *90210*, *Party of Five* was—and continues to be—regarded as 'quality' prime-time drama. Described in its inaugural season by *TV Guide* as 'the best show you're *not* watching' (Slate 1996: 10), it won a prestigious Golden Globe award for the Best TV Drama of 1995 ahead of the likes of *ER*. In the same year it also won a Humanitas Prize for its depiction of positive social values—an award which reinforces earlier comments made in this chapter concerning the broadly constructive, responsible and largely non-threatening nature of much contemporary youth programming.

The show's rather strained premise, which sees the five Salinger siblings left to fend for themselves following their parents' death in a car accident, did not augur well. *Party of Five* 'reeked of high concept plotting' (Owen 1997: 144), appearing from the outset to promise little more than equally glutinous measures of melodrama and syrupy moralism. The prospect of a rather worthy and preachy show notwithstanding, the removal of parental figures from the outset undoubtedly proved an attractive draw to teen viewers, effectively counter-balancing any initial resistance many might have felt towards it.[10] Of equal significance to an increasingly sophisticated and demanding demographic was the undoubted high quality of both the writing and the acting. Acknowledging this, *Time* magazine christened the show 'a *thirtysomething* for teenagers and young adults' (Slate 1996: 10), further reinforcing the link between the clutch of nineties teen dramas and their adult-oriented progenitor.

Party of Five's writing team was adamant that the show should tackle the many problems facing the Salingers as directly and unsentimentally as the network would allow. As co-writer Amy Lippman acknowledges, the show has consistently dealt with 'some dark issues and grim overtones' (ibid.: 12). In addition to the obvious emotional struggles the orphaned children have had in coming to terms with their parents' untimely deaths, *Party of Five* has explored drug abuse, teen pregnancy and abortion, HIV and AIDS, juvenile delinquency, and alcoholism. All this on top of the more typical crises each of the young Salingers has had to face as they grow older. Lippman and her fellow writers were also keen to avoid stereotypes. With this objective in mind they created characters like Charlie, the oldest but initially least responsible sibling, and the non-maternal oldest daughter, Julia. By series five, the combination of the broad range of ages represented by the show's principal protagonists and those non-teen-specific issues tackled was working to take *Party of Five* out of the realm of the 'teensomething'. As the elder Salingers entered the working world, embarked on 'serious' relationships, and in a couple of cases even got married, it became apparent that the show was moving at pace into narrative spaces occupied by adult dramas.

Parental Discretion Advised—Dawson's Creek as Teen Drama Par Excellence

At the time of writing, *Dawson's Creek* is arguably the highest profile teen drama on American television. Initially turned down by the Fox network, who feared it was too similar to their *Party of Five*, the show premiered on the fledgling Warner network on 20 January 1998. Critics argued that an aggressive and cynical multi-million dollar pre-publicity campaign focusing on the principal actors' movie-star looks, the creative involvement of 'hot' Hollywood script-writer Kevin Williamson (*Scream*, *I Know What You Did Last Summer*, and *Scream 2*), and the promise of plenty of teen sex accounted for the show's higher-than-might-be-expected Nielsen ratings.[11] In contrast to *My So-Called Life*, *Dawson's Creek* has been almost universally condemned by adult critics, who tend to see it as little more than an over-heated melodrama lacking the 'startling "Hey, that's me" emotional resonance' of the former (Millman 1998: web). If—as one reviewer gratefully declared—*Party of Five* offers blessed relief from youth TV's raging 'hormonal gulch' (Loynd 1994: 30), then the 'hyper-ventilating [. . .] Freudian misadventure of boiling libidos' (Richmond 1998: 71) that many seek to argue is *Dawson's Creek* arguably returns its teen audience to just such a place. In appearing to concentrate all of its characters' energies on sex and relationships to the near-total exclusion of other issues that might be expected to intrude on young American lives, critics have argued that the show risks descending into the self-conscious campy territory staked out by shows like Fox's *90210* offshoot *Melrose Place*. Episodes entitled 'Carnal Knowledge' and 'Sex, She Wrote' did little to dispel the perception that *Dawson's Creek* was sex-obsessed. Fifteen-year-old Pacey's much-heralded first series' sexual relationship with his high school teacher, Ms Jacobs, probably did not help either. However, the show's subsequent re-scheduling from the original 9 to 10 p.m. (EST) slot it occupied in its first season to the earlier 8 to 9 p.m. 'family hour' it occupied in its second would appear to suggest that the show billed as 'the frankest depiction of teenage sexuality ever seen on the small screen' (Fretts 1998a: web) is perhaps not nearly so threatening to the nation's moral well-being.

Dawson's Creek might not introduce 'issues' as explicitly as some of its predecessors, but it is marked by an intelligence and seriousness that clearly confers membership of the teensomething roster upon it. In stark contrast, for example, to a teen-utopian-Hughesian world of adolescent pleasure and liberating hedonism at all costs, *Dawson's Creek* rarely shows its teens enjoying themselves.[12] In fact, theirs often seems a world of perpetual crises and angst, in which youthful *joie de vivre* is noticeably absent. As one critic of the show noted, in contrast to the wise-cracking, full-blood[i]ed and vivacious characters featured in Warner's other big teen drama success, *Buffy the Vampire Slayer*, the young protagonists in *Dawson's Creek* come across as rather morose and jaded.

Once again, certain key ingredients are combined to concoct what is almost the perfect recipe for the nineties teen drama. Set in the photo-genic fictional Massachusetts coastal town of Capeside, *Dawson's Creek* centres on the coming-of-age traumas of a mutually protective circle of four 15 to 16-year-old friends and high school classmates: Dawson Leery (James van der Beek), Pacey Witter (Joshua Jackson), Joey Potter (Katie Holmes), and Jen Lindley (Michelle Williams). As with the character of Angela Chase in *My So-Called Life*, the dilemmas of Dawson Leery provide this show with its focal point—and sometime focalizer—around which/whom the lives and loves of the friends can revolve. At fifteen years old, Dawson is a Spielberg-obsessed, would-be movie director, but with more of a talent for talking than film-making. Much like the similarly aged Holden Caulfield in J. D. Salinger's novel *The Catcher in the Rye*, Dawson loves nothing better than to analyse. The show's official website describes him as 'a charmingly obsessive and passionate' young man. Yet, in this 'outlandishly analytical milieu' (Richmond 1998: 71), Dawson is not a 'freak', since all the Capeside teenagers demonstrate the same precocious willingness to dissect their own and others' lives. As an example of this, in one episode the equally thoughtful Joey explains to the pre-teenage sister of a schoolfriend that whilst growing up is never easy, it is made bearable by those rare and special moments which help alleviate all the pain and suffering. Joey is fifteen years old. In *Dawson's Creek*, then, the viewer is 'emersed in the teen equivalent of a Woody Allen movie—a kind of *Deconstructing Puberty*' (ibid.: 71).[13] Dawson in particular is crippled by a near-debilitating introspection—resulting in an 'inertia' which he himself typically acknowledges as a 'profoundly unattractive' trait. Of course, the teenager's propensity to contemplate his or her own metaphorical navel is both a recognized facet of the adolescent experience and an established fixture in many youth narratives.[14] As *Entertainment Weekly*'s Ken Tucker pointed out in an otherwise unfavourable piece, 'one of the best things about the show is that it's not afraid to make its young protagonists look the self-absorbed hypocrites teens can so often be' (Tucker 1998a: web). Although it is certainly the case that Dawson and his peers possess an almost unnatural gift for verbalizing their innermost thoughts and feelings—to the extent that we might argue that it is the scriptwriters and not their characters who speak to us—it is also the case that such verbosity merely works to position them in a line of teen protagonists stretching all the way back to Alcott's Jo March and Twain's Tom Sawyer. Those who criticize the show's wordiness are missing a crucial point about both *Dawson's Creek* specifically and teen narratives in general. Since adolescence is arguably the most self-absorbed of all life stages, texts which examine the teen's propensity to self-obsess— or which, as Joey says of Dawson, 'spend all [their] time analysing [their] sad adolescent lives'—are surely guilty of little more than nailing down the adolescent experience.[15]

In *Dawson's Creek* the teenager's struggle to narrate that is featured in so many youth texts is here symbolized and, in part, actualized through Dawson Leery's film-making—a process through which he can seek to assert some measure of control and authority over/in the world. As an example of the drive for self-expression and articulation, it stands as an archetypal facet of the youth narrative—a variation on those texts in which youthful narrators aspire to be writers carefully attempting to construct a world in their own language. We might look at Dawson's film-making, then, as evidence of the desire 'to order the world, to exercise power and to control aspects of reality' (Campbell and Kean 1997: 230). Dawson's film-making projects frequently centre around self-definition. They are autobiographical, therapeutic and entirely consistent with aims of adolescent narrators for whom 'to write [or film] is to control material and empower the self' (ibid.: 230). In the episode 'High Risk Behaviour', for example, we see Dawson hashing his entire relationship with Joey into a movie script; and in 'His Leading Lady', this teenage auteur is casting for a Joey-esque lead for his autobiographical film.

In addition to exploring the need for self-definition and expression, the *Dawson's Creek* remit clearly includes an examination of the collision between youth and various manifestations of authority. Typically, these centre around the young characters' frequent clashes with parents and educators. In the case of the clash between parents and children, however, what is most immediately noteworthy is the extent to which the task of 'teaching and preaching' is one more than likely to be carried out by the latter in a effort to improve the behaviour of the former. Far from coming across as a study in teen delinquency, it often appears that it is in fact the adults of Capeside who are the delinquents being observed here.[16] Even the show's doomed teen villain, the vindictive Abbie Morgan, has a dysfunctional family life to account for her behaviour. Writing in *Time* Michael Krantz commented that:

> Williamson's kids may talk like therapists but they act like guarded and wounded 15 year-olds whose cell phones and videotapes stand in for a sadly absent adult institutional authority.
>
> (in Crosdale 1999: 127–8)

Similarly, Williamson himself has pointed out that although his teen creations appear to have 'all the answers [. . .] their behaviour is that of a 15 year-old, inexperienced and not so sure of their next step' (Johnson 1998: web).

Whilst Dawson must struggle to come to terms with his parents' failing marriage and eventual decision to separate, his closest friends face arguably more difficult tasks in dealing with parents who patently fail to match their offspring's demands. It is thus ironic, given the critical mauling the show has received for its perceived portrait of teen immorality, that what comes across most forcefully in *Dawson's Creek* is the commitment each of the main players displays towards the sanctity of family and the sheer amount of energy they expend in seeking to demonstrate this commitment. For example, arguing with Mr McPhee over what is best for the mentally ill Andie, her boy-friend Pacey is ultimately forced to concede that family overrides 'the whole support system' friends can provide and reluctantly accepts that she must leave Capeside to receive the best medical attention her father can supply. As further evidence of such commitment, in 'Reunited' we witness Joey and Jen's well-meaning and semi-successful attempt to engineer a meeting between Dawson's estranged parents, Gail and Mitch, with the hopeful intention of making them see the error of their adulterous ways. This highlights the way in which it is the kids who act as active 'fixers' and seekers of stable family environments.

Far more than sex, it is the family that obsesses Dawson and his friends, as they battle to sustain meaningful relationships in the face of near constant parental shortcomings. In this way, we could argue that *Dawson's Creek* explores territory not dissimilar to *Rebel Without A Cause*, particularly in delivering the apparent message that it is parents and not their children who need to mend their ways. As in *Rebel*, *Dawson's Creek* exposes parental failure to the harsh gaze of teens who remain convinced that the ideal is workable in practice. Just as Jon Lewis has argued that Nicholas Ray's genre-defining movie ultimately functioned to 'reinscribe the family ideal' (Lewis 1992: 27), so *Dawson's Creek* appears to engage in similar work in the 1990s. In the closing episode to the show's second season—'Parental Discretion Advised'—Dawson confronts Joey's father over the latter's return to drug-dealing. Urging the just-paroled Mr Potter to give the criminal life up for good, Dawson proceeds to deliver a lecture about family obligations and love to a man more than twice his age who in his defence pleads for some consideration of life's 'greys'. However, like Jim Stark in *Rebel Without A Cause* before him, Dawson is committed to honesty at all costs—a commitment which sees Mr Potter back behind bars by the episode's close, but which also results in him losing the love and friendship of on/off girlfriend Joey, who berates Dawson for seeing the world in 'black and white' and finds him responsible for ruining her chance of rekindling a meaningful father–daughter relationship.

Here then, Dawson exhibits the archetypal teen protagonist's qualities of naivety and idealism that peers and elders alike can find infuriating. 'I don't understand how someone can be so self-aware and yet so utterly clueless', says an exasperated Joey to Dawson in an early episode; whilst Mitch Leery passes judgement on his son's idealism by pointing out to him that '[i]n reality, people have flaws'. One of the show's key plotlines is surely Dawson's exposure to these 'flaws'. By the end of the second series, Dawson's construction of a white picket fence outside his girlfriend's house still tells the viewer more about his own continued commitment to innocence and a desire to return to simpler times than it does about the strength of his love for her. Clearly, it means so much more to Dawson—a character described as a 'reality rejecter' by one of the show's perceptive young fans.

A faith in the sanctity of family life lies at the very heart of *Dawson's Creek*. As might be expected, the episode that closes the show's second series seeks to resolve at least some of its loose ends by reasserting this faith. Following a falling out that has resulted in her moving away, Jen Lindley, for example, returns to her grandmother's house seeking her guardian's 'support not [her] judgement'. With Jen's plea for a family answered by her grandmother's tears and hugs, this particular narrative strand is—for the time being—resolved. Throughout the first two series, Pacey and his sheriff father have battled over what the former sees as the latter's lack of affection and the latter views as the former's wilful rebellion. In the episode titled 'Uncharted Waters', Dawson and Pacey take a fishing trip with their respective fathers which rapidly becomes a forum for the boys to air their grievances over parental failings and in particular dysfunctional paternal relationships. During the course of the trip Pacey is constantly belittled or ignored by his father, who he begs in desperation to love him unconditionally irrespective of his shortcomings. Yet, Mr Witter becomes so drunk that his son's appeal passes him by. Pacey catches the day's largest fish; but in a moment that typifies his attitude toward his son, his father merely lets him keep the fish with the crushing observation that it will probably be the sum total of his life's achievement.

Somewhat predictably, Pacey's relationship with his father comes to a head in series two's curtain-call episode, 'Parental Discretion Advised', when Sheriff Witter verbally and then physically assaults his son in front of his work colleagues. Humiliated, Pacey fights back, knocking his father unconscious with a punch that finally alerts Mr Witter to the error of his parenting ways. 'I deserved your punch,' he tells an angry Pacey. Crucially, he admits he knows very little about his son. The key line here is surely his admission that 'I've not been the kind of dad you can *talk* to', since being unable to *talk* is one of the greatest 'crimes' in *Dawson's Creek*.

Joey's discovery that her father is back dealing drugs prompts a similar father–child confrontation, in which the elder person is positioned as the prospective recipient of any lessons learned. When Joey asks her father why he has once again jeopardized their future as a family unit, Mr Potter claims he did it to make money for them all to live as a family. Mr Potter tells his daughter that he is 'haunted by the knowledge that I've failed you', and admits that he is 'weak'. Like Pacey's father, his real crime is perhaps that he too cannot or will not 'open up' to others and express himself.

The cathartic value of *talking*, together with the superior status conferred upon those who can actually do it, is further emphasized when Dawson hands out advice to his mother on how to handle her failing marriage. What is of interest here is perhaps not so much the nature or quality of that advice, but rather the illuminating fact that Gail Leery actively seeks advice from her neophyte son. In a genre-defining inversion of expectation, all three parent–child confrontations described here show teenagers acting as responsible counsellors to errant and/or confused adults.

On one level it might be possible to argue that *Dawson's Creek* exposes and passes judgement upon the Boomer values of the generation who grew up in the 1960s and 1970s.[17] Certainly, it is the children who display a greater commitment to ideals that might well label them more conservative than those who are their elders (but in the context of the show's value-system hardly their 'betters'). In 'Alternative Lifestyles', for example, Dawson is appalled to discover that his parents are contemplating an open marriage, following the disclosure of Gail Leery's infidelity. In his hysterical attack on Hollywood, Michael Medved accuses it of 'promoting promiscuity [. . .] maligning marriage [. . .] encouraging illegitimacy and handing over control to kids who know best' (Medved 1993: 147). He argues that contemporary popular culture helps 'poison relationships between parents and children', since:

> [N]o notion has been more aggressively and ubiquitously promoted in films, popular music, and television than the idea that children know best—that parents are corrupt, hypocritical clowns who must learn decency and integrity from their enlightened off-spring.
>
> (ibid.: 147)

However accurate this assessment might appear to be, given what occurs week-in-week-out in many 'teensomethings', it hardly stands as a major narrative departure. The idea that children 'know best' has always been a staple of pre-electronic mass media youth texts. It is, furthermore, arguably rooted in a national myth dating back to the emergence of the Republic, in which independence itself was figured as a youthful attempt to break free of the parental grip of the British. Notwithstanding this, Medved's attack on the formula which pits 'evil parents vs. enlightened kids' (ibid.: 148) surely misses the point. As a close analysis of *Dawson's Creek* demonstrates, nothing could be further from the truth. Those critics of the show who would argue that it is disrespectful of adult authority and an advertisement for teenage promiscuity unaccountably overlook the obvious—namely, that for all the superficial trappings of rebellion on display, the young Capesiders are a fairly moral bunch and that they are in fact earnest advocates of traditional ideals, values and institutions. Once again, a useful comparison might be drawn with the movie *Rebel Without A Cause*, in which the teenage protagonists appear 'more moral, more upstanding and law-abiding than anyone else' (Biskind 1983: 200).

Whilst Medved accuses teen-targeted shows of depicting 'young people as creatures who cannot possibly restrain their lustful impulses' (Medved 1993: 115), *Dawson's Creek* cannot be found guilty of this charge. For all its *talk* of and about sex, the show actually demonstrates what Medved in fact calls for when he urges Hollywood to acknowledge that teen attitudes towards sex are both 'complex and conservative' (ibid.: 115).[18] Perhaps no greater illustration of this can be found in the juxtaposition between a theme tune entitled 'I Don't Want to Wait' and the fact that through a combination of choice and circumstance Dawson does. Commenting on Dawson's virgin status, Joey points out that 'there are popes who have had more [sexual] experience'. Yet, such one-liners aside, the show does not lionize the sexually experienced teen. Pointedly, the teen with the most sexual experience, Jen Lindley, regrets that she was 'sexualized way too young'. Whilst there is, therefore, some accuracy in Pacey's semi-serious assessment of his best-friend Dawson as the last of a dying breed—'You take in stray animals. You help old ladies across the street. You just say no. You *are* Jimmy Stewart'—given the opportunity, each of the main protagonists demonstrates a similarly old-fashioned commitment to the view that sex without love is meaningless. Emphasizing this, *Dawson's Creek*'s 47-year-old producer, Greg Prange notes that, whilst:

> it was daring of the show to tackle the fact that Jen lost her virginity at the age of 12, [. . .] the generation of teens we have today are more conservative. I think it was wilder when I was a teen than it is now.
>
> (quoted in Crosdale, 1999: 139)

Yet, in keeping with many youth texts down the years, *Dawson's Creek* mixes liberal and conservative values that are themselves reflective of the teenager's own set of often conflicting desires and emotions.

The linked episodes 'To Be or Not To Be . . .' and '. . . That is the Question' cover more conventional ground, in featuring an archetypal show-down with school authority, emergent sexuality, and that staple of many youth texts, the idea(l) of personal sincerity or integrity. With the possible exception of the distracted Pacey, Dawson and his friends are conscientious students who worry about their grades and future employment prospects.[19] As the self-explanatory episode 'All-Niter' demonstrates, they are academically self-motivated. When class-mate Jack McPhee is forced by his English teacher, Mr Peterson, to read out loud a confessional poem with apparently homosexual overtones as punishment for in-class indiscipline, he can only get so far before embarrassment gets the better of him and he runs out of the classroom close to tears. The following day, with rumours and innuendo concerning Jack's sexuality flying around the school, Mr Peterson once again forces Jack to read his poem. This time Pacey intervenes and, supporting his friend, asks the teacher why he 'gets off on tormenting' his pupils. Ordered out of the class for insubordination, Pacey spits in Peterson's face before exiting. Hauled before the school principal and asked to apologize, he refuses—

> Making a student cry, embarrassing him, stripping him of his dignity was not right. And while I respect this system, I do not respect people like you, Mr Peterson. I don't.

As a result of his principled stand he receives a week's suspension. Whilst Pacey admits that spitting at his teacher was wrong, he is determined to expose what he sees as his teacher's bullying, and this determination eventually pays off when diligent research uncovers Peterson's violation of numerous pedagogical rules. The outcome is entirely consistent with the show's inversion of the traditional adult–child power axis, as Pacey's discoveries result in Mr Peterson's 'decision' to opt for early retirement rather than face the possibility of a public reprimand.

The poem and the very public debate it generates forces Jack McPhee to admit to his homosexuality. Jack's coming-out also brings into sharp focus yet another instance of parental failure, as his father flatly refuses to accept his son's sexuality, but instead promises to get him all the 'help' he needs by urging him to see a professional about his 'problem'.

On one level, *Dawson's Creek* is undoubtedly a slick and 'soapy' example of Hollywood product. Yet, as the 'edgiest depiction of teendom since *My So-Called Life*' (Sellers 1998: web), it is clear that for many of its young fans it can—and indeed does—function more constructively at the critically undervalued level of emotional realism.[20]

Conclusion

In *Teenagers and Teenpics*, Thomas Doherty concludes his examination of Hollywood's post-war drive to tell and sell the teen experience with an assessment of teenpics at the tail end of the 1980s:

> Up against a parent culture that is ever more accommodating and appeasing, ever less authoritative and overbearing (not to mention present) the teenage rebel faces a problem [. . .] never anticipated. [. . .] One of the most fascinating undertones of teenpics since the 1960s is their palpable desire for parental control and authority, not adolescent independence and authority. [. . .] Parents today are more likely to be condemned for being self-centred, weak, and uncertain than for being overbearing, intrusive, or present. [. . .] In a culture of loose rules and relative morality, the teenage rebel has lost his best foil. [. . .] Today's teenpic hero is more often a weird or wimpy one, more liable to flash watery eyes than snarling lips. He is a hapless kid seeking direction, not a tough rebel fleeing restriction.
>
> (Doherty 1988: 237)

Doherty's definition of the archetypal teenpic plot and its main protagonist could apply to the television dramas discussed here. He might well, for example, be describing Dawson Leery or even Angela Chase when he refers to a 'hapless kid seeking direction'. Yet, the contention that 'teensomethings'—like big-screen teenpics—privilege a 'consciousness [that] is emphatically adult' (ibid.: 236) should be problematized, if not openly challenged. For whilst these are not revolutionary texts, neither do they advocate acquiescence. Close readings would suggest that they are more complex and less resolution-driven. As viewers, we are not simply delivered to a point at the close of each episode with the efficacy of adult values demonstrated, proven and our wayward teens tamed. Like Dawson, it appears that viewers and critics alike must come to terms with the 'greys'.

Allied to this point, one of the principal reasons for the pangenerational appeal of shows like *Dawson's Creek* and *My So-Called Life* is surely that many of the values usually ascribed to youth have become indistinguishable from those espoused by mainstream adult society. As Doherty himself observes, from the 1960s onwards youth comes to be increasingly defined by a 'movement [. . .] away from a term denoting chronological age or a developmental phase [. . .] toward an ever more ephemeral experimental realm', which as it 'progressed upward, not downward' becomes 'a concept not a chronology' (ibid.: 232). Thus, teenage culture becomes the more inclusive *youth* culture and membership swells.[21]

A brief look at today's schedules confirms that, much as in Hollywood where movies appear to be 'geared unequivocally and unapologetically to the young' (ibid.: 233), a similar transformation has taken place in American TV in the 1990s. It too has become an increasingly 'juvenilised industry' (ibid.: 235). However, part of this chapter's brief has been to suggest that such juvenilization should not be regarded as necessarily detrimental to television's general well-being or representative of a 'dumbing down'. Just as recent teenpics like *Cruel Intentions*, *10 Things I Hate About You*, *Go* and *Clueless* display far greater energy, wit, and acting and writing talent than many contemporary adult movies, so 'teensomethings'—their small-screen siblings—exhibit such qualities in equal measure. In this instance, juvenilization does not have to mean infantilization.

Notes

[1] In his book *Demographic Vistas* David Marc defines demographics as a 'name of a social science that purports to describe audiences for a particular cultural item, in terms of salient marketing characteristics—age, sex, income level, education level, religion, race, etc' (Marc 1996: 216).
[2] In comparison, ABC's average viewer is aged 35, NBC's 39, and CBS's 48.
[3] Nielsen surveys confirm that girls aged 12–17 and boys aged 12–17 (in this order) remain the demographic units that watch the *least* television.
[4] Predating the arrival of Fox by some five years, cable channel MTV demonstrated the economic viability of an exclusively youth-oriented service; and, whilst ratings were comparatively low compared with those garnered by the major networks, MTV was arguably all about *who* was being reached and not how many.
[5] The charge that teen shows like *Beverley Hills 90210* and *Dawson's Creek* glamorize what they profess to caution against is a familiar criticism levelled at youth texts down the years. In the 1950s, for example, movies like *The*

Blackboard Jungle, *The Wild One* and *Rebel Without A Cause* met with similar attacks.

6 The ease with which Winnie Holzman moved from scripting this show to writing *My So-Called Life* lends support to such a view.

7 It is also worth pointing out that *thirtysomething* was itself a highly successful example of a show clearly targeted at a potentially lucrative-to-advertisers niche audience. As National Public Radio critic Elvis Mitchell wryly observed, 'I've never seen such a blatant pitch to demographics outside Saturday morning TV' (Feuer 1995: 61): Demonstrating the rewards to be had from homing in on a specific demographic, *thirtysomething* surely paved the way for the unapologetic narrow-casting signalled by shows like *My So-Called Life*.

8 There were rumours that Claire Danes's unwillingness to sign a new contract helped hasten and harden the network's resolve to cancel a show which garnered respectable ratings in a highly competitive Wednesday evening slot. It should be noted here that *My So-Called Life*'s Nielsen numbers were as healthy as those currently are for both *Party of Five* and *Dawson's Creek*.

9 December 1998 Nielsen ratings placed *Party of Five* 11th with American teen viewers.

10 *Party of Five* replicates the basic premise found in S. E. Hinton's 1967 novella *The Outsiders*, in which the three Curtis brothers struggle to remain a family unit after their parents are killed in a road accident.

11 December 1998 Nielsen ratings for *Dawson's Creek* showed that it was ranked 5th among teenage viewers. With all four shows placed ahead of it on the ratings non-teen specific, *Dawson's Creek* can justifiably claim to be *the* current number one made-for-teens show. Its total audience numbered on average between 6 to 7 million people, confirming healthy cross-generational appeal. Crucially for advertisers and sponsors, research revealed that the show was ranked 1st among teenage girls—traditionally the most elusive demographic.

12 This could be considered a little unexpected, given that Kevin Williamson is on record as identifying John Hughes as his 'hero'.

13 Dawson Leery even sounds like Woody Allen at times.

14 See Chapters 4, 5, and 6 in particular.

15 Creator Kevin Williamson has acknowledged that his characters sometimes 'talk like they've had ten years of therapy', but is adamant that this 'heightened' dialogue does not go above the heads of the show's young audience.

16 In this it is reminiscent of *Rebel Without A Cause*, which focused at length on parental shortcomings. In his book *The Cinema of Adolescence*, David Considine argues that the movie diagnosed the state of the middle-class, suburban family, as opposed to dealing with working-class, urban delinquency. Indeed, it is reported that a full-page advertisement for the movie placed in *Variety* ran with the headline: 'Maybe the police should have picked up his parents instead!' Writing in the *Motion Picture Herald* in 1957 Walter Brooks observed of the

America that JD movies purported to reflect that 'it's hard to tell if our problems are with adult juveniles or juvenile adults' (in Doherty 1988: 230).

17 Whilst Howe and Strauss identify a tendency to bemoan the excesses and downright selfishness of Baby Boomers as a characteristic of Generation X, this chapter is not concerned with the ultimately reductive practice of seeking to pigeonhole millions of Americans. However, if it were, it should be pointed out that the likes of Dawson Leery and his friends do not qualify for 'membership' of Generation X by birthdate, since they fall outside the commonly accepted 1961–81 band. Americans born from 1982 onwards have been tagged members of the Millennial Generation (see Introduction).

18 Medved should also take heart from the comments of TV critic Bruce Fretts, who in defending *Dawson's Creek* against charges of an unhealthy sex-obsession, wrote: 'Frankly, I'm more concerned about America's youth aping *South Park*'s foul-mouthed cartoon hooligans than the comparatively wholesome *Creek* kids' (Fretts 1998b: web).

19 It is tempting to view the class clown Pacey as Huck Finn to Dawson's Tom Sawyer. After all, Pacey is more of an outsider figure—under-achieving at school, abused at home, socio-economically 'beneath' his best friend, and sexually experienced at the hands of a woman more than twice his age. By the close of the second season, however, Pacey is shown knuckling down to his studies and relishing his first 'A' grade term paper, and crucially being 'civilized' by the love of a good woman in the shape of Andie McPhee.

20 Viewer feedback registered on the show's official and unofficial websites confirms a high level of interaction and identification with the characters and their dilemmas. Producer Paul Stupin has gone so far as to admit that such feedback can 'help plan how we're going to proceed' (in Crosdale 1999: 136).

21 Typically, Michael Medved blames the 1960s for Hollywood's obsession with and uncritical valorization of all things 'youth', and its concomitant advancement of—what he calls—'the principle of puerile power' (Medved 1993: 151). For Medved, 'the anti-adult messages that characterised that era have remained a fixed and prominent feature' of Hollywood's output (ibid.: 155).

Bibliography

Baker, M. (1993) 'Age old questions', *Broadcast*, October 8: 26–8.

Barnouw, E. (1990) *Tube of Plenty: The Evolution of American Television*, New York: Oxford University Press.

Bindas, K. and Heinman, K. (1994) 'Image is Everything?: TV and Counter Culture Message in the 1960s', *Journal of Popular Film and Television* 22(1): 22–37.

Biskind, P. (1983) *Seeing is Believing*, New York: Pantheon.

Campbell, N. and Kean, A. (1997) *American Cultural Studies: An Introduction to American Culture*, London: Routledge.

Crosdale, D. (1999) *Dawson's Creek: The Official Companion*, London: Ebury Press.

Doherty, T. (1988) *Teenagers and Teenpics: The Juvenilisation of American Movies in the 1950s*, London: Unwin Hyman.

Du Brow, R. (1986) 'Youth Must Be Served', *Channels of Communication* 6(1): 69.

Fetterley, J. (1973) 'The sanctioned rebel', in D. Kesterson (ed.) *Critics on Mark Twain*, Coral Gables: University of Miami Press.

Feuer, J. (1995) *Seeing Through the Eighties*, London: British Film Institute.

Fretts, B. (1998a) 'High school confidential', *Entertainment Weekly*, January 1, website.

—— (1998b) 'Remote patrol—keeping a watch on TV', *Entertainment Weekly*, April 3, website.

Garrett, S. (1990) 'Dear Doctor Youth', *Broadcast*, May 4: 29.

Goodwin, A. (1994) 'Ideology and diversity in American television', in R. Maidment and J. Mitchell (eds) *The United States in the Twentieth Century: Culture*, Milton Keynes: Open University Press.

Hill, D. (1988) 'Tailor-made TV for the Teens', *TV World* 11(8): 84–5, 126.

Howe, N. and Strauss, B. (1993) *13th Generation: Abort, Retry, Ignore, Fail?*, New York: Vintage.

Johnson, T. (1998) 'Dawson's Peak', *TV Guide*, March 7–13, website.

Kellner, D. (1995) *Media Culture: Cultural Politics, Identity and the Politics Between the Modern and the Postmodern*, London: Routledge.

Kile, C. (1993) 'Recombinant Realism/Caliutopian Re-Dreaming: Beverley Hills 90210 as Nostalgia Television', *Bad Subjects*, October, website.

Lewis, J. (1992) *The Road to Romance and Ruin: Teen Films and Youth Culture*, London: Routledge.

Loynd, R. (1994) 'Party of Five', *Variety*, September 5–11: 30.

Mahler, R. (1989) 'Teen Ed', *Emmy* 11(5) 10–12.

Marc, D. (1997) *Comic Visions: Television Comedy and American Culture*, Oxford: Blackwell.

——(1996) *Demographic Vistas: Television and American Culture*, Philadelphia: University of Pennsylvania Press.

McElvogue, L. (1993) 'Fox hounds the networks', *Broadcast*, October 8: 40–2.

Medved, M. (1993) *Hollywood vs. America: Popular Culture and the War on Traditional Values*, London: HarperCollins.

Millman, J. (1998) 'Dawson's Crock', http://www.salon.com/ent/tv/1998/03/cov_16tv.html

Owen, R. (1997) *GenX TV: The Brady Bunch to Melrose Place*, New York: Syracuse University Press.

Oswell, D. (1998) 'A question of belonging: television, youth and the domestic', in T. Skelton and G. Valentine (eds) *Cool Places: Geographies of Youth Cultures*, London: Routledge.

Paterson, E. and Thompson, T. (1996) 'Teenage rampage: young 'uns go for it', *Time Out* 1340, April 24: 18–22.

Rapping, E. (1987) 'Hollywood's Youth Cult Films', *Cineaste* 16(1–2): 14–19.

Richmond, R. (1998) 'Dawson's Creek', *Variety* 369 (10): 71.

Roth, L. *et al.* (1982) 'Images of Adolescence', *American Film* 7(4): 32–5, 71.

Seiter, E. *et al.* (1989) *Remote Control: Television, Audiences and Cultural Power*, London: Routledge.

Sellers, J. (1998) 'Screenings and Screamings: Do You Believe the Hype', *React*, February 9, website.

Silverstone, R. (1994) *Television and Everyday Life*, London: Routledge.

Slate, L. (1996) 'Surprise Party', *Emmy* 18(4): 10–12.

——(1986) 'Telling the Truth About Sex', *Emmy* 8(1): 21.

Spring, J. (1992) *Images of American Life: Movies, Radio and Television*, Albany: SUNY Press.

Sunila, J. (1988) 'Take Two thirtysomethings and Call Me in the Morning', *Emmy* 10(3): 20–3.

Tucker, K. (1998a) 'Crippled Creek', *Entertainment Weekly*, January 23, website.

——(1998) 'Dawson Creaks', *Entertainment Weekly*, May 22, website.

Turner, G. (1993) *Film as Social Practice*, London: Routledge.

Twitchell, J. (1992) *Carnival Culture: The Trashing of Taste in America*, New York: Columbia University Press.

Watson, M. (1998) *Defining Visions: Television and the American Experience Since 1945*, Fort Worth/Orlando: Harcourt Brace.

Wax, R. (1991) 'teensomething', *Emmy* 13(5): 37–40.

A note on materials

Dawson's Creek is easily available on compilation video tapes, *The Best of Dawson's Creek Volumes 1 and 2* (1998), Columbia/TriStar Home Video.

Websites

http://www.dawsons-creek.com
http://www.foxworld.com/po5/show.htm
http://www.geocities.com/TelevisionCity/Studio/4809
http://UltimateTV.com

EIGHT
The Body's in the Trunk: (Re-)Presenting Generation X
Jon Lewis

> For us, everything seemed normal. I remember wondering why people
> were surprised that prices were going up. I thought, that's what prices did.
> Some people were dismayed that America was losing the war in Vietnam,
> but to me it seemed like America had always been losing the war. Some
> people were scared that George Wallace was running for president, but he
> ran every time, didn't he?
>
> (Jefferson Morley, on being twentysomething in 1988)
> (in Ritchie 1995: 103)

A statistical abstract on the 1990 US census contains a surprising piece of
data: there are almost 80 million people out there in the United States
born between 1961 and 1981. At present, this 'Generation X' accounts for
approximately 30 per cent of the total US population, exceeding the Baby
Boom generation by about 10 million people (Ritchie 1995: 16–17).

But despite its size—and its potential as a political and economic
force—those born after the boom are widely regarded as a lost generation.
You see them on the bus, on the street, in class, lost in a kind of escapist
void, tuned in to their *personal* electronic devices: their gameboys, their
walk- and disc-mans. Back in their rooms, dorms or apartments, they
spend hours trolling, interacting anonymously, impersonally on the
world wide web. Unlike the sixties hippies, who are anathema to most
Gen-X'ers, there are no claims made to a communal *counter*-culture.
Gen-X'ers tune out to waste time. Such is the ironic limbo of slacker
culture.

Richard Linklater's *Slacker* and Kevin Smith's *Clerks*, the two indie films that first focused on this Gen-X slacker culture, suggest that the dominant condition of youth today is an aimless locomotion from one grungy rental unit to the next, from deep sleep to a job that requires little more than a pulse-rate and maybe a sense of humour. Young people find irony if not pleasure in such an aimless existence, these films suggest, because monotony may well be better than what, for them, comes next. Generation X, if we take seriously their re-presentation in the popular media, is a big, dispirited bunch. They've seen the future on film, in popular magazines, and on TV and it doesn't seem to have much to do with them. For Generation X, the twenty-first century promises a series of part-time, dead-end service jobs, broken marriages and sexually transmitted diseases. American companies have through most of Gen-X's young adulthood committed themselves to downsizing and sub-contracting production overseas. The booming US stock market, low inflation and low interest rates of the late 1990s have proven out the *economic* wisdom of this new *American* economy. The economic success of the war-time and Baby Boom generations was built upon a fundamental selfishness and shortsightedness. And this success has come very much at Generation X's expense.

Sex has become not so much a battlefield as a minefield. One hears a statistic on TV all the time: a woman over thirty has a better chance of getting struck by lightning than finding a mate. The statistic may or may not be true, but it is nonetheless widely accepted. Witness the popularity of *Friends*, *Sex in the City*, and *Ally McBeal*, TV shows about the absurdity and/or impossibility of 'settling down' and the struggle for fun let alone happiness in the nineties. One in four Gen-X'ers lucky enough to have sex will get a dose at least once before 1999 comes to a close. The percentage who might get something life threatening like HIV is, for all of us young or not, just too scary to contemplate.

In a 1992 essay titled 'Slacking Toward Bethlehem', Andrew Kopkind ruminated on the strange cultural fix of Generation X:

> The domestic and economic relationships that have created the new consciousness are not likely to improve in the few years left in this century, or in the years of the next, when the young slackers will be middle-agers. The choices for young people will be increasingly constricted. In a few years, a steady job at a mall outlet or a food chain may be all that's left for college graduates. Life is more and more like a lottery—is a lottery—with nothing but the luck of the draw determining whether you get a recording

contract, get your screenplay produced, or get a job with your MBA. Slacking is thus a rational response to casino capitalism, the randomization of success . . . if it is impossible to find a good job, why not slack and enjoy life?

(Kopkind 1992: 187)

A UNESCO report published ten years earlier projected just such a dire future not only in the US but world-wide. 'The key words in the experience of the young,' the report concludes, 'are going to be: "scarcity", "unemployment", "ill-employment", "anxiety", "defensiveness", "pragmatism", and even "subsistence" and "survival" itself' (Unesco 1981: 17).

A Hotel in the Poconos

In May 1961 at a resort hotel in the Pocono Mountains, the American Academy of Arts and Sciences held its annual conference; the conference theme: 'the challenge of youth'. To meet that challenge, conference organizer Daniel Bell invited a veritable who's who of American academe: Harvard's Erik Erikson, Talcott Parsons and Kenneth Keniston; Yale's Jay Lifton; and from the University of Chicago, Bruno Bettleheim and Reuel Denney. The conference and the subsequently published papers—*The Challenge of Youth* (1965a)—marked the American academy's first significant examination of youth culture after the Second World War.

The professors assembled by Bell spoke with some authority about the young people in their college classes, many of whom would eventually take part in the anti-war and civil rights movements on campuses nationwide. A second youth subculture, few of whom would ever set foot on a college campus, was even more interesting to the conference participants. These delinquent youth were increasingly in the news in the late 1950s and early 1960s and there was considerable anxiety in the adult population for someone somewhere to come up with a cure. At least three of the conference participants, Erikson, Keniston and Bettelheim, spoke directly to this growing anxiety developing a new discipline: adolescent psychology. But as these academics began to study teen deviance and delinquency, a cure became a lot less certain than the problem's cause.

Erikson discussed *the challenge of youth* in terms that would soon come to characterize the field:

Youth shares with other groups, such as women and old people, the fact
that the role assigned to it by nature has been elaborated by cultures as a
set of differences from some standard human being, the norm, of course,
being usually the normal adult male. The group is then judged on the basis
of what it is not and will never be, or is not quite yet, or is not anymore.

(Erikson 1965a: viii)

Erikson's notion of adolescence as a transition stage was hardly original.
But his larger contention that youth might better be understood as an
oppressed minority in search of definition, equity, or at least common
decency ably refuted conventional wisdom at the time. Erikson introduced
the notion that complex social factors impacted upon the psychology of
youth and in doing so suggested that the problems faced by fifties and
sixties teenagers were mostly their parents' fault. Like most of the other
conference participants, Erikson focused specifically on the post-war,
Baby Boom generation. But his psycho-social model for the study of youth
has proven resilient, even prescient. His work reads as if it were written
specifically about and for Generation X.

Social Problem Teen Movies, 1955–1984

In the 1955 teenpic *The Blackboard Jungle*, a policeman confronts a teacher
who has just taken a beating. The cop asks him to identify the assailants,
most of whom are students in his class. But given the times—the Hollywood blacklist is still a going concern—naming names is just not an option
. . . For a hero at least. The teacher's silence at first frustrates
the policeman. But he too understands that ratting out a couple of bad
kids promised to do little to solve the problem of teen delinquency. In
terms strikingly similar to those later posed by Erikson, the policeman
ruminates: 'I've handled lots of problem kids in my time—kids from both
sides of the tracks—they were five or six years old in the last war—father
in the army —mother in the defense plant—no home life—no church
life—no place to go—so they form street gangs . . . maybe kids are like the
rest of the world today—mixed up—suspicious—scared'(ibid.).

    The film's gang leader, Artie West, appreciates the cop's social com-
mentary. He fully embraces the notion that he is but a product of his
times. On the street with his teacher as a robbery takes shape before them,
West waxes philosophical: 'A year from now the army comes along and
they say Artie West you get on a uniform and you save the world and you

192 The Radiant Hour

get your lousy head blown right off. Or maybe I get a year in jail—maybe when I come out jail, the army they don't want Artie West to be a soldier no more—maybe what I get is out.' West's acceptance of his role as a metaphor not only in the plot of the film but in the larger 'problem of generations'[1] staged in post-war American culture appears at the time to be a cop-out. He's a thug with a leather jacket who has watched too many social problem movies about teenagers. Hollywood and the larger culture it serves was already impatient with his kind. Within the year, Hollywood would lampoon him and the entire genre of social problem teen films with the Jerry Lewis vehicle, *The Delicate Delinquent*, a film which renders absurd Erikson's notion that delinquents are made and not born. What social problem after all could possibly explain Jerry Lewis?

Six years later, the supple delinquents in *West Side Story* at once dramatized and satirized the tendency on the part of sociologists and psychologists to blame the adult generation for the sins of its young. In a song played for laughs, 'Gee, Officer Krupke,' the white teen gang, the Jets, muse on their delinquent behaviour. While the song undercuts the seriousness of race-based urban delinquency depicted in the film, it reveals the ways in which the academic/professional discourse on troubled youth had entered into the larger adult mass culture. (As Marx has suggested, history plays out first as drama, then as farce.)

'Dear kindly Sergeant Krupke,' the Jets sing, 'you gotta understand/ It's just our bringing upke/That gets us outa hand/Our mothers all are junkies/Our fathers all are drunks/Golly, Moses, naturally we're punks/ Gee, Officer Krupke, we're very upset/We never had the love every child outa get/We aint no delinquents, we're misunderstood/Deep down inside us there is good.' Later in the same song, the Jets acknowledge the absurdity of social causality: 'Dear kindly social worker/They tell me get a job/Like be a soda jerker/Which means like be a slob/It's not I'm anti-social/I'm only anti-work.' Still later in the number, a Jet sings, trying to sound like a female social worker, 'These boys don't need a job/They need a year in the pen/It aint a question of misunderstood/Deep down inside them they're no good!' While the Jets effectively lampoon those who attempt to understand them from afar, they also do well to expose the absurdity of a key Hollywood generic assumption that bad teens can be cured by (tough) love, by understanding, by some adult (played by a movie star) taking the time to understand and help them.

Such a generic convention is evoked once again in all its simple-minded absurdity in the 1984 Gen-X film *Repo Man*. Leaking blood all over the floor of a convenience store he has just tried to rob, Duke attempts to pay off the scene with a vague reference to Artie West via Erikson *et al.*: 'The lights are going dim—I know a life of crime led me to this sorry fate—I blame society—society made me what I am.' The film's sardonic hero, Otto, a former pal, attempts to pay off the scene in terms appropriate to a generation that has heard this speech before. 'You're just a white suburban punk,' Otto reminds Duke, 'just like me.' With his last breath, Duke affirms the obvious: 'Ya, but it still hurts.'

Back to the Poconos

Youth, Erikson maintained, is best described by what it is not, i.e. not adult, not a child. Alienation, he maintained, was merely a logical, even instinctive response to such an unstable identity. Erikson regarded an essential paradox at the core of teen alienation—a desire for separation from one's parents that is accompanied by a need for their continued approval and love; an affirmation of diversity in opposition to the con-formist adult world tempered by a single core value, fidelity, to one's peers with whom one comes to identify and conform. 'Fidelity is a virtue and quality of adolescent ego-strength which belongs to man's heritage,' Erikson wrote, 'but which—like all basic virtues—can arise only in the interplay of a life stage with the individuals and the social forces of a true community' (Erikson 1965b: 3).

Youth's search for 'something or somebody to be true', Erikson argued, revealed larger social problems inherent in post-war American adult culture. The adult generation's refusal or inability to provide youth with security, truth, and fidelity compelled young Americans to search for those core values elsewhere. When that search proved futile, a variety of forms of dysfunction were the inevitable result. 'It is the young,' Erikson observed, 'who, by their responses and actions, tell the old whether life as repre-sented by the old and as presented to the young has meaning' (ibid.: 24).

Kenneth Keniston, at the time of the conference a lecturer in Social Relations at Harvard at work on his magisterial study, *The Uncommitted: Alienated Youth in American Society* (1965b) placed the blame for such a disaffected, disillusioned youth firmly on an adult society gone corrupt, selfish and soft. Noting that 'estrangement is increasingly chosen' and not imposed through force or contracted like a disease, Keniston lamented the absence of role models and discernible rites of passage into adulthood. The net effect of this estrangement, Keniston concluded, was an artificial extension of adolescence, an acceptance of marginality and transition as a state preferable to the supposed stability of adulthood. 'When a young man sees no possibility of becoming like his parents, then their world is so remote that it neither tempts not threatens him,' Keniston wrote, 'it [is not] that their parents are poor role models (for a poor model is still a model of what not to be), but that parents are increasingly irrelevant as models for their children' (Keniston 1965b: 203–5).

In *The Uncommitted*, Keniston wrote:

> A complex and heterogeneous culture like our own of course offers many different paths to acculturation; but insofar as ours is a culture, these paths share common, socially learned assumptions about what is important, meaningful and right. When this learning is incomplete, as with alienated subjects, we can speak of a failure of acculturation. On the most conscious level this failure of course involves the explicit rejection of most of the fundamental tenets of the American way of life.
>
> (ibid: 197).

For Keniston, alienation is, when we are talking about teenagers, both the nature of *the* and the nature of *our* age.

Keniston's insistence on the social rather than simply or solely psychological dimension of teen alienation foreshadowed and foregrounded the Birmingham School's view of anomie as a politically conscious, albeit inarticulate refusal, a stylized attempt on the part of youth to oppose the basic values of the official, adult culture.[2] Though Keniston saw acculturation as a necessary and inevitable stage in human development—the Birmingham crowd are far more romantic in their celebration of youth's *rituals of resistance and refusal*—he was anxious to acknowledge why teenagers after the war systematically rejected adult culture. 'Alienation is a response of individuals especially sensitized to reject American culture,' Keniston wrote in the conclusion to *The Uncommitted: Alienated Youth in American Society*, 'and it is in part a response to social stresses, historical losses, and the collective estrangements in our shared existence' (ibid.: 391).

Premature Cynicism: It's the End of the World as We Know It and I Feel . . .[3]

If there is a collective unconscious—a 'collective estrangement' in a 'shared existence'—for Generation X it is the stuff of *bad TV*, the line-up on Nick at Night,[4] for example: *Gilligan's Island*, *Green Acres* and *Happy Days*. Such a collective appreciation, even fascination with rerun television is affirmed—at once celebrated and parodied— in a number of Gen-X films. In *Reality Bites*, for example, the slacker-roommates recall episodes of *Good Times* with startling clarity. But while they seem to know enough to see the absurdity in this shared knowledge—why is it that, after four years of college, this is what they know—they miss the point that *Good Times* was about black people and they're white, and that the black people on *Good Times* were, as the title song chimed, 'movin' on up', and that they are totally stuck in the slacker spiral of downward mobility. Missing from the sort of knowledge that might win them a game of Trivial Pursuit is any sort of cultural context. They know what happens in every episode of every bad TV show, but they don't seem to know or care about what any of it means.

When Vicki, the most successful of the roommates—she is an assistant manager at The Gap (where 'there are a hundred different ways to fold a shirt')—has an AIDS scare, she puts it in context to a scene (with her as a guest star) that might appear on TV: 'it's like I'm watching some crappy show like *Melrose Place* and I'm the new character, I'm the HIV AIDS character and I live in the building and I teach everybody that it's OK to talk to me, it's OK to be near me and then I die and there's everybody at my funeral wearing halter tops.' When a romance and job possibility turn sour for Lani, Vicki's roommate, she muses; 'I wonder why things can't just work out . . . like on *The Brady Bunch*.' It proves to be a question worth asking when Troy, Lani's eventual paramour, points out that 'Mr Brady [actor Robert Reed] died of AIDS'.

It isn't that Gen-X'ers can't distinguish between their shitty lives and bad TV, it's just that the distinctions are subtle, contextual, beside the point. Solutions to the bad stuff all around them are available someplace in that vast archive of TV resolutions that crowd their minds. Dysfunctional behaviour, then, emerges not from within but from bad choices at the archive, bad plotlines to which, unlike TV, no neat solution seems readily available.[5]

Take, for example, *River's Edge*, a depressingly realistic teen picture based on a well-publicized teen murder in Milpitas, California. The Milpitas killer, Jacques Broussard, killed his 14-year-old-girlfriend, Marcy Conrad, and then invited his friends to view the body. They poked the corpse with sticks to make sure he was not playing a practical joke on them, then kept his dirty secret from the cops, parents, teachers, everyone except their peers. In Milpitas, the kids *kept the faith*; the body was discovered eventually by authorities and the killer was arrested fairly soon thereafter. In the film, Matt, a reluctant teen hero, has a crisis of conscience and goes to the cops. At the core of the little drama in both stories is the code of fidelity—what Erikson was anxious to view as the primary *value* of youth. But even that core value is diminished by the shared consciousness of Gen-X's *TV Nation*.

In *River's Edge*, Lane, the most eccentric of the killer's friends, endeavours to cover up the crime. His sense of loyalty is culled from his favourite TV shows: *Starsky and Hutch* and *Mission Impossible*, dated shows about urban crime and Cold War espionage Lane confuses and conflates with the reductive little histories he's heard on the evening news. 'It's people like you,' he tells the increasingly existential killer, 'who are selling this country down the tubes. No sense of pride—no sense of loyalty. Why do you think there are so many welfare cases? Why do you think Russia is gearing up to kick our asses?' At the peak of his excitement over the cover-up of the crime, Lane again finds a reason to defend his friend in the confused array of images and plots flitting about in his head: 'It's like a fuckin' movie when a good friend gets in potentially big trouble. Now we have to deal with it. We've got to test our loyalty against all odds. It's kind of exciting. I feel like Chuck Norris.'

While Lane finds the core value of youth in the plots of the films and TV shows he has otherwise confused in his memory, the girls who journey to view the body are struck by their inability to feel as much at the death of their friend as they've felt watching even bad TV melodramas. 'I cried when that guy died in *Brian's Song*,' one recalls in embarrassment, 'you'd think I'd at least be able to cry for someone I hung around with.'

While the teens in *River's Edge* fail to establish a critical or ironic distance from the trash they consume in movie theatres and on TV, the college-educated twentysomething slackers in *Reality Bites* can't seem to shake a pervasive critical, ironic distance that keeps them from enjoying life. That distance persists in their 'real lives' where, as the title denotes, the real stuff of their lives 'bites'.

At a job interview, Lani is asked by a prospective employer to define irony. The word has so much meaning for her—it so completely and complexly characterizes her life—she can't put it into words. 'It's not a noun,' she says, 'it's a condition.' In frustration, she concludes that the term eludes definition, but she 'knows it when she sees it'. Lani doesn't get the job and not because she can't define irony but because she can't recognize it. Though she's unemployed and largely unprepared for the world of work, Lani is overqualified and that in and of itself, the inter-viewer tells her, is ironic. Back at her pad, she tells Troy about the botched interview. 'Irony,' he reminds her, 'is when the actual meaning is the opposite of the literal meaning.'

One Last Presentation in the Poconos

'In today's society,' remarked University of Chicago professor of educa-tional psychology Bruno Bettleheim in 1961, 'there is no pattern for the transition from young to old.' In the absence of a discernible rite of passage into adulthood, there was instead a disconcerting competition between the old and the young—a phenomenon that came to be known as 'the generation gap' in the late 1960s.

At the root of this generation gap was a growing suspicion prompted by significant shifts in Western culture from the nineteenth to the twentieth century. According to Bettleheim, the older generation's ties to its young derived from 'an emotional need to see its way of life continued by the coming generations' (in Erikson 1965: 92). But with the advent of a technological, fully twentieth-century society, few adults had so 'intimate a feeling for their life's work.' The adult generation's growing disillusion-ment and disaffection—the anomie fifties cultural historians like David Riesman, C. Wright Mills and William Whyte had observed in the adult workplace—proved a disconcerting legacy. The shifting post-war American society—the unsettling of American culture by the Baby Boom, the Red Scare, the flight to the suburbs and the accompanying subcultures of prosperity and leisure, a rising divorce rate and a seeming 'sexual wilderness' chronicled first in scientific terms by Drs Kinsey *et al.* and then in more hysterical prose by popularists like Vance Packard[7]—disconnected adults from the very society they had once fought to protect and sustain.

A growing commitment to higher education in the US after the Second World War vastly expanded the population on college campuses nation-wide. This emerging university subculture, fuelled first by return-ing vets on the V.A. (Veterans' Administration) plan and then even more dramatically by the post-war prosperity of the 1950s and early 1960s, was on its surface a good thing. A better educated population promised a more effective and thoughtful democracy and a workforce well tooled and suited for an increasingly global economy. But while parents publicly extolled the possibility of a better life for their children, they did so at the expense of culturally specific rites of passage and psychologically significant stages in psycho-social development.

The younger generation's rite of passage into an adult world worth occupying depended to a degree on the competition of the younger generation for control over a political and economic culture controlled by their elders. When one's elders show little confidence in or affection for what they and their parents had made of the world, Bettleheim argued, it was no small wonder that adolescents felt disconnected, disillusioned, alienated. 'You cannot test your own strength and vitality,' Bettleheim wrote, 'the very things you feel most dubious about as an adolescent, when all you can push against is a vacuum . . . Without something definite to push against, youth feels lost' (in Erikson 1965a: 92). In the end, it is pointless for youth to rebel—an activity Bettleheim aligned with the staging of and the emergence out of the Oedipal conflict—when they 'do not know what to fight for' (ibid.:106).

Bettleheim observed that post-war youth's instinctive pursuit of goals —diploma, marriage, job, etc.—was further problematized by the previous generation's unwillingness to surrender its ties to youth. The Second World War had interrupted youth for many men and women. The cult of play and selfish consumption inherent in suburban leisure culture seemed to Bettleheim a form of psycho-social compensation. But, Bettleheim cautioned, this leisure culture came at the expense of America's truly young and transitional.

In compensation for their own troubled and prolonged transition into adulthood, the Boomer generation has hung onto its youth even more tenaciously than their parents. Even a cursory look at the popular media reveals this continued extension of Boomer youth culture. Radio stations now format classic (sixties and seventies) rock. TV shows and movies are demographically shot to suit Boomers as they age through the century.

The seeming inaccess to a mass mediated expression of their own youth culture(s) is exacerbated for Gen-X'ers by constant reminders of how much worse things will be for them when they, indeed if they ever come of age. Widely felt fears of economic recession and downward mobility and the seemingly inevitable collapse of social security have made the psycho-social generational fix observed by Bettleheim in 1961 all the more acute for Generation X.

There were thirteen workers for every one Social Security beneficiary in 1949; 3.4 to 1 in 1990; and there will be just 1.9 to 1 in 2030 (*Forbes*, November 1988: 225). There is plenty of time for young people to get into the workforce. But once they get in, they may never get out.

According to a *Details Magazine* survey conducted in 1993, most twentysomething adults find it difficult to fully establish economic independence. Only 26 per cent of Gen-X adults took no money from their parents. 40 per cent counted on their parents for 'emergencies only,' 24 per cent for doctor and dentist bills, 24 per cent for car insurance, 16 per cent for rent, 16 per cent for clothing and 10 per cent for car payments. Another 7 per cent received a weekly allowance—an American cultural practice designed primarily to teach *children* the value of money (Ritchie 1995: 152).

Two Different Eighties Teen Films, Two Gen-X Role Models, The Same Future

Two of the principal characters in *Repo Man*—Otto and his nerd sidekick Kevin—are introduced stacking and pricing generic food cans in a mini-mart. Kevin mindlessly sings a TV jingle: 'I'm feeling 7-Up! Feeling 7-Up!' as he finally gives in to Otto's impatience with the task at hand. Work gives way to play and the boys are fired by their outrageous and outraged boss.

The next scene is set at a party where Duke steals Otto's girlfriend. Forlorn, sort of, Otto exits the party only to wander the 'bad neighbourhoods' of downtown LA. Against a backdrop of a poisoned-air sunset, Otto begins to sing. It's a Black Flag song—a late LA punk standard—but the message is equally well suited to the tasks at hand: stacking cans, repossessing cars, working all sorts of dead end jobs: 'We don't want to think about anything else/We don't want to know/We're just dedicated/ To our favourite shows: *Saturday Night Live*, *Monday Night Football*, *Dallas*, *Gilligan's Island*, *The Flinstones*.' The next scene finds the two young men seated on a doorstep in the rain contemplating the future. Kevin is perusing the want-ads. 'There's room to move as a fry-cook,' he suggests to an unimpressed Otto, 'in two years I'll be assistant manager. It's key.'

Such diminished expectations are repeated in a far more upscale picture released two years later: *Ferris Bueller's Day Off*. Unlike Otto and Kevin, Ferris lives a life of suburban privilege. He's not only rich but popular and charismatic, that rare teenager who somehow transcends cliques and sports to be popular more or less because he's cool. But like Otto and Kevin, he's got his issues and they're practical as opposed to global. 'Life moves pretty fast,' he tells us in the beginning of the film, 'If you don't stop and look around once in a while you can miss it. I do have a test today . . . It's on European socialism. I mean, really, what's the point? I'm not European. I don't plan on being European. So who gives a crap if they are socialists. They could be fascist-anarchists. It still wouldn't change the fact that I don't have a car.'

While cutting school—high school, he reminds us, is 'a little silly'— Ferris and his friends drive into the city in a borrowed Ferrari and play-act as adults. The act mostly fails. The car eventually ends up underwater. The head waiter at a posh restaurant kicks them out. When they decide finally to just be kids, the day turns out all right. During a German-Day celebration downtown, Ferris mounts a float and lip synchs Wayne Newton's 'Danke Schoen' as pretty young women in leiderhozen can't help but join the party. Ferris's friends see him on the float and marvel at his *chutzpah* and his ingenuity. But just as the song changes to the classic rock song 'Twist and Shout', Ferris's friends look to the future. 'What do you think Ferris will be when he grows up?' his girlfriend ponders. 'A fry cook,' his best-friend replies without a moment's hesitation.

That two such different young men might share the same low-rent future is made all the more disconcerting when one considers the number of eighties teen films that render comical the economic bind faced by Gen-X adolescents. Comedy, after all, hinges on shared expectations, shared understandings. In *Fast Times at Ridgemont High*, a variety of teenagers gain status through service-oriented mall jobs. A good job is where one might meet cute guys or girls or get to watch movies for free. The young man we come to like the best—he takes care of his sister when she has an abortion and keeps her secret from their parents and later becomes a hero by foiling a robbery at a mini-mart—aspires only to a future in management in the fast food industry. His alter-ego, the film's slacker/surfer hero, Spiccoli, thinks little about the future. Though he barely graduates, Spicolli gets lucky. In a lucky accident, he saves Brooks Shields' life and wins brief celebrity and a wad of dough. He wins the lottery, sort of, but it proves only temporary as he squanders the money in a desperate effort to forestall adulthood.

Films that focus on twentysomething Gen-X adults in the workforce similarly present little hope for Gen-X teens. In *Reality Bites*, Lani at first works at a local TV station as a production manager on a morning talk show assisting a host who hates her. When the host refuses to acknowledge her efforts—when he refuses to treat her with the same deference that her teachers, tied to the Gen-X educational priority on 'self esteem', had to—she ditches the job and decides to move on. But finding another job proves traumatic. Lani won't even contemplate a career folding shirts at The Gap or waiting tables. When her parents refuse to help, she turns to the tube for solace and for a message about the future from the folks at the Psychic Connection Network. Lani runs up a phone bill she can't pay calling the network's 900-line, then, making matters worse, she attempts to raise money to pay the phone bill by pumping gas for strangers, paying with her dad's credit card, and pocketing the cash. The gas station gig is not really a job. The cash she earns—sort of like what happens when you work— puts junk food on the table and keeps the phone connected for another month. But in the end, the scam only adds to her tab with her parents.

Gen-X adults do find work, at least on the big screen. But while they have money and their own stuff, they are mostly lonely, socially (sometimes sexually) dysfunctional and unhappy. For many of them, work has failed to fully accomplish a transition into adulthood. Their extended adolescence is visually rendered on screen as it is on the streets. We see these gainfully employed twentysomethings still tied to their personal electronic devices: cell-phones and lap-tops top the list, but walk- and disc-mans, Nintendo hand-units, are still in use. The only difference for them between youth and adulthood is there's less time to waste. The personal electronic devices more and more come to mediate their struggle for fun. For example, in *The Truth About Cats and Dogs* and *Denise Calls Up* there's erotic play on the phone. In *sex, lies and videotape*, as the title suggests, *getting off* requires first *turning on* a machine. While the film chronicles a series of infidelities it does so only to suggest that film-making and viewing is a more intimate and personal enterprise than sex. In this age of STDs, the film comes to a close without much hope for the more randy characters; their lives are ruined and they deserve it. But things turn out OK for the two characters who seem to like sex the least.

Work, if you can get it in a Gen-X film, is a trap. After a while you end up like your parents. In *Big Daddy*, for example, virtually everyone's either a lawyer or a doctor—even Adam Sandler. Through most of the film, Sandler doesn't practise law; indeed he tries his hardest not to work at all. He lives off a bogus insurance windfall and works one day a week in a tollbooth. By the end of the film, fatherhood puts him in a suit and tie. He's finally doing what he was trained by all that higher education to do. We see him in the film's brief coda attached to a cell-phone, like his friends at the start of the film, still trying to get away from work long enough to hug his kid.

As in *Big Daddy*, several of the twentysomethings in the Seattle-set

Singles are successful at work. There's an engineer and a doctor and two state workers in the professional–managerial ranks. The crowd at the apartment complex—a sort of *Melrose Place* for a rainier clime—also features a couple of losers: a dreadful musician moonlighting as a delivery man and a young woman caught in the quintessential Gen-X trap; she's a waitress at a coffee shop, earning just enough money to pay back her college loans, hoping someday to make enough to get her breasts done.

In *Party Girl*, the title character, Mary, is a dedicated slacker. Her skills, by her own accounting, suit her present interests: throwing rave parties at remote sites, wearing clever mis-matched couture outfits (mostly pilfered from friends' closets at parties), having fun, putting off adulthood. 'You know what I'm good at,' she confesses to a friend, 'maintaining when I'm fucked up, partying, making stuff up, having fun.' After she meets Moustaffa, a falafel vendor who taught school in his native Lebanon before emigrating to the United States where he falls hard into the Gen-X service economy, Mary begins to think about growing up, about making some sort of passage into adulthood. 'Maybe I'll open an aerobic studio,' she muses, looking around her spacious Soho loft. But while she's got the space, she knows nothing about fitness and, she laments, her clothes are all wrong. Mary wonders if she might someday be an actress, a clothing designer, a writer, an investment banker. But she is quickly daunted by the fact that she needs talent and/or expertise to do any of these more appealing jobs.

Moustaffa suggests she might, at least at first, set her sights a bit lower and tells her the story of Sisyphus. Though she is hearing the fable for the first time, she understands the story all too well. 'It's depressing,' she says, readily appreciating that work, in and of itself, is meant to depress. Later she tells the story to her male roommate Leo, a dance club DJ. He doesn't get the point of the story; he is after all still trying to make a career out of an extended adolescence (spinning records at nightly parties). Mary attempts to explain the story to him. 'It's a metaphor—to life.' 'It's a drag,' Leo quips, determined to put off such a sorry fate. 'I think I'm an existentialist,' Mary says, finding it all kind of funny, 'I really do.'

It is meant to be at once ironic and revealing that at the end of the film Mary decides on a career in library science. After all, she never reads, and her brief career as a clerk and stacker in a New York City library is a disaster. From the start, she can't get the hang of the Dewey Decimal System, though her aunt Judy, her boss, tells her that a trained monkey learned the system 'in a matter of hours'. Later she breaks into the library to have sex with Moustaffa. Judy finds out and fires her. The film ends in

Mary's apartment as her friends host a surprise birthday party for her, complete with a male stripper. Unaware, Mary has set up a meeting with Judy to try to get her job back. Mary arrives just minutes before her aunt. She enters the apartment in a conservative business suit; she at least looks the part she plans to play in the future. 'I want a career in library science,' she announces to her friends who are dancing to records spun by Leo. Mary tries to kick the revelers out and win back Judy's trust. But it's too late. Judy enters just as the stripper has completed his act. 'I want to go to graduate school,' Mary announces as everyone continues to dance: the stripper, her roommates, Mary (who tosses off her conservative suit jacket), even Judy. The party in *Party Girl* is the stuff of the mean-time—the transition between adolescence and whatever these days comes next.

http://thesite.org . . .

thesite.org is a popular Gen-X web-page. It lists, under the category 'education and work,' four growth fields: film and television, information technology, pharmacy and travel and tourism. This seems on the surface good news for Generation X. Preparation for careers in these fields may well require *experiences* they've all had: watching a lot of movies and TV, playing with and on the computer, 'maintaining' while stoned or drunk, getting the most out of a road trip or a summer job filling out that dog costume greeting folks at some theme park. Things may not be so bad for them in the future after all.

Of the four growth fields, easily the most glamorous is film and television. But entry into that field remains of the four listed above the most difficult, mysterious, even hazardous. But the long odds and the possibility of living fast and dying young only add to the attraction and glamour.

In the summer of 1999, the biggest film with Gen-X audiences in the U.S. was *The Blair Witch Project*. The film tells the story of three film students who disappear under scary circumstances. On its surface, *The Blair Witch Project* seems to suggest that the three students die because they fail to take the stories they hear about the witch seriously. But that's not the half of it and that's not why the film is, at this writing, poised to surpass *American Graffiti* as the biggest box office indie film of all time. The mistake the students make is one of ambition; they take too seriously what their little film might mean and pay dearly for the very pretension and ambition characteristic of so many of their real-life peers. The film's telling irony is that the grainy, jerky, hand-held images in the film are not only effectively chilling, they reveal the absurdity of the students' dreams of Hollywood discovery and future celebrity. The film that's found in the woods after their disappearance is convincing *because* it looks bad enough to have been shot by a student film-maker. But while the three college students end up dead in the movie on screen, young filmgoers are far more likely to invest in the other fantasy told by the film: that if you've got the right gimmick and like $60,000, there's a chance you too can make it big in the only town worth making it big in America these days. Eduardo Sanchez and Dan Myrick, who co-produced and directed the film, got their little hand-held pseudo-documentary screened at Sundance and then masterfully distributed by Artisan. They made a film, sold it, and got rich and famous. And they didn't even have to intern anywhere!

For those without a $60,000 horror picture earning more than $100 million at the box office, the internship route has become a popular strategy. But the odds of making it off the intern circuit are not much shorter than those faced by the likes of Sanchez and Myrick. My students know this, so many of them are hedging their bets with business classes and seminars, informercial tapes and web-sites that teach them networking and people skills. Exactly what it will take to make it in Hollywood in the twenty-first century, it seems, will have nothing to do with making movies.

John August, one of the few former interns to emerge as a creative player in the industry, offers an interesting case in point. He's anxious to tell aspiring film industry players to find a safer, saner career, that the chances of making it in Hollywood are slim. What wannabe film-makers are apt to miss in August's success story is that he has made it not (only) because he was an able intern, a savvy little player, but because he has talent, he can write. His script for the Gen-X black comedy, *Go*, is deft and complex. The screenplay tracks a single fateful night in the lives of a number of young characters all of whom, in the heat of a moment, make decisions that screw up their lives, maybe forever. August has made it where most aspirants are doomed to fail. Once you have your script produced, you really do have it made in Hollywood. But even with such success, August is hardly sold on life in LA. Though he can afford to recall his life as an intern with detached amusement, in a recent issue of *Entertainment Weekly*, August reminisced: 'I was an intern for a top Hollywood exec. We were waiting for the elevator and she took off her sunglasses, reached over, untucked my shirt, and wiped off her sunglasses without ever looking over at me' (August 1999: 31).

For more on the subject of Hollywood internships, there is *Swimming With Sharks*. Ostensibly an intern's revenge fantasy, the film opens with a reference to *Sunset Boulevard*. If we get the allusion, we are led to believe that we are watching a film narrated by a dead man destroyed by a corrupt industry. But unlike the hero of the Billy Wilder film, things end happily (albeit ironically) enough for the intern: he's not only not dead (face down in a pool, or figuratively dead in the industry), he's got his own office and the freedom to act as badly as his former boss. Guy, the film's college-educated hero, succeeds not because he's smart (he is) or because he's learned a lot of useful stuff in school (he hasn't; he learns more the first day on the job), but because he displays an ability to maintain his cool even after he kidnaps and tortures his boss, a vicious Hollywood executive named Buddy Akerman who clearly deserves what he gets in the film. Aside from the fantasy-revenge stuff, *Swimming With Sharks*, albeit comically, exposes the day-to-day absurdity of Hollywood business and the role so many interns so willingly play in hopes of getting ahead.

Guy's first day on the job begins badly. He parks in one of twenty empty spaces only to discover that he's chosen the one space reserved for an important female producer. Then he meets Akerman, an executive VP on the rise at the fictitious Keystone Studios. Guy's first assignment is to fetch coffee with Sweet and Low as his boss hurries off to a meeting. He returns with the coffee and a packet of Equal, which he points out contains the same basic ingredients as Sweet and Low. Still he is summarily dressed down: 'I asked you for Sweet and Low and you bring me Equal,' Akerman bristles, 'That just won't cut it here. Do me a fucking favour: shut up, listen and learn. I know this is your first day on the job and you don't really know how things work here. So I will tell you: You—have—no—brain. No judgment calls are necessary. What you think means nothing. What you feel means nothing. You are here to protect my interests and serve my needs. While it seems like a little thing to you—when I ask for a Sweet and Low—that's what I want and it is your job to see that I get what I want.'

When I show my students *Swimming With Sharks*, they find Buddy at once funny and familiar. Work is after all just work. Internships and entry-level gigs involve stupid tasks that a chimp could master in a couple of hours. At least in Hollywood, the weather's nice.

206 The Radiant Hour

It's Better for Girls

In *Kicking and Screaming*, a film which focuses on a group of recent college graduates, the world of work looms somehow still in the distance. Degrees in hand, they are all daunted by previous generations whose success strikes them as at once impossible and exceptional. Otis, who plans to go to graduate school in Milwaukee but chickens out in favour of a temp job at Video Planet, assesses the future in terms of a past he knows only in fragments (of the sort picked up on TV): 'I've done a little research. We all know how old Mozart was when he did all that . . . and Keats, big poet, was already dead by 24. And Tracy Austin was tiny when she started doing all those things on the tennis court'. When Otis gets a second interview at Video Planet—it's daunting when even the local video store has enough applicants to have a first and second cut—his media expertise is put to the test. The store owner asks him about his influences. Otis offers the gospel according to the *Cahiers du Cinema*: 'Samuel Fuller and all the other ones.' The reply gets him the job, and gets him the same start in the industry as Gen-X *uber*-film-maker Quentin Tarantino. But he never gets the hang of the boss's shelving system; the job is actually too hard for him. The titles are organized by genre, which at Video Planet tend toward the idiosyncratic: animal buddy pictures, terminal illness pictures, etc. The video-store job convinces Otis to get on the plane to Milwaukee; graduate school can't be as bad as work.

During his brief stint as a clerk, Otis decides to keep up with his education. He forms a book club with his friend Chet, who is a bartender and a perpetual student. But it falls apart when Otis never gets around to reading the first book. Chet, who does the assigned reading, is an amiable slacker. He puts off adulthood by accumulating credit hours but never fulfilling specific graduation criteria. Skippy, another of Otis's friends (who foolishly graduates), decides to use the money he's earned over the summer to re-enroll. When Miami, his soon to be ex-girlfriend expresses impatience with the decision—she like the other women in the film, is ready to move on after college—Skippy feigns an interest in 'Scandanavian Literature', and other such esoteric classes he never got around to taking the first time through.

Max, the group's cynic (and that's saying a lot given how cynical they all are) applies for a job as an intern in the philosophy department. In the meantime he keeps to a rigid schedule: the same bar, the same time every day. The 'internship thing', itself a transitional gig, is also on the horizon for another recent grad, Grover. His dad arrives for a visit and tells him that his new girlfriend works at *The New Yorker*. But the job, which isn't even really a job, it's an internship—there's a difference of course; jobs pay money but have no future, internships pay little if any money but hold the promise of a career—carries with it, its own considerable baggage. If he takes the job he will be indebted to his dad's much younger new girlfriend. He will have to live all too near to this new couple in the very sort of day-to-day dependence he had gone to college to avoid.

Grover's dilemma only serves to support Max's worst anxieties about the future: 'Eight hours ago,' he muses at a post-graduation party, 'I was Max Belmont, Senior, English Major . . . [suddenly] all my accomplishments are in the past.' When summer break ends and a new crop of students arrive to take his place, Max laments: 'What I used to write off as just a bad summer could now potentially turn into a bad life.' Later, he muses: 'I wish we were just going off to war . . . or retiring.' In despair as much over his own inaction as to the daunting nature of the future, Max waxes existential: 'I enter wake up and go to bed in my date book as if they were two different events.'

The young men in the film are as daunted by sex and relationships as they are about work. Soon after graduation, Max begins a relationship with a much younger working-class girl named Kate. When she turns seventeen, he remarks sarcastically: 'Well now you can read *Seventeen* and get all the references.' She knows he's making fun of her, but chooses instead to be optimistic: 'See,' she replies, 'it isn't so bad.'

Through much of the film, Grover pines for Jane, a former girlfriend he met in a Creative Writing seminar. In a flashback, we see a moment from their first class together. She is critiquing Grover's story: 'All the characters spend all their time talking about the least important things— you know, like what to have for dinner or who's the best looking model in the Victoria's Secret catalogue.' Jane is at once smarter, more talented and more practical than he is, a point made clear in their first exchange. 'They put a lot of time and work into that catalogue,' he deadpans. But she just doesn't get why he is trying so hard to be stupid. 'All that thought and energy put into Saturday morning cartoons', she adds; 'I think it's depressing.'

At the post-graduation party, Jane tells Grover she's going to Prague to study fiction writing. He has no plans for the summer, for next year, forever and he's crestfallen. The one thing he sort of knew he wanted was company. He is so stuck in the slacker, Gen-X, post-grad rut, he can't even fathom a move as big and consequential as a year abroad. When he summons up the courage to ask her to stay, he wonders aloud why anyone would ever want to go to Prague. She reminds him that he's never been there, really never been anywhere, to which he responds: 'I haven't been to Prague, but I know that thing—I know that stop shaving your armpits, read *Unbearable Lightness of Being*, fall in love with a sculptor, now I realize how bad American coffee is thing.' Jane reminds Grover that in Prague it's beer, not coffee that's a whole lot better than it is here in the states, and basically shrugs off his plea. Finally, in desperation, he makes reference to Prague's most famous one-time resident, Franz Kafka, a muse for all Gen-X'ers who have bothered to read him. 'Prague,' he says; 'you'll come back a bug.'

All of the women in *Kicking and Screaming* know what they want. Jane goes to Prague because the experience will do her good. While she is away, Grover stumbles his way into a freshman woman's dorm room. She wants what they've ostensibly come up there to get, but he gets cold feet. As he stammers a series of lame excuses, she takes off her shirt and says: 'Come on, be romantically self-destructive with me.' He's still not sure: 'Look, I'll sleep over,' he says, 'but I won't do anything.' She frowns and won't take no for an answer. She calls him 'a pussy' and as the roles completely reverse, she pushes him down on the bed and, as she tugs at his belt, adds: 'look woman, take off your skirt.' The camera finally cuts away, but only after it becomes clear that they are finally going to *do it*.

While gender equity, even in the bedroom, is still the stuff of Hollywood fantasy, the data suggests that things have changed and for the better for the young women of Generation X. As of 1993, 53 per cent of all BA and MA degrees were awarded to women. While the professions—law and medicine, for example—are still mostly male, the percentage of law and medical degrees awarded to women suggest a dramatic change for the future. In 1990, 34 per cent of all medical degrees and 42 per cent of all law degrees went to women—this compared to 1960 when only 5 per cent of the MDs and 2.5 per cent of the JDs went to women. In 1960, women comprised just over a third of the workforce; today it nears fifty per cent (Ritchie 1995: 34–5) Between 1980 and 1989, women aged 25–34 saw their average income increase by 62 per cent. Over the same period, average incomes increased by only 41 per cent for men (ibid.: 47). The data explains the recent backlash against Affirmative Action in conservative American politics. It also explains the anxiety level of so many young men in college today.

Discovering Japan

By 2015, Hispanics (Mexicans, Cubans, Puerto Ricans and other Latinos) will outnumber African-Americans in the US and become the single largest minority in the nation.[8] In several large cities in the South and Sunbelt—Miami and Los Angeles, for example—Hispanics already outnumber Anglo-whites. And while Hispanics comprise just 9 per cent of the total US population, they comprise a significantly larger percentage of Generation X. The median age of Hispanic Americans is 26. They are the youngest of all census-designated population groups (ibid.: 55).

The burgeoning Hispanic population has been represented on television and on film with fairly consistent reference to three significant political and social problems: bi-lingualism (in schools, in neighbourhoods, on TV), immigration (of the illegal and unregulated sort) and criminality (racial gang violence and illicit drug running). Like African-American youth, Hispanic youth is represented as a problem to be solved, as a problem complicated by the very cultural differences that define *their* culture as somehow distinct from *ours*.

The fastest growing ethnic group in the US today is Asian-American; between 1980 and 1990, the Asian-American population has grown by 108 per cent. But this burgeoning population is less a problem to be solved than a market to be served. According to a *USA Today* poll, roughly one-third of all Asian-American households earn more than $50,000 a year—this compared to 29 per cent of white households and 13 per cent of Hispanic households. The success of this ethnic group in the US economy seems the result of a collective family emphasis on higher education. Twenty-one per cent of all Asian-Americans have completed four years of college as compared to 13 per cent of all Americans—this despite the fact that many speak English as a second language (ibid.: 57). The success of especially the Japanese in the US and the ascendant Japanese economy in the 1970s and 1980s explains why a lot of young Americans are looking to the Pacific Rim for the secret of success in the 1990s. Ironically, the Japanese seem to be looking back at us more and more these days as their economy is showing signs of age: recession, inflation, trade problems, (youth) unemployment.

The term Generation X dates most directly to Douglas Coupland's 1991 novel: *Generation X: Tales For an Accelerated Culture*. It is first mentioned in the book in a workplace vignette set in Japan. Andrew, the novel's sort-of hero and narrator, is working for a teeny-bopper magazine in Tokyo as part of a half-year intern/exchange programme. One day,

Andrew is invited by the magazine's boss, Mr Takamichi, to have a drink in the executive suite. The invitation gets Andrew in some hot water with his Japanese co-workers. The rigid nature of the Japanese workplace has locked many of them into jobs they hate with little or no chance of even an afternoon's break for a drink with the boss. They are part of the *shin jin rui*—what the Japanese newspapers have labelled 'new human beings', a generation lost to dead-end jobs. The *shin jin rui* are convinced, with some good evidence to support their convictions, that things will be worse for them than it was for their parents. Andrew tells Mr Takamichi that a similar generation resides across the Pacific, 'but it doesn't have a name—an X generation—purposefully hiding itself. There's more space over here [in the US] to hide in—to get lost in—to camouflage (Coupland 1991: 56).

Coupland's novel is glib and prescient. A quick scan of some of the chapter titles reveals the novel's dominant themes. 'The Sun is Your Enemy', 'New Zealand Gets Nuked Too', 'Remember Earth Clearly', 'Plastics Never Disintegrate' and 'MTV Not Bullets', all point to natural or man-made disasters (the hole in the ozone layer, nuclear and atomic weapons, the accumulation of indisposable waste, racially drawn urban violence) caused by the carelessness of previous generations. So far as the novel is concerned, future disasters abound. Some are just bad luck: 'Await Lightning'. Others are just a matter of time and/or the times: 'December 31, 1999' and the final chapter, 'January 01, 2000'. Other chapter titles offer commentary on life, such as it is, for those young, American and lost: 'Our Parents Had More', 'I Am Not a Target Market', 'Quit Your Job', 'Dead at 30 Buried at 70', 'Purchased Experiences Don't Count', 'Why Am I Poor', and 'Define Normal' (ibid.: v–vi).

Coupland leaves the most telling account of this generation lost in and to America for a secondary character to tell. Dag is from Buffalo, New York—America's first 'ghost city', which 'one fine 1970s day' lost its industrial core to cheap labour overseas and across the border to the north in Canada. Dag finds in Buffalo's sad little history a metaphor for his condition as a Gen-X slacker. He traces his peculiar Gen-X anomie to his early youth spent watching Lake Erie freeze, wandering the few malls that were still open, eyeing stuff he couldn't buy and/or couldn't use (ibid.: 29–30). As he tells his story to Andrew, Dag cannily observes:

> there invariably comes a certain point where youth fails us; where college fails us; where Mom and dad fail us . . . But my crisis wasn't just the failure of youth but also a failure of class and sex and the future and I *still* don't

know what. I began to see this world as one where citizens stare, say, at the armless Venus de Milo and fantasize about amputee sex or self-righteously apply a fig leaf to the statue of David, but not before breaking off his dick as a souvenir. All events became omens; I lost the ability to take anything seriously.

(ibid.: 30)

Dag drops out and like Andrew wakes up one morning in the desert southwest 'where the weather is hot and dry and the cigarettes are cheap' (ibid.: 31). There, in the barren landscape, on the outskirts of a series of affluent senior citizen enclaves carved into the Mojave and quite near where the military tests its nuclear hardware, Andrew and Dag await an end to a life they've had so little time or opportunity to enjoy.

The Body in the Trunk

After watching a lot of movies about Generation X, I am struck by a curious but nonetheless indicative genre convention: the body in the trunk. From *Repo Man* to the recent twentysomething nightmare *Very Bad Things*, the logic of disaster suggested in Coupland's table of contents has taken on the form of a dead body in the trunk of a Gen-X'ers car. In *Repo Man* it's some sort of radioactive mess, maybe not even a body really. But in more recent films it is the accidental victim of some careless or unlucky act, some moment of pleasure cut short by the cosmic consequences that seem to attend the struggle for fun in these last days of the twentieth century.

In *Jawbreakers*, it's a friend killed accidentally in a birthday prank; in *Heathers*, a series of little acts of revenge that end badly and deadly; in *Go* it's a stranger who stupidly walks behind a moving car driven by two guys already in a world of trouble. Life and death are cheap I suppose, that's part of it. But really it's the possibility, no the inevitability, of the unlucky accident that lays in wait for Generation X. Theirs is not just a future in the suburbs that might suck. For them there is some unlucky victim out there waiting to fuck up their future once and for all. The body in the trunk has become the literal and figurative moment of truth in Gen-X films, a rite of passage into adulthood or oblivion, which, as suggested in *Very Bad Things*, may well be the very same thing.

The bachelor party revellers in *Very Bad Things* leave behind their boring jobs and their hectic suburban lives (noisy kids, cloying wives, impatient girlfriends) for one last young, white and single play in Las Vegas (the destination of so many twentysomething road-trips in Gen-X films: *Swingers, Go, Very Bad Things* to name just three). It's a bad idea from the start; the women in the film all tell them so. It's clear they are just boys all *playing* at being free, at being young, at having no real responsibility to anyone or anything except maybe their own fun.

A stripper/prostitute comes to their hotel room and things turn ugly fast. Sex these days seldom comes without its consequences. The prostitute is killed during a bout of wild sex. The young men are forced to suddenly sober up to the fact that their lives, what's left of them, hinge on two things: (1) what they do with the body and (2) what they do as a group, as friends, to cover-up the crime when they return home and resume their lives.

It is important that they fail on both counts. The first death requires a second, a security guard from the hotel stumbles upon the body and they kill him too. After the second murder, the rite of passage for these young men involves not only disposing of a body killed by accident, but a second killed with premeditation and on purpose. When they return home, paranoia gets the better of them. They're all so selfish, so uncertain, they can't really trust each other. By the end of the film, the few men who have not already fell victim to revenge and paranoia are reduced by yet another unlucky accident to wheelchairs, denied entry into an adult world they came so close to joining.

The final scene of *Very Bad Things* seems an object lesson in the strange generational fix of America's *shin gin rui*. Failing the entrance exam into adulthood—failing to dispose of that little problem in the trunk without falling apart intellectually, morally, psychologically—the young men are reduced to dependent little children. And they find in that regression a particularly telling little moral: to be forever young, after doing such very bad things, is to be stuck forever in some terrible suburban nightmare, fed through a tube, unable to speak or cry out, nursed to their deaths by a woman who is not really their mother.

Notes

1   This the title of Bruno Bettleheim's *Challenge of Youth* conference presentation and the title of his essay published in Erikson's anthology. The essay will be discussed at length later in this essay.
2   For more on the Birmingham School approach, see: *Resistance Through Rituals*,

edited by Stuart Hall, John Clarke, Tony Jefferson and Brian Roberts (London: Hutchinson, 1976), Dick Hebdige, *Subculture: The Meaning of Style* (London: Metheun, 1979) and *Hiding in the Light: On Images and Things* (NY: Routledge, 1989), Angela McRobbie, *Feminism and Youth Culture: From 'Jackie' to 'Just Seventeen'* (Cambridge, MA: Unwin Hyman, 1991) and (maybe less obviously) Simon Frith, *Sound Effects: Youth, Leisure and the Politics of Rock and Roll* (NY: Pantheon, 1981). [Editor's note: this approach is also discussed in the Introduction to this collection.]

3   The first half of this intertitle is taken from: Kenneth Keniston, 'Social Change and Youth in America', p. 202. The second half is from a song by the Gen-X band REM.

4   Nickleodeon, a basic cable channel on most systems in the US programmes entertainment for children during the day and screens reruns of *classic* sixties and seventies sitcoms at night.

5   It is worth adding here that many elementary schools in the US these days deal with disciplinary problems in terms of *good* and *bad* choices. In schools clinging fast to the mantra of self-esteem, there is no such thing as a bad kid, just good kids who seem to make bad choices. Young adults surviving this contemporary education are wont to view life in the same terms. They are never bad or lazy or thoughtless or cruel or even murderous; it's always just a matter of making the wrong choice instead of the right one.

6   David Riesman, *The Lonely Crowd* (New Haven, Connecticut: Yale University Press, 1950), C. Wright Mills, *The Power Elite* (NY: Oxford University Press, 1956) and *White Collar* (NY: Galaxy Press, 1956), and William Whyte, *The Organization Man* (NY: Anchor, 1957).

7   See: Alfred Kinsey, Wardell B. Pomeroy, and Clyde E. Martin, *Sexual Behavior in the Human Male* (Philadelphia: W.B. Saunders, 1948), Alfred Kinsey, Wardell B. Pomeroy, Clyde E. Martin and Paul H. Gebhard, *Sexual Behavior in the Human Female* (Philadelphia: W.B. Saunders, 1953) and Vance Packard, *The Sexual Wilderness* (NY: David McKay, 1968). Also of relevance and interest on the subject: William Masters and Virginia E. Johnson, *Human Sexual Response* (Boston: Little, Brown, 1966).

8   This is a deceiving statistic in that 'Hispanic' is a category used by the US census that includes a variety of very different Spanish-speaking South and Central American, Mexican and Caribbean immigrants.

Bibliography

August, J. (1999) 'The It List', *Entertainment Weekly*, Summer, p. 31.
Bettleheim, B. (1965) 'The Problem of Generations,' in E. Erikson (ed.), *The Challenge of Youth*, New York: Anchor Books.

Coupland, D. (1991) *Generation X: Tales For an Accelerated Culture*, New York: St Martins.

Erikson, E. (ed.) (1965a) *The Challenge of Youth*, New York: Anchor Books.

——(1965b) 'Youth: Fidelity and Diversity,' in *The Challenge of Youth*, New York: Anchor Books.

Keniston, K. (1965a) 'Social Change and Youth in America,' in E. Erikson (ed.) *The Challenge of Youth*, New York: Anchor Books.

——(1965b) *The Uncommitted: Alienated Youth in American Society*, New York: Oxford University Press.

Kopkind, A. (1992) 'Slacking Toward Bethlehem,' *Grand Street*, no. 44.

Ritchie, K. (1995) *Marketing to Generation X*, New York: Lexington Press.

Unesco (1981) *Youth in the Eighties*, Lausanne, Switzerland: Unesco Press.

Filmography

The Blair Witch Project (1999), directed by Dan Myrick and Eduardo Sanchez, Artisan Entertainment.

Fast Times at Ridgemont High (1982), directed by Amy Heckerling, MCA/Universal.

Go (1999), directed by Doug Liman, Tri Star Pictures.

Kicking and Screaming (1995), directed by Noah Baumbach, Trimark Pictures.

Party Girl (1995), directed by Daisy von Sherler Mayer, First Look Pictures.

Reality Bites (1994), directed by Ben Stiller, MCA/Universal.

Repo Man (1984), directed by Alex Cox, Edge City.

River's Edge (1987), directed by Tim Hunter, Island/Hemdale Film Corporation.

Swimming with Sharks (1994), directed by George Huang, Trimark Pictures.

Very Bad Things (1998), directed by Peter Berg, PolyGram.